ANYWHERE WITH JESUS I CAN SAFELY GO.

Worthy Words for the Journey

KAREN M. LAND

Anywhere With Jesus I Can Safely Go.
Worthy Words for the Journey
by Karen M. Land

Printed in the United States of America.

ISBN 9781498432566

Scripture quotations taken from the Nelson Study Bible, New King James Version (NKJV). Copyright © 1979, 1980, 1982 by Thomas Nelson, Inc. Used by permission. All rights reserved.

www.xulonpress.com

Anywhere With Jesus I Can Safely Go!

Through this Life's 'Valleys' and its 'Mountaintop' experiences...,
"He will never leave you or forsake you." Hebrews 13:5

"Life with Christ is an endless hope; without Him
a hopeless end." – Unknown

KAREN M. LAND

Table of Contents

Introduction

*T*his book was written with the intent to help people make wise choices and take steps towards Jesus. I found that when you decide to give your life to Jesus, you might as well say "goodbye" to being popular. You won't necessarily get "high-fived" or a "pat-on-the-back" when you decide to give your life to Him! After all, this world chose to crucify Jesus! I wish that someone would have told me these things early on...but I had to learn them the hard way. God has walked with me through the pain of homelessness, AIDS, rejection, loneliness and financial ruin. He has brought peace to my broken heart, and healing to my soul! He has heard my cries for help and placed divinely and strategically appointed people around me to love, mentor and teach me. It has taken awhile for the lessons to "sink in", however, once I made the decision and told God that, *"I didn't want anyone in my life unless God wanted them there" things* started to change! He led me to my precious husband, David, and in November of 2009 we were married. In the safety and comfort of my marriage and relationship with God- and David, my heart slowly began to heal.

After we were married, David told me the following things about myself when we were dating. He said, "Yes, you looked like you were a little 'beat up'...and that you weren't going to put up with any 'crap', but I felt that God was showing me that you were the love of my life!" Since then, I cannot begin to thank God enough for the amazing, loving and accepting family that He has surrounded me with! The speed of my healing has been a process of God's design. It has been totally based on my own desire and motivation for healing...and God's wisdom to not give me more pain than I could handle. I remember devouring every "self-help" book in sight... and going to counselors to get E.M.D.R. therapy. As my healing was accelerating...so was the pain. I was asking God a lot of questions... and slowly began to come to the realization that my entire purpose on this earth was to glorify Him. **(Matthew 6:33 – "But seek first the kingdom of God and His righteousness, and all these things shall be added to you.")** It wasn't to be a millionaire, a celebrity or anything like that...but it was to have Him be in charge of my life... wherever that would take me! I needed to be obedient to do whatever He was asking me to do! I prayed that He would show me what He wanted me to do to further His kingdom. As I spent more time at the feet of Jesus, I began to feel an overwhelming desire to jot down scripture and spiritual encouragement so that it could be of help to others. As I spent more and more quiet time with God, I felt that He was asking me to send daily texts of encourage to my friends, family and our home group.

This book was birthed as a result of the multiple texts that went out every morning to these amazing family, friends and acquaintances. They didn't judge me for punctuation mishaps, grammatical errors or for anything else. They allowed me to practice writing for God's glory! Instead, they just sent back wonderful texts... expressing their appreciation that someone cared enough to create and send out encouragement.

AS you read these devotionals, I hope that you are impressed with the importance of taking **'EVERYTHING'** to God. In James 4:2, God says, **"...Yet you do not have because you do not ask!"** I have started talking to God everywhere I go. As a result, He has spoken to me in very unlikely places- such as the shower, and in the moments that I would sit in my favorite recliner. There were even times when I would hear his voice above the bustle of work...or while I was out on my road bike. His loving voice has become the most exciting and exhilarating thing to hear and experience in all of my life!

God has made it very apparent to me that He wants "Freedom" from pain for all of His children!! He has a plan for YOU!!! My prayer is that you will take EVERYTHING to God...and surrender it all to Him so that He can turn it into something beautiful! The best way to live is to "Remember that Jesus is with you everywhere you go!"

Dedication

This book is dedicated first to my amazing Heavenly Father who has taken up residence in my heart and utterly is changing me. He is turning my pathetic "mess" of a life into a "miracle"! And secondly, to my husband, David, who has brought great healing, love and purpose back into my life. It is because of His tender, unconditional love, acceptance and commitment to me, that I have fully come to know healing and victory in the love of Jesus Christ! Thank you precious David, Mari, Donna and Steve! I thank Nick, my son, for his dedication in getting my website up and running and my daughter, Britanny, for her wonderful encouragement and support!

A big "Thank-You" and hugs to Sharon Rose and her husband, Gary for their support with the pre-editing of this book. Additional thanks to Hope Cottage and Stephanie Boardman for her support to not only myself, but all of the women, men and children that are going through homelessness and times of crisis. Mel and Carol Brewster, God's face shines upon you! Thank you for allowing me to give my testimony at your church! A big thank you to all of those friends, family, home group, and others who have given support and encouragement to finish this book! God has blessed me with the gift of your friendship! May God's face shine upon you!

Chapter 1

About...
"Control and Pride"

I believe that Pride and Control are major culprits in keeping us under a shroud of ignorance. This harsh reality has caused an utter sadness inside of me that I have not been able to shake. I confess to you today, that we are all *"way too comfortable"* in our own little lives. We don't like to be pushed out of our comfort zones. We like to be in total control...and don't like to "sweat"! We avoid pain, inconvenience, loss and discomfort at all cost! Many times we make bad choices and then we blame others or God! ...Really?

Will we allow the pain or tragedy that we experience to lead us to healing or wholeness,... or will it make us a bitter and angry person? The choice is ultimately yours and mine. Will we start asking God what we are supposed to learn from our trials... or will we become bitter and start complaining about how life is not fair...and that it is all God's fault...and why didn't this happen to my neighbor down the street? Our Heavenly Father is waiting for our "total surrender"!

I guarantee... it is a small price to pay for the joy and inner peace of knowing Jesus Christ! Our pain can be used as blessings to melt and mold us into the kind of people that God can use. Can we let go of the "control" that we think we have and bury our "pride" at the foot of the cross? WOW!... maybe if we give up our pride and control, we will have a shot at our own amazing relationship with our Creator, Jesus Christ!

The following is a short story that I heard and then shared with my staff one day. It went something like this:

There was once a young boy who came to stay with his Grandparents for the summer. He and his cousin were walking home from the field where they had been helping their grandpa put up hay. They decided that it would be a little faster to take a short-cut to get home to the farmhouse because they were tired and couldn't wait to taste grandma's fried chicken. Soon, however, the two boys came upon a fenced pasture area that had a sign on it that read, *"ABSOLUTELY NO TRESPASSING"...and then in very small print- the boys read aloud, "If you decide to cross this pasture to the other fence, you must make it in less than five seconds to keep Roscoe the Bull from beating you to the other side!"*

Why do we think that we are so good at making decisions and choices for ourselves? In real life...we do not always get the "fine print messages" that describe what our consequences will be! Instead, we barrel ahead...making one decision after another without the help of Jesus...or anyone else for that matter. The big mistake is that we don't bother to get to know God, our creator, who knows us from the inside out...and knows the outcomes of our lives- from the beginning to the end! Jesus will definitely give us the wisdom and insight into the "fine print messages" of the crossroads and decisions of our lives! We only need to start asking Him and then prepare to listen and wait in silence to hear His voice.

Matthew 7:13 & 14, "Enter by the narrow gate; for wide is the gate and broad is the way that leads to destruction, and there are many who go in by it. Because narrow is the gate and difficult is the way which leads to life, and there are few who find it." (This also indicates that if 'everybody is doing it',...then you might want to think twice before you go along for the ride.)

Psalm 63:8, "My soul followeth hard after Thee; Thy right hand upholdeth me."

A.W. Tozer, in his book, "In Pursuit of God", pgs 13 & 14, says, "God is a person, and in the deep of His mighty nature He thinks, wills, enjoys, feels, loves, desires and suffers as any other person may. In making Himself known to us, He stays by the familiar pattern of personality. He communicates with us through the avenues of our minds, our wills and our emotions. The continuous and unembarrassed interchange of love and thought between God and the soul of the redeemed man is the throbbing heart of New Testament spirituality." This intercourse between God and the soul is known to us in conscious personal awareness. It is personal: it does not come through the body of believers (the Church), as such, but is known to the individual, and to the body (the Church), through the individuals which compose it."

"To have found God and still to pursue Him is the soul's paradox of love, scorned indeed by the too easily satisfied religionist, but justified in happy experience by the children of the burning heart." A.W. Tozer, In Pursuit of God, pg 15.

Who is "really in charge" of your life?

Many times it seems that our Heavenly Father will stand back and let us "knock ourselves out", so to speak, until we come to our senses and realize that He has all of the power and strength, and we are nothing without Him.

2 Cor. 12:9-10 "And He said to me, 'My grace is sufficient for you, for My strength is made perfect in weakness.' Therefore most gladly I will rather boast in my infirmities, that the power of Christ may rest upon me. Therefore I take pleasure in infirmities, in reproaches, in needs, in persecutions, in distresses, for Christ's sake. For when I am weak, then I am strong."

How many times have you gotten to the end of your rope? What did you do...sit down and cry? Did you get angry? Did you call a friend? Did you cry out to Jesus for help? I was raised in a household of "stubborn German individuals". My role models were the ones that modeled the good work ethic and the stubborn, "never give up" approach. My parents were the "Pull yourself up by your bootstraps" kind of people. I rarely saw them ask for help from anyone...so it has not come very naturally. It also seemed that our home had an unspoken rule of "perfection"... which I found can become a curse... and eventually ruin your life.

Even though my parents did their best with what they had been given, in light of these things, I was not shown how to "live out" my belief in God. I grew up in somewhat of a "Calvinistic", Seventh–day Adventist Faith. I know that we did pray growing up, however, I don't know that my parents actually "believed" that God could answer their prayers. I didn't know that I could ask Him for the little things in life... like when I was afraid- or when I lost my keys. It seemed that I was raised believing that God didn't want to hear about the details of my day...that my opinion didn't count...and that I was to be "seen and not heard".

I have learned a lot of things about God since then. After years of searching and questioning every belief that I ever had...these are the things that I am absolutely sure of and I know! I know that our Heavenly Father loves to hear from you and me. He loves to make the impossible possible. He wants to be the **first** person on our list of people to talk to. He left His Holy Bible as a book of instruction in wisdom. And I know that the Bible will never become "outdated" or "obsolete"! It is very relevant to the world and situations that you and I face every day. The bible has wisdom on multiple topics such as sex, raising children, marriage, work and much more!

These are also some of the other things that I have learned about His character. Feel free to add your own to this list about God as you get to know and understand Him!

-He typically shows up when there are no other possible solutions.

-He can repair a car or patch it up and make it run at our smallest cries for help.

-He can heal His children from their illnesses and infirmities, if it is part of His plan and will.

-He can heal wounded hearts from divorce, death, rejection and family secrets.

-He can provide your next meal when you have nothing to eat.

-He can sell a house when the market is not good.

-He can make your money stretch farther, if you give Him the first 10% of your income.

-He is a counselor. His Holy Word is all healing. Those who read it daily will heal and become whole.

-He is our protector. His angel warriors are always by our side to offer protection and safety.

Our prayers are what activates this protection.

"Dear Father, You are everything to me! You are the air I breathe; You are the joy and laughter in my life. Lord, without your guidance I wouldn't be where I am today. Thank you for Your steadfast love. Jesus, I can't do this day without You! Help me to surrender every part of my life to you each day! Amen"

Does God really want us to be controlled by our feelings and emotions of our past?

The answer is "No", God does NOT want us to be controlled by our feelings! How often have we said, ***"I just don't feel like it?"*** There are times and situations when each of us can be driven by our emotions. Emotions, however, can serve a dual purpose. They can serve as <u>warning signs</u> or <u>red flags</u> that tell us when danger is near, when we need to get more rest or even when we need to eat a more balanced diet, get more exercise, or spend quality time with our families or our creator. There are times when our emotions are a "release" for stressful situations. However, in most situations, in order for us to progress through the grieving process, we need to be angry, cry, be depressed and feel the hurt so that we can move forward with our lives into more joyful moments. If we continue to push our feelings aside and don't deal with them... then we have the potential of becoming very depressed, withdrawn, angry or explosive people without realizing it. In this case of suppressing our emotions, we may not realize that by suppressing our emotions...we can be robbed from a joyful and productive life. Our fear or unwillingness to address painful issues from our past can keep us from getting to where God wants us to be! There are times when we don't fully understand the things that drive us. It can be things that we are aware of... or not. I have learned that the human mind can block out painful times in our lives...even up to ten years and more! The huge hurdle may appear as we are trying to figure out what emotions are running our lives, or why they have such a grip on us. If we cannot find the underlying cause through a little bit of research... such as...asking yourself, "Is it hormonal in origin", "does it remind us of something hurtful or painful in our past"...or have I been under a lot of stress lately"...then we most likely need to be consulting our Father in heaven, (who is the great counselor), and possibly making an appointment with a professional counselor.

Have you heard of multi-generational sin or perhaps heard of some-one's great grandmother coming "out of the closet" with mistakes or sins of the past? These sins of sexual promiscuity, sexual abuse, physical abuse, murder, poisoning, torture, incest and more... can possibly exist in one's family and may come from several generations up the line without our awareness of it. Even though we like to think that our past is perfect, it may surprise you at how many things start coming out when sitting in silence before Jesus ...or in the office of a counselor. Grandparents, parents...or even great grandparents can pass down multi-generational sin that might be affecting our lives today. And yes! There is something that we can do about genera-tional sin and even mental illness and other fears that have been passed down for generations. You can STOP it in it's tracks with a little help!!

A few years ago I attended a thirteen week prayer conference that really opened my eyes to a lot of the strategies of the devil. There was one week that was especially interesting. The topic one week was on "Free Masonry". After this presentation on "The Free Masons", I was horrified at the prospect that my grandfather was a "Free Mason". This practice was very popular...and continues to be cloaked in mystery and deceit. In order to join the Free Masons, its joining members must recite certain incantations or chants in Latin. These oaths are "curses" that the joining members, unbeknown to them, are taking upon themselves and their families. As I indicated, most of the time, the men who join have no idea that these Latin words that they are reciting are "curses"! These curses can be reversed if you believe in Jesus Christ! All you need to do is ask Jesus Christ to remove these curses from you and your family and from any future generations! The Free Masons are ultimately worshiping the Devil- without open knowledge of any of it! After watching this documentary on its origin, its practices and the horrific things that happened and continue to happen in this cultish setting, our presenter had our entire class pray and ask Jesus Christ, the only Living God to remove all of the curses from each of us if we were exposed to the Free Masons or had family members that were involved. We prayed and asked that these curses be removed...and that if anyone up the line in our generations was involved- that God would remove these curses and restore them and our entire families to the wholeness that He wanted for us!

It is my belief that we can get to a place of healing and wholeness by getting on our knees and asking God to begin the process of healing in our lives. There are only a few requirements for this process to work and be effective!

1. The first requirement is that you have a desire to be whole.
2. The second requirement is that you ask God to show you what to do...and that you "Believe" that He can and will do it! Ask Him to begin to make you whole! (Read the story of healing in Mark 10:46-52.)
3. Thirdly, I encourage you to start reading God's Holy Word. God's Word has never lost its wisdom. It has never become

obsolete! It will level out your emotional "ups and downs." (II Timothy 3:16)

4. Keep asking for God's help and waiting and listening for His answers! Keep searching for guidance from God's Holy Word and asking for wisdom. God will lead you!

I have spent a fair amount of time on my knees begging that God heal my heart and make it whole. I have also asked Him to stop the generational sin that might have been passed down to me on a subconscious level. We don't have to be slaves to our feelings, to substances, to the past, or to anything or anyone for that matter! Negative people require 'things' or 'people' to make them happy. Most of the time, people who are controlled by their feelings or emotions do not care about anyone but themselves. It is not fun to be around people that feel life is "all about me."

Philippians 4:13 "I can do all things through Christ who strengthens me." Paul says we are to rely on God to make us happy and joyful. God is capable of healing our lives and brokenness from the past.

We have a choice and can choose how we will handle and react to every situation that comes our way. We can choose **not** to join the ranks of the following emotional mind sets:

-exploders
-stuffers
-avoiders
-confronters
-controllers

-manipulators

-blamers

-liars & cheaters

-drama mamas

It seems as though this world continues to raise up generation after generation of self-serving adults who don't even know how to "make it" in life because they were never required to control their emotions or discipline their minds.

I was told that I should be "Seen and Not Heard" as a child... so, I wasn't sure that it was safe to express my feelings to God or anyone else for a while. This possibly contributed to me feeling like a "zero" and most likely added to low self-esteem. As I grew into adulthood, I became a stuffer of my emotions until I finally would explode.

I have finally realized that my parents were no longer in control of my life...or my emotions—I am! This has happened for quite some time until I realized how I was affecting those around me. One of the most difficult things to do, is to take a step back and look at yourself. This is not a fun activity, but can be a life-saving one! I have asked a handful of loyal friends to tell me what they were seeing in me...and to be honest and truthful. Now that I am married, I have also enlisted my husband's help to give me feedback! He is a great sounding board! I have asked Him to be honest with me and to tell me if I am grumpy, irrational, and hormonal or way out there! My desire is to be a better person with God's help... and not a bitter, "fly-off-the-handle" person that God cannot use!

25

Our reactions and attitudes can make or break us! Our attitudes can make or break friendships, marriages, a church... or even the company we work for!

Our world places way too much "clout" on feelings–and should be placing way more trust in the God that we serve. Feelings should be somewhat of a warning, red flag, or indicator as to how we should handle things. However, there is never a time when they should be allowed to run our lives. God expects us to discipline our emotions in such a way that we grow and begin to realize that we are His children and our main purpose in this world is to make life a little more bearable for those around us.

Today's reminder is that our feelings are a very important part of the recovery process, however, learning how to balance feelings with appropriate action is where it is at!

"Dear God, I pray that You continue to mold me and help me to see myself clearly. Please bring Godly people into my life that can speak truth and wisdom when I need it most. Help me to be accountable to You and to not allow my emotions to control me. I want to grow into a mature, loving adult who can be molded into someone useful with a servant's heart. Amen"

*Did you know that you should **NEVER** underestimate God's ability to act in <u>your life</u>?*

"Be encouraged for I know the plans I have for you, says the Lord, Plans to prosper you and not to harm you, plans to give you hope and a future." Jeremiah 29:11

We all have the tendency to underestimate God's abilities to work through us. We put God in a box of our own making, and according to our own experiences. In scripture, we are told that Moses didn't feel that he was capable of leading the children of Israel out of Egypt. He didn't know what God's plans were for him at the time. Then there was David, the shepherd, who didn't feel that he was qualified to be king. We also read in the Bible about Joseph, who was also sold as a slave, was imprisoned for a while and eventually became the ruler of a mighty nation and saved the nation from starvation and famine. What is it that you might be doubting about God's plans for you? ***God isn't asking you to trust your own abilities…He is asking you to <u>trust HIS</u>!***

"God doesn't call the qualified, He qualifies the called!" – Unknown.

As I turned the radio on this weekend and was getting out of the shower I was listening to David Jeremiah. He suddenly said, ***"Some of you are settling for so very little when your Father wants to give you so much!"*** I can't even begin to tell you how many times I have wanted to do things my way, and then realized that God's way would have turned out a whole lot better! There is a certain story about God's blessings being compared to a warehouse that had shelves

27

full of unopened gifts. The story was about all of the gifts and blessings that we have not received because we either didn't ask or we were too stubborn and wanted to do it our way. Perhaps there exists some level of unforgiveness that might be keeping us from receiving His blessings. How tragic that we think that we can 'RUN THE SHOW' better than God!

Matthew 6:33 "Seek ye first the Kingdom of God and His righteousness, and all these things shall be added unto you!"

Remind yourself today to stop letting old fears, limiting ideas and doubts stop you from discovering your strengths and talents. Today, by letting go of these bad thoughts and habits ...I will give myself opportunities to learn something wonderful about myself!

*"Argue for your limitations, and sure enough, they define you!"– Richard Bac*h

"Dear God, please help me to rely on Your strength and not my own! I feel so puny and unworthy at times! Please cover me with Your robe of righteousness and fill me with Your love, kindness, compassion and every good thing that comes from You! Fill me with Your Holy Spirit and mold me into the person that You would have me be! I pray that You would pour out Your Holy Spirit and Your Blessings upon me. I pray these things in the precious name of Jesus Christ. Amen"

Do you want to hear God laugh? ...Tell Him your plans!

Did you know that God wants us to plan and think ahead? However, He asks us to "surrender the control" portion of our lives to Him. That means that we may be required to learn to become flexible if He asks us to change things up. And when we do plan in advance, we always need to remember that God needs to be consulted when doing the planning!

James 4:13-16 says, "Come now, you who say, 'Today or tomorrow we will go to such and such a city, spend a year there, buy and sell, and make a profit'; Where as you do not know what will happen tomorrow. For what is your life? It is even a vapor that appears for a little time and then vanishes away. Instead you ought to say, 'If the Lord wills, we shall live and do this or that." But now you boast in your arrogance. All such boasting is evil."

Proverbs 16:3 says, "Commit your works to The Lord, and your thoughts will be established."

Our Heavenly Father wants us to consult Him daily with the issues of our lives...no matter how BIG or how SMALL they are. Interestingly enough... I have been found guilty of telling God how He is supposed to answer my prayers, change certain situations... and sometimes, even "zap" certain individuals who have wronged me. The funny part is that this is part of our Christian growth. In persisting with prayer and communicating with God, His Holy Spirit convicts us where we have been wrong in our prayer life and our thought life. As we slowly begin to reform our prayers and the way we approach our Father in Heaven... A transformation takes place. We begin to give and surrender more and more of our own fears and control over to God. This in turn, builds our trust in Him as we watch God do miracles and make beautiful and unbelievable things out of our mediocre lives!

Proverbs 16:9 says, "A man's heart plans his way, but The Lord directs His steps."

Picture this, – You are behind the wheel in the car of life. You are new at learning how to talk to God and trust Him. Jesus is in the passenger's seat. He is talking to you. You are winding up a hill on the interstate and a MAC truck comes and tries to run you off the road that you are traveling. As you see this MAC truck coming straight at you, you yell, "Jesus, save me!" In that moment, Jesus reaches over and takes the wheel of your life. He commands His angels to take charge of the oncoming truck and keep it from hitting you. With your eyes tightly shut, He guides your car to safety. Once the oncoming attacks and threats are over, you decide that you want control of the wheel again.

Your Heavenly Father will always be there to run your life and take over the wheel. He just needs your permission. He is a gentleman and will never force His ways upon you. He tells us that He will never leave us or forsake us. (Hebrews 13:5). We humans are so thick-headed and stubborn. We endure divorce, job loss, and lack of sleep, homelessness, cancer, car accidents, loss of friendships, multiple health issues and even more before we begin to learn to trust our Heavenly Father with our lives. How tragic that it takes us so long to trust our lives in His capable hands.

"He who trusts in The Lord, happy is he." Proverbs 16:20

God wants you to flourish! He has blessings and victory for your life that you may never know until you ask Him to take over. (Matthew 7:7). Asking God to take over is not a sign of weakness... but a hallmark of strength and trust!

"Never underestimate God's ability to act in our puny lives!" -Jaimie Rasmussen (Senior pastor at SSBC in Scottsdale, AZ)

"Dear Father, I beg forgiveness for trying to plan my life without asking You first. I know that when trying to plan for the future, I will now say, "If it is Gods will... I will go here or do this." Lord, You have created me. You know the beginning from the end. You know which basketball team or football team will win each season... and I have no idea. You are the true source of all wisdom and understanding. You have created me and I will give my life to You and ask that You direct it as You see fit. I know that all I am guaranteed is today. Lord, please take control of today and use me to help others. Amen"

Did you know that it is considered "Prideful" when we try to live our lives independent of God?

"Any life that is not lived out in willing dependence on God is motivated by pride." -Derek Prince

"Whoever exalts himself will be humbled." Matthew 23:12

The very subtle deception of "pride" is the desire to be "independent" of God. Lucifer fell into this trap of thinking he was better and more powerful than God. Isaiah 14:12-21. Millions of people today are guilty of the sinfulness of "pride". The boastful pride of this life is living as if it is "all about me"!

Instead ...our goal as true "Children of God", could be portrayed as living our lives with God at the center of everything. The results of pride are always predictably the same, ending in rebellion and disaster! Pride and rebellion never go with obedience. Pride is a barrier that keeps God from working inside of our hearts and lives. The story of the prodigal son in Luke 15:11-32 reveals a young man who is self-centered, independent and self-sufficient. Sadly, these are all traits that our world looks on as "admirable". We must be intentionally God-centered in order to escape this trap of deception. God did get this young man's attention through trials and troubling times. Through similar trials and hardships...many a man or woman who has forgotten God has been stopped in their tracks and had to re-evaluate their ways. *"Blessed is trouble when it directs ones' heart back to God."- E.M. Bounds*

"Dear Father, my heart is breaking because I know that I am guilty of trying to run my life without You. I am horrible at relationships and Lord, I don't really know how to run my life. I need your guidance and direction. Please remind me that You are the One who created me. You own all of my possessions and my family is Yours and You know my heart and needs better than I do. Lord please show me what You want me to learn from all of this trouble. Please take the Pride out of my heart...and anything else that is not of You. Amen"

Were you aware that Pride can prevent us from having a relationship with our Heavenly Father… and will keep us from being effective leaders?

It seems that "stressful situations" do not build character, however, they bring out the "pride" and other things that we have not given to God. King David knew this very well. **Psalm 10-13 is David's conversation with God about being a sinful human. "Create in me a clean heart, O God, and renew a right spirit within me. Do not cast me away from Your Presence, and do not take Your Holy Spirit away from me. Restore me to the joy of Your Salvation, and uphold me by Your Generous Spirit. Then I will teach transgressors Your ways, and sinners will be converted to You!"**

Contrary to popular opinion, most of the time, "stress" does not build character unless we are made aware of our ***"Unsanctified…or bad character traits"*** during the process. Most of the time, in our blind human state, we are unable to see our own areas of weakness, and don't listen to others if they hold us accountable and point out these weaknesses.

Pride is usually the greatest offender. It can be a roadblock to restoring marriages, families, friendships and even church disagreements or disputes. Pride can even prevent us from growing spiritually and may eventually keep us from a relationship with God.

"Pride goes before a fall" Proverbs 16:18

33

"But avoid foolish and ignorant disputes, knowing that they gen-erate strife (stress). And a servant of The Lord must not quarrel, but be gentle to all, able to teach, patient, in humility correcting those who are in opposition, if God perhaps will grant them repen-tance, do that they may know truth, and that they may come to their senses and escape the snare of the devil, having been taken captive by him to do his will." 2Timothy 2:22-26

There are times when we all end up being stressed out at times and say things that are not thoughtful or respectful. It is a won-derful thing to have our loyal friends come alongside us and hold us accountable. The spirit of sincere humility and apology goes a long way! We cannot treat those around us with disrespect and careless-ness and not expect it to come back on us somehow. Each person that surrounds us has gifts and talents that God has bestowed upon them. Maybe they have come to you or me for mentoring...or maybe for guidance...perhaps for us to help them develop their talents and grow their hearts. We cannot help others or build them up if it is done in an unloving, ridiculing or demeaning way. These lovely ones have been entrusted into our care to "grow".

Psalm 51:17 says, "The sacrifices of God are a broken spirit, a broken and contrite heart— These, oh God, You will not despise."

You may wonder, why God loves a broken spirit and a contrite heart. **Because He is unable to use a proud and arrogant one.** Let me explain. There was a time in my life when I felt like I was "All That and a Bag of Potato Chips"!!! Early on in my thirties, I didn't realize that God was on the throne, and that He was actually the ONLY One that puts leaders into place. He also showed me that He was able to "dethrone" leaders as fast as He could put them into leadership–based upon their obedience and willingness to listen to His bidding. Little did I know that He is and was the only One that has the final say... And He is the only One that is worthy to be praised! I somehow began to grasp this as I was "dethroned" time after time...because I thought that it was "All about me"! It is true that 'The Teacher keeps coming back until the lesson is learned'!

Amazing things get accomplished when nobody cares who gets the credit! John Maxwell talks about leadership in his book, "How Successful People Lead". He says that all leaders must pass the trust "Trust Test". This involves 6 things:

1. Model and live consistency of character. Solid trust can only be developed if people can trust you all of the time.
2. Honest Communication. This means that your words and your actions must match.
3. Value transparency. If you are open and honest- admitting your weaknesses, people will be able to better relate to you.
4. Exemplify humility – people won't trust you if they see you are driven by ego, jealousy, or a belief that you are better than they are.
5. Put others first.
6. Fulfill your promises. One of the fastest ways to break trust is to fail to keep your commitments.

Zig Ziglar has it all straight in this statement, *"If you will help others get what they want, they will help you get to where you want to be."*

"We will know Peace when the "Power of Love" overtakes the "Love of Power".–Unknown

"Dear Father, I pray that You please take over my heart and mind and don't ever leave! I pray that you bring humility into my heart! I pray for Your blessing, strength, protection, and wisdom. Lord, move into my heart today. Please forgive me for my prideful self-focus and help me to keep my heart and eyes turned upon You! Please remind me that I can do nothing without You, and that You deserve all of the credit! Amen."

Chapter 2

"About...
Hope, Value and Joy"

*H*ave you ever marveled at the fact that the little children in Africa have more joy and hope in their lives than we do? Have you ever stopped to ponder what would happen if you didn't have a house, a car, or all of the possessions that you now have? I believe that we could possibly be filled with a lot more joy... and much less stress! However, the interesting thing that I found when faced with homelessness- was an inner peace that I can't even describe to you! It was in the knowing that my Heavenly Father was always there...and that He would never leave me or forsake me!

A.W. Tozer states this concept so eloquently! He says, **"The way to deeper knowledge of God is through the lonely valleys of soul poverty and abnegation (self-denial or self-sacrifice for the sake of other's benefit) of all things. The blessed ones who possess the kingdom are they who have repudiated every external thing and have rooted from their hearts all sense of possessing. These are the "poor in spirit". They have reached an inward state paralleling the** outward circumstances of the common in the streets of Jerusalem. That is what the word poor, as Christ used it, actually means. These blessed poor are no longer slaves to the tyranny of "things". They have broken the yoke of the oppressor; and this they have done- not by fighting, but by surrendering. Though free from all sense of possessing, they yet possess all things. 'Theirs is the kingdom of heaven.'" From his book, The Pursuit of God, pg 23.

What happens when life has lost its joy, its hope and you feel that you no longer have value? These are clearly symptoms of a huge lack of balance that could lead to depression and ruin. It may mean taking some time off from the frantic path that you have travelled to find the joy, hope and meaning that God has intended all along! It may involve re-examining your life, your past, your motives and your purpose, however, I guarantee that in the silence and fear of your quest, you will most likely find what you are looking for!

Matthew 6:33 & 34, "But seek first the kingdom of God and His righteousness, and all these things shall be added to you. Therefore do not worry about tomorrow, for tomorrow will worry about its own things."

"Life with Christ is an endless hope; without Him a hopeless end." – Unknown

Do you realize that you have someone to live for? ... His name is "Jesus Christ!"

Have you ever heard the song, "My Hope is built on nothing less than Jesus blood and righteousness..."? He died for our sins, changed the "odds" that were against us, and promised that He would never leave us or forsake us!

Psalm 71:5 "For You are my hope, O Lord God; You are my trust from my youth."

Some time ago, before leaving Nebraska, as I was teaching at a community college, I had the privilege of taking my students to a Center for addictions and substance abuse. I will never forget the bronze statue we saw. Our tour guide explained that this life-sized sitting bronze statue of a homeless man was created by a local artist. Then she said, "Now, look at his eyes. Do you see anything different? Notice how empty and vacant his eyes are?" As we all looked closer, it was very apparent how hopeless and empty this homeless man looked. The woman went on to explain that in their program, they were able to help individuals through the pain in their lives that they were trying to medicate with substances like alcohol, drugs, or sex. She said, "We show these people that there is hope for their addictions and they can and do have a purpose in life...and they are loved."

I realized that I had been in the same boat! It is scary to admit that I probably looked just as hopeless as this bronze statue. There was so much loss, pain and rejection in my life. I had gone through divorce, job loss, relationship loss, and became destitute and homeless. My own family had even tossed me aside like an old worn out shoe.   If someone were to look at me, I felt like there was no way that I could hide my sadness and brokenness. I had struggled with depression and prayed that God would help me through this difficult time. I was on my knees, crying out to God asking Him to help me. There were countless days when the evil one would whisper negative suicidal thoughts in my ear…, and believe me, it was tempting to just end the pain. I found great comfort in uplifting praise music and CD's that I had in my car. I also began to battle these evil thoughts with God's promises of hope, help and healing in His word. I finally realized that God's Holy Word started to make more sense… and I asked that God would show me how to live my life on this earth.

Before I truly found Jesus, I had told myself that "IF" I was successful, pretty and perfect at everything, I would be happy and loved by everyone around me.   That, however, was the furthest from the truth. My desire for "perfection" drove me a little crazy. When I was faced with "alone time or silence",… I really didn't know what to do with it. I realized that I didn't enjoy being alone! I didn't like being alone with myself. It seemed that during these times that the old tapes of doubt, shame, insecurity and dread would play in my head. Consequently, during my "alone" times I would run and do various things **instead of talking to God or reading the Bible…or instead of "being still", I would resort to:** (Does this sounds like you?)

- Clean the house from top to bottom.
- Turn on the radio or TV to drown out the silence.
- I would go work out or go for a jog.
- I would call up a friend and talk with them on the phone.

- I would volunteer to take food to someone in need or bake something for my family.
- I would do yard work.
- I would take a long drive around the neighborhood.
- I would go shopping.

These things were not ultimately bad things to focus my time and energy on; however, they kept me from filling my life with things that would bring me closer to Jesus Christ. I was not comfortable being alone with myself. I really didn't know who I was in Christ and I didn't love who I was or who God had created me to be. I didn't know how to begin my relationship with Jesus. I knew that something was missing in my life–and I really didn't know what "it" was!

Psalm 46:10 "Be still and know that I am God."

Below are a few things that will point you in the right direction if you are seeking God and having a hard time hearing Him because of all of the distractions: (they may take from a month or two ...or even up to several years to implement- depending on your level of commitment and determination to "hear God's voice". Remember, you are creating a whole new habit and way of thinking and living.) ***Start asking God, "What is it that is keeping me from hearing your voice?"***

1. ***Try eliminating all unnecessary activities, duties and noises from your life.*** Ask yourself if it is really necessary–or if it will help your relationship with God. I found that it was necessary to cut out T.V. entirely for a few years. Now David and I will record some of our favorite programs and watch them on the weekend.

41

I have decided to not listening to much on the radio, unless it was Christian Radio that pointed me to Christ. Because I wanted to grow towards Jesus more than anything else and didn't want anything to separate or distract me from Him. (You will need to discover what works to discipline your life.)

2. ***Carve out daily "quiet time" with Jesus.*** If the only time you have is 5 o'clock am before the kids wake up, or before work starts, then do it! Go to a spot somewhere in your home where you are comfortable and will not be distracted. I know that on many an occasion that God has spoken to me in the shower or while I was in my favorite recliner. What a blessing to begin to hear His voice speaking wisdom into your life! You won't regret it! This is a great way to begin to hear God talking to you!

3. ***God's word is His will. If you want to know your creator on a personal level, you will need to read up on Him in the Holy Bible that He left for us.*** There is tremendous wisdom and power when Gods word is implemented into our mediocre lives! God's word can transform any life into something beautiful! You might wish to consider memorizing scriptural promises that pertain to what you are going through. (B.I.B.L.E. is an acronym for 'Basic Information Before Leaving Earth'.)

4. ***Start talking to God about everything that is on your heart.*** He wants to be a part of your life! Look up promises in the bible for every worry or concern that you have. There is usually a topical index in the back of most bibles. Look up the things that are bothering you. Ask God to guide you, give you wisdom, and pro-tect you! Then wait in expectation for His answer to you! God loves you so very much! He wants more than anything in this

world to heal the painful memories, abuse, abandonment and neglect in your life!

God's Holy Spirit is poured out in power upon those who dare to take baby steps forward in faith. The minute that we say, "Father, I believe that you will handle this situation...and move forward in faith". HE WILL SHOW UP!!! (He always does, however, it is in His time and in His own way!)

You must remember that*," **You are valuable and loved! You are a child of the King!".*** This life begins to have true meaning and purpose once we stop focusing on ourselves and put God in charge!

"Dear God, My hope in this life is entirely based on You! I don't want to feel like my life is a mere existence! I claim my inheritance as your child this day! Please show me how to break the strongholds of pain that keep me from talking to You. Please show me your love and heal my wounded heart. I want to live my life to glorify and honor You! Amen"

Did you know that Jesus died for you? You are NOT disposable!!

Does it seem to you that our world, at times, views humans as "disposable assets"?

Relationships and people were at one time considered our world's most valuable resource! Now, in today's world, it seems that if you make one false move or one mistake in the workplace ,....soon you find yourself replaced with someone that can do things more perfectly. What has happened to, "teaching people how to do their jobs and mentoring one another, instead of expecting instant perfectionism?"

So, what is happening to our values today? Are we becoming a society that is so self- centered, perfectionistic and focused on our own needs... that we are unwilling or unable to love or journey and grow with others? Are we unwilling to help others heal? Are we so busy that we are "inconvenienced" by those who may need us to help carry their burdens for a short while? Are our own plates and backpacks so filled with the demands and cares of this world that we are unable to love ourselves ...much less anyone else?

I really believe that we all tend to get a little "apathetic" about things when we get too busy or overloaded. That is a serious problem if "Apathy" truly is described as the opposite of "Love". We begin to feel that we are so overloaded that we do not have the energy or the time to intervene in the lives of those around us. This is also another strategy of the Devil. He wants us to think that we won't be happy unless we are going through life at a pace that is not healthy. You and I need to seriously re-evaluate our lives if we do not have the time or the desire to love our selves or others.

Matthew 9:35-38 Talks about how Jesus went about all the cities and villages, teaching in synagogues and healing every sickness and every disease among the people. It says in verse 36, "But when He saw the multitudes, He was moved with compassion for them,

because they were weary and scattered, like sheep having no shepherd." He then mentioned to His disciples, "The harvest is plentiful, but the laborers are few. Therefore pray the Lord of the harvest to send out laborers into His harvest."

In a recent sermon, our Pastor Bob spoke about how we should be loving others from the overflow of love in our hearts. Some days, however, it does not seem that we have enough energy to make it through the day and meet the needs of our own families! I pray for an outpouring of the Holy Spirit into our lives that we may be filled with love, compassion, and a passion for others! My hope is that we begin to love ourselves enough to re-prioritize our lives and find fulfillment in doing what God has asked us to do! ...After all, our purpose on this planet is to make others' lives a little more bearable!

Galatians 6:2-3 "Bear one another's burdens, and so fulfill the law of Christ. For if anyone thinks of himself to be something, when he is nothing, he deceives himself."

Matthew 24:12 "And because lawlessness will abound, the love of many will grow cold."

"Dear Father, I pray that you would pour out a triple portion of your Holy Spirit into my heart! Fill me with the unconditional love, compassion, discernment, wisdom and endurance to help carry the burdens of others around me! Help me to see their wounded hearts and pick them up with Your help and carry them to safety! Dear Father, teach me to love others as You do! Teach me to have

the patience to journey with others. Thank you for taking my place on the cross. Amen"

Did you know that value and respect are essential to lead a well-adjusted and meaningful life?

Matthew 10: 30-31 "But the very hairs of your head are numbered. Do not fear, therefore; you are of more value than many sparrows."

In fact, these two attributes are becoming extinct in our homes and also in the workplace. It seems to be that pride and self ("It's all about me"), are the main culprits. To what lengths are you willing to go to attain value and respect? Brooks and Dunn sing a song entitled "Husbands and Wives" where they sing, "Pride is the chief cause of the decline in husbands and wives." It seems that marriages are declining because husbands and wives don't want to give value or respect to their soul mate. It seems as if people are afraid to value and respect one another as God has truly asked us to.

John Maxwell, author of "How Successful People Lead", states that in order for a leader to develop authentic relationships, the leader must be authentic. This means that they must admit their mistakes, own up to their faults and recognize their shortcomings. Sure, you can stay guarded and never get hurt, but then you will never have the chance to have deep, rewarding relationships that will enrich your life and the lives of others. It will limit the amount of influence and usefulness you will have in this life. Being guarded will put us in the wrong camp along with our very self-focused world.

Recently, a co-worker came up and said, "It feels so great to be appreciated!" It took me off guard for a second, and as tears welled up in her eyes and mine- we gave each other big hugs and again verbally expressed our mutual appreciation for each other. Wow! What a wonderful place to be! It leads me to believe that there will be no dictators in heaven. Our Heavenly Father is not only the ruler and creator of this universe, but He is also very relational! He loves you because you are you! He continually is saying, "Please come to Me, all I want to do is love you! You are valuable to Me!"

The whole chapter of Psalm 139 talks of his intimate knowledge of you and me!

"Oh Lord, You have searched me and known me.
You know my sitting down and my rising up;
You understand my thought afar off.
You comprehend my path and my lying down,
And are acquainted with all my ways.
For there is not a word on my tongue,
But behold, O Lord, You know it altogether.
You have hedged me behind and before,
And laid Your hand upon me.
Such knowledge is too wonderful for me;
It is high and I cannot attain it." (Psalm 139: 1-6 NKJV)

Know that you are valued, respected and loved by your Heavenly Father. He gave His very life for you!

"Dear Father thank you for loving me and valuing me as your Child! Even though I have suffered at the hand of abusive and wounded people, it is so great to know that You have a plan and a purpose for my life! Thank you for giving me value and dying for my sins! Dear Lord, Jesus, help me to believe in Your unconditional love for me! Amen."

Did you know that the Joy of The Lord is our strength?

That is right, a relationship with Jesus will make our hearts joyful! There is a certain old hymn that sings of the joy of The Lord and how our Joy in being His child becomes our strength!

In 1 Thessalonians 2:19-20 Paul says," For what is our hope, or joy or crown of rejoicing? Is it not even you in the presence of our Lord Jesus Christ at His coming? For You are our glory and joy!"

Joy is a huge part of being a child of God! I remember reading an article about an experiment that a physician had done with her patients one day. One day she concluded that most of the patients that she saw in the hospital and nursing home were lacking one thing...and that was joy! As she made her rounds, she intentionally asked each one of them, "What is it that brings you joy?" Her conclusions, unfortunately, were that over 90% of her patients didn't even know what might bring them joy. They were depressed and hopeless. Our lives without Jesus Christ are hopeless indeed! We are here on this earth to build our relationship with Jesus Christ! If we fail to do so…we will experience a certain "hell on earth" the Bible describes as "eternal separation from our Creator."

Oprah also did an experimental show on "Back to the Basics" where people lived with very little luxury, much like the pioneers who settled in our country. At the final conclusion of this show, most of these families that lived like the pioneers didn't want to come back to our culture as we know it today. They found that having to work very hard together in order to live had bonded their families so much closer together. There didn't seem to be any disciplinary issues that a little hard physical labor couldn't remedy. All of the hard physical labor and time spent together was exactly what the doctor ordered.

What is it that brings you joy? Have we lost the simple joy of living for Jesus? Have we become way too self-absorbed?

"We are only truly alive when serving others"-Rabbi Shmuley

"Dear Father, please bring back the Joy of living for You! Help me to never forget that I am only truly alive when serving others and glorifying You! Remind me daily, that it is our acts of kindness and generosity towards others that feed our souls and make our hearts grow bigger! My joy comes from living for You, Jesus! Amen"

Is your wounded heart robbing you of Joy?

This morning I got up early to read and chose one of Charles Stanley's books, "Living the Extraordinary Life". In chapter two, Stanley spoke of a time in his late 40's where he felt something was lacking in his walk with The Lord. He began to search his heart for anything that might be hindering his relationship with God, but was left with only a keen awareness of the void in his heart.

He then called four of his closest friends together and asked them for their help. The first night that they met, Stanley said that he shared every piece of personal information he could remember with his friends, talking for more than eight hours. Later, he stayed up all night filling seventeen legal-sized pages full of more intimate details of my life. The following morning, Stanley met with them again and shared more personal information he could remember with his friends. After some reflection, one friend asked Stanley to elaborate on the death of his father, who had died when he was 9 months old. After Stanley finished, he was asked to close his eyes. Then his friend said, "Picture that your father has just picked you up in his arms and is holding you. What do you feel?" Stanley said, "I cried, I felt loved, warm and secure. I had never felt the amazing depth of my heavenly Father's love until then." Sometimes we need to reach out and get professional, Christian help to deal with the pain from our past. If we can do this, God will reward our search for healing and heal our hearts!

For years, just like Stanley, many of us likely have experienced a distant and joyless relationship at some point with our Savior, almost as if some personal sin was keeping Him away. However, this is the biggest lie and strategy that the devil uses today! Nothing can separate us from our Heavenly Father's love!

God's word says, **"For I am persuaded that neither death nor life, nor angels nor principalities nor powers, nor things present nor things to come, nor height nor depth, nor any other created thing, shall be able to separate us from the love of God which is in Christ Jesus our Lord." Romans 8:38, 39**.

Paul talks of a time where Christians lost their Joy of living because it became "All about the rules". Jesus, our Lord has wiped that slate clean and has proclaimed, "It is truly all about your relationship with Me!"

"Dear Father, heal my heart and continue to swoop me up in Your arms and hold me. Continually remind me today and always that it is not about the rules, but it is about my relationship with You. Please remind me to keep looking up at You so that I am obedient and every ready to act when one of your children is needing support! Amen"

Did you know that the very lack of encouragement can hinder a person from living a healthy and productive life?

-"When a person feels encouraged, he can face the impossible and overcome incredible adversity."–John C. Maxwell.

-Encouragement is "Oxygen to the Soul"–George M. Adams

-Poet T.S. Elliot asserted: "Half the harm in the world is done by people who want to feel important."

Maxwell tells a story in his book, "Becoming a Person of Influence", about a school teacher who had taught the third grade and had also taught junior high math. She mentioned that one Friday in her classroom, things didn't feel right. She had been working on a new concept all week and had sensed that her students were growing frustrated with themselves and each other. She asked her students to take out 2 sheets of paper and write each student's name down, leaving some space between each name. She then had each student think of the nicest thing they could say about each of their classmates and write it down. It took the remainder of the class period for the students to complete this assignment. However, they handed in their assignments one-by-one. Over the weekend, the teacher combined each list. She then gave each student their list of attributes that Monday morning. The students were notably excited about the positive things that each had accumulated.

....Years later this school teacher had been asked to attend the funeral of one of the boys that had been in her math class. This young man, Mark, was killed in Vietnam. After the funeral, Mark's parents came up to his math teacher and said, "When Mark was shot–he had this on him. We thought that you would like to see it." Marks parents then unfolded an old rumpled list of his strengths and attributes. As his classmates gathered around, they each started confessing that they also had kept their lists and placed them in photo albums or kept them in special places.

We never know the impact our encouragement may have on someone's life. When people are made to feel secure, important, and appreciated, it will no longer be necessary for them to whittle down others in order to seem bigger in comparison.

"Dear Father, help me to treat others as I would want to be treated. Help me to "Believe" in someone and help them find the path that You would have them walk! Lord, please help me to always find ways to encourage others to live the best life they can and to trust in You! Amen"

"What" or "Who" is your hope in?

Are you discouraged or depressed? Where does your "Hope" lie? Is it grounded in something or someone Rock solid? Is your "hope" in your own ability? Is your hope in a certain football team, soccer team or basketball player? Do you feel as if you are invincible? Are you trying to be "superman" or "superwoman"? What are your Hopes and Aspirations in this life?

Psalm 25:5 "Guide me in your truth and teach me, for you are God my Savior, and my hope is in You all day long."

Hebrews 6:19 says, "This hope we have as an anchor of the soul, both sure and steadfast, and which enters the Presence behind the veil."

Do you believe that if you do everything perfectly that you will be successful?

What is the hope that you hang your hat on when everything around you is crumbling?

What keeps you going and motivated to put one foot in front of the other day after day?

Have you heard the hymn, "My hope is built on nothing less than Jesus' blood and righteousness"? This hymn was written by Edward Mote, who grew up in London, England, the child of innkeepers. At the age of 16, he genuinely became a converted follower of Christ after being mentored by a cabinet maker. The rest of his life was a testimony to his love and purpose for Christ. He became a pastor and wrote many hymns! The lyrics of this hymn are as follows. They are full of hope!

> My hope is built on nothing less
> than Jesus' blood and righteousness.
> I dare not trust the sweetest frame,
> but wholly lean on Jesus' name.

Refrain:
> On Christ the solid rock I stand,
> all other ground is sinking sand;
> all other ground is sinking sand.

2.   When Darkness veils his lovely face,
> I rest on his unchanging grace.
> In every high and stormy gale,
> My anchor holds within the veil.
> (Refrain)

3.   His oath, His covenant, His blood
       Supports me in the whelming flood.
       When all around my soul gives way,
       He then is all my hope and stay.
       (Refrain)

4.   When he shall come with trumpet sound,
       O may I then in Him be found!
       Dressed in His righteousness alone,
       Faultless to stand before the throne!
       (Refrain)

"Life with Christ is an endless hope; without Him a hopeless end." – Unknown

Jesus Christ is the ONLY One that has full control of your life! Here is how I know! I was at a crossroads in my life. I knew that I had to choose… either to reach out to Jesus and grab His hand… or to end my life of misery. I began to make choices to trust God… instead of just staying and wallowing in the misery and dysfunction. I wanted to get healthy, to have a joyful life of hope. I left everything that was familiar and started over. I began questioning every value that I ever had. I started reading the Bible and every book that I could get my hands on that might help me get through the pain. I could see the hypocrisy of how I had been brought up believing that God was all about the rules. I saw that the words of many friends and family that I was spending time with… didn't match their actions. This caused me to start looking at my own life- and I decided **that I didn't want to be a hypocrite.** I asked that God would help me be a woman of my word...and that I would also be a woman of action. I wanted my words and my actions to match up.

- I started praying to God every time I was fearful or anxious.

- Every time I lost my keys, my phone, or wasn't sure if I had enough money for food... I ran to God.

- I ran to Him with every moment of anger, discouragement and sadness when friends, family or coworkers tried to make life miserable.

- I ran to Him with my joblessness, health issues, problems with my children, and when my car was out of gas and I had no money. I found with every predicament, situation or crisis, that I started asking God what I was supposed to learn from it. Don't EVER give up when this life is way too stressful and caving in on you!!! Reach out to your Father in Heaven!   Pray and ask Him to send someone to help you through this dark time in your life!   He will!

Isaiah 40:31 "...But those who hope in The Lord will renew their strength. They will soar on wings like eagles; they will run and not grow weary, they will walk and not be faint."

If you are not in a good place today and the old thoughts and tapes are playing in your mind...the ones of discouragement, unworthiness, or possibly telling you that you are not valuable or that no one loves you... this is a SPIRITUAL BATTLE for your very soul!! (Ephesians 6:12-13)! Negativity does not come from God!

Follow these steps to shake the old tapes of negativity!!

1. Tell yourself to STOP thinking those thoughts that are not pure and wholesome! Negative self-talk is not from God.
2. Rebuke the devil and tell him to leave and stop feeding you lies!
3. Find a Godly person to pray with you and for you. Find someone to hold you accountable. You will need people to journey with you...and mentor you. Pray and ask God to send someone like this into your life! ...He will!
4. Ask Jesus to come into your heart and mind. Tell the Devil that you are a child of Your Heavenly Father.
5. Remember, if you are tempted to take yourself out of this world... or you possibly think that you are not valuable. Just remember that your life was never yours to take. Your Heavenly Father created you in His image and loves you so much that He died on the cross for you!
6. Get out of your isolation. (The Devil loves to attack you when you are alone, tired and vulnerable.) Start going to church, praise services and reaching out to others for help! You were made to fellowship with others and talk about your pain. We were made to need each other! Go have coffee with a friend.
7. Start memorizing Scripture and promises to replace the negative thoughts. Scripture is the only way to win this spiritual battle!

(2 Timothy 2:7 "For God has not given is a Spirit of fear, but of power and of love and of a sound mind."). 2 Timothy 3:16 says, "ALL SCRIPTURE IS GIVEN BY INSPIRATION OF GOD, AND IS PROFITABLE FOR DOCTRINE, FOR REPROOF, FOR CORRECTION, AND FOR INSTRUCTION IN RIGHTEOUSNESS..."

Whatever your story is today... Know that you are loved, valuable, and that God created you with a defined purpose! God doesn't create "junk"!!!! Start asking Him to show you what His purpose is for your life! Your hope is in Jesus Christ! He is NOT dead! He is alive and performing miracles in people's hearts and lives today! Let Him show you His love for you!

I encourage you to listen to one of Steven Curtis Chapman's new songs, 'Glorious Unfolding'. I encourage you to look it up on "You-Tube" and listen to the encouragement that he sings about! He wrote this whole album after his daughter was accidentally killed by his own teenage son when he backed over her with his vehicle. You will be encouraged, amazed and brought to tears... Because, just as Steven Curtis Chapman's song says, "Your journey is just beginning...this is only the beginning!!

"Dear Father, thanks for Your ever present hand in my life! Please continue to guide me and make my path very apparent. Give me hope for today and strength for tomorrow. Help me to always have an expectant HOPE in You! When life gets really tough and unbearable... Help me to turn to Your Holy Word for encouragement, peace and instruction. Please continue to walk beside me through these storms of my life! Amen"

Did you know that "Joy" is not a feeling, but a state of mind?

Nehemiah 8:10 says..."Do not sorrow, for the joy of The Lord is your strength." *(Strength here, refers to a place of refuge, safety, and protection)*

Just prior to saying this, Nehemiah, the governor, had just witnessed Ezra, the scribe, reading the book of the Law of Moses to the Israelites. The Israelites continually said, "Amen," with their faces bowed to the ground. Verse nine says that, "they wept and mourned, for after hearing the high standards of the law, they realized their low standing before God. Nehemiah, Ezra, and the Levites were undoubtedly glad to see the conviction of the Israelites; however, they wanted the Israelites to get past their feelings and communicate with and worship God. They directed the people to fellowship and share with one another their sins and joys in true worship to their creator." Wow!! It sounds like a big counseling session where God's healing was alive and well. He did instruct the Israelites that He no longer wanted them to be in mourning. He instructed them to be joyful in the Lord! Our Savior did this, because He wants us to be joyful, thankful and grateful in all things...even trials...and even when we have made poor choices and are paying the consequences!

The powerful secret of joy is that even when Paul and Silas were bleeding and thrown in jail, they began to sing and be grateful and joyful. This very act of praise in the midst of persecution, unleashes God's power!!! Amazing isn't it?!! (You can find this story of Paul and Silas in Acts 16:16-40.)

I know this is difficult to do, however my friend, don't let your past, anything in the present or any future concerns or anxieties steal your joy! I remember several occasions when I was robbed of the "Joy" of The Lord. On one particular occasion, I remember the feelings that came over me. I had been living with a couple in their home after giving up my apartment due to increased rent and low salary. I had been renting a room from them for 400.00 per month, helping with groceries, and cleaning the house. However, my job was terminated, and I was not able to pay them for the last month. I was actively looking for work, however, little did I realize, even though the agreement was that everyone would be honest and open about things, the wife had not come to me, but expressed to another mutual friend that she wanted me out of their home. I suspected that there was a margin of jealousy involved and she didn't like the fact that I was at their home so much while I was looking for a job. She had expressed to another friend that she was getting to the point of doing bodily harm to me.

I had no idea that this was transpiring. My friend, Kara, phoned me and told me she was on her way over. She mentioned that she needed me to pack up clothes, shoes, and stuff that I would need because I was coming to live with them. She said, "I will fill you in when I get there." In a state of shock, I started packing and throwing shoes and clothes into a laundry hamper. The tears started coming. I sat down on the bed and instead of praising God for Kara and a way out... I had a pity party about having no one and nowhere to go! I didn't look at what God was doing! All I felt was rejection, abandonment, and a huge lack of human love and acceptance. I was so grateful for the offer of shelter that was given to me by this wonderful woman and her husband with such compassionate hearts! I owe them so much for their kindness and generosity!

Our Joy is a God-given gladness found when we are talking to God daily. He truly is our Refuge and Strength!

"Dear Father, thank You for the Joy and peace-of-mind that you give! I so depend upon Your Strength and Your Promises to fill my heart so that fear, doubt, anxiety, rejection and depression cannot creep in and overwhelm me. Help me to remember to praise You and be joyful in You – even if I don't know where I will live or what my assignment will be! I pray that You fill my heart and soul with the joy and peace of mind that You will never leave me or forsake me! Amen"

Did you know that Jesus Christ is risen...and He is the only God that is still alive today?

"There is no medicine like hope, no incentive so great, and no tonic so powerful as the expectation of something better tomorrow!"
-Orison Swett Marden

The first of the Ten Commandments listed in **Deuteronomy 5:7 says, "You shall have no other Gods before Me."** There are many in this world today that dabble in Buddhism, Chakra, and worship many other Gods. The problem with this is that God goes on to say that He is a jealous God. There is a story that is told in 1Kings 18: 17-46 that tells a story of the battle between the false Gods of Baal and the true God, Jehovah. It is a great read and tells of the inability of the false Gods of Baal to have the power to do anything! Elijah, However, called on the name of God, the great Jehovah,...and fire came down and consumed the sacrifices that were upon the altar. The fire not only consumed the sacrifices, but also consumed the water that was around the altar. I encourage you to read the story and you will see that our Savior, Jesus Christ, is the **only God** that has risen from the dead and is deserving of our worship and praise! The irrefutable facts exist that point to a "living God" that has power over death! There is no other God like our God!

I can't think of a more exciting conversation to have about our God and Savior!!!! It is difficult to fathom that Jesus sacrificed his own life for me and YOU...then He rose from the dead! *Our GOD is the only God who has conquered the grave and is alive and well today!!* You may have seen the recent movie, "God's not dead!" This movie is an incredible tribute to God and His power to act in our lives! It portrays the battle that faces many college students today in the secular world. Our God can still win our battles today! It is our job to 'Believe' that He can!

Jesus is our only source of life, hope, and strength. Our job is to call on His name, the name of "Jesus"! He is always willing to turn our lives into something beautiful!

"Jesus, thank you for your unselfish sacrifice for my sins. I thank You for dying on the cross for me. Thank You for never giving up on me! I ask You to take up permanent residence in my heart! Change me

from the inside out and please take the other Gods in my life and replace them with You! Amen."

Did you know that our days are numbered,...and we need to live out each day with Hope, Joy and Purpose?

Ecclesiastes 3:1, 2. "To everything there is a season, a time for every purpose under heaven: A time to plant, and a time to pluck what has been planted."

Each one of us will die someday. However, our greatest tragedy is not death itself, but life lived without purpose. My father-in-law recently passed from this earth and as one woman so eloquently put it, "he graduated into heaven". So, naturally, the topic of our human mortality has been at the forefront of my mind. It is true that many times, we do not consider what our true purpose is until we are on our death bed. I am hopeful that you will take some quiet moments to have conversation with your creator. Ask Him to bring you great joy into your daily living, and to show you what your purpose is in this life.

In Rick Warrens book, "What on earth am I here for", he says," Hope is as essential to our lives as air and water. You need Hope to Cope. "

Dr. Bernie Siegel found he could predict which of his cancer patients would go into remission by asking them, "Do you want to live to be one hundred?" Those with a deep sense of purpose answered an emphatic, "Yes"! The American people struggle with their sense of purpose in life. Currently our society has an unbalanced emphasis on productivity, overstimulation and lack of balance. Caffeine use is at an all-time high. Depression is running rampant among young and old. Primary causes are due to a lack of balance, lack of sleep, lack of feeling valued and nurtured. On a recent radio broadcast of Charles Stanley's, he said that a young man in his 20's had told him, "I feel like a failure because I'm struggling to become something, and I don't even know what it is. All I know is how to get by. Someday, if I discover my purpose, I will feel like I am beginning to live." Charles Stanley stated in his broadcast, that his prayer for his children is that they will find their purpose early in life so that they won't waste their years on futility.

Charles Stanley, in one of his radio broadcasts has mentioned the following steps to help guide you to find your purpose in this life:

1. Has God brought you through some horrific trials or near death experiences? Pray and ask Him to open your eyes and show you your purpose in this life.
2. Do you have a passion to help other people? If so, how could God utilize you in this area? Pray that God will give you a testimony that will touch many hearts for His kingdom.
3. What things are you passionate about? Pray for passion in your life- because without it, it is even hard to get out of bed in the morning. Meaningless work wears us down, saps us of our strength and robs us of our joy.
4. Knowing your God-given purpose will prepare you for eternity and a life with God. These things are usually beyond the disposable trophies that can end up in the trash, degrees or

accomplishments that no one cares about, or any amount of money that might make us feel like a VIP for a very short time.

In Erickson's stages of Life- the most difficult stage is "integrity vs despair". Which typically hits us around our 70's to 80's. This is when we look back on our lives and ask ourselves, "What did I do with my life?" "Did I help anyone or impact their lives...or was my time totally wasted as I was trying to make ends meet?" "Was I selfless... Or selfish?" "Did I get upset if someone inconvenienced my schedule...or did I clear my own schedule to accommodate someone else's needs?" I encourage you to start spending some quality time with God. Ask Him to use your life to impact others. Ask Him for what you need. He will!!

"Dear Father, I am so very sorry that my life has gotten so far out of control. I pray that You would forgive me for making poor choices. Lord, I ask that you show me what your purpose is for my life. I know that I have not spent much time talking to You, however, Lord, if there is any hope or purpose for my life, I pray that you open doors and make it very apparent. Please help me find purpose in life before I am too old. Lord, help me to fix my eyes upon You. Amen."

Chapter 3

"About...Pain, Suffering and Crisis"

At some point in our lives, we all come to realize that this life is not without pain, suffering and hardships. As God's children we can expect it! However, I was not told, mentored or forewarned by a soul that the Devil would be on my tail like a fly on flypaper! This is in fact what began to happen in my life when I stopped being a Christian in word and started being a Christian of action. It seemed as though all of my so-called, "Christian friends" became very scarce when I walked away from my beautiful home on 5 acres, and filed for a divorce. Even my own family was more than happy to toss me out like a worn- out shoe. The bible says that we can expect these things to happen.

1 Peter 4:12 & 13 says, "Beloved, do not think it strange concerning the fiery trial which is to try you, as though some strange thing happened to you; but rejoice to the extent that you partake in Christ's sufferings, that when His glory is revealed, you may also be glad with exceeding joy."

"The truth will set you free, but it will not be pain free!" –
Jewish Carpenter

The brutality of "pain" is that it is not pleasant, however, the friends
that dare to journey with you to this place are ones that will last a
lifetime. Many times the pain and discomfort of suffering and crisis
are the only things that are able bring us to our knees and crack
open our hearts of stone.

**A.W. Tozer said it so eloquently in his book, Pursuit of God, pg 28
& 29.** He tells of Abraham's story of God asking him to sacrifice his
only son. God was truly testing Abraham's heart and his priorities.
Through the extreme pain that Abraham went through- as his son
was lying on the altar ready to be sacrificed- an angel was sent to
keep him from killing his son with a sword. This was Abraham's crucible of fire! **Tozer's interpretation of what God said after this trial
was this; "It's alright Abraham, I never intended that you should
actually slay the lad. I only wanted to remove him from the temple
of your heart that I might reign unchallenged there. I wanted to
correct the perversion that existed in your love. Now you may have
the boy, sound and well. Take him and go back to your tent. Now
I know that you fearest God, seeing that thou hast not withheld
thy son, thine only son, from Me."**

What is it that is causing you to have pain and suffering in your life?
Is it your own poor choices, generational sin that was passed down
through the generations...or just your plain and simple lack of integrity and wisdom? Have you caved in to peer pressure ...and are you
even aware that God's Holy Word has all of the instructions for living

life to the fullest on this earth? How has God been trying to get your attention? Whatever you are going through right now- is your personal journey of 'wrestling with God'. It cannot be done by anyone but you! ***What a blessing when our pain brings us to our knees... because only then do we truly see our need for Jesus Christ!***

Dear Father, I am so very tired of the pain and suffering in my life! Please show me where it is all coming from and what I need to do to change things! Take this pain in my life and use it to change me from the inside out. Lord, show me what I need to learn from this so that I can be a light in the darkness for others that will go down this same path of suffering. I pray this in the precious name of Jesus, Amen."

Have you ever wondered why it seems that God waits to show up until we are desperate or experiencing pain?

Deuteronomy 4:29 says, "But you will find Him if you seek Him with all your heart and with all your soul."

...The truth is, sometimes we don't call on Him until it is painful and there is no way out.

Researchers have proven that we humans are much more likely to remember the painful events in our lives than the 'smooth-sailing' events. Dr. Larry Crab states in his book, "Connecting", that total strangers can bond much faster if facing an adverse event together. Bill Hybels, in his book, "Courageous Leadership", talks about how our 'crucible' moments in life can be so important in keeping us humble and useful people to God and society.

I know that there have been numerous occasions when God chose to allow me to sweat profusely and pray in desperation for Him to show up. God wants us to be "desperate" for Him. He created everything about our nature, and He knows that if life is nothing but sunshine and smooth-sailing, that we will not be well-rounded, humble or obedient people..., and we will not grow in our trust of Him. Our heavenly Father is very relational...and wants us to trust Him and believe in Him 100%.

I remember one of these "crucible" moments in life where I wasn't sure if I was going to land on my feet or just take a nose dive. One weekend, while at church, I had an amazing answer to prayer! I had driven all week on nothing but fumes in my gas tank. My prayer had been, "Dear Father, Please fill my gas tank with Your Holy Spirit." "I believe that You are able to make my car run- even though I have no money for gas!" My little car had literally operated on air that entire week. As I sat in the church pew, ready to get up and sing, I remember having asked God to provide for my needs- because it would be another week before I would be able to put gas into my car. As I sat there listening to the pianist and turning my heart towards God, this wonderful woman in her 50's slipped into the pew behind me and discretely handed me a twenty dollar bill. I remember my heart being so thankful. I turned to her with tears in my eyes and whispered, "Thank you for your kindness!" God can provide for His children's needs without us taking an ad out in the paper. When I asked her later about what prompted her to give me twenty dollars, she just said, "I know that you are in a very difficult time in your life right now and God directed me to give this to you today." Wow!! God didn't intend that we sit out on street corners with cardboard signs, rob a bank, prostitute our bodies or sell drugs to get our needs met. God is fully aware of your needs, and if you start asking Him, He will not let you down. He becomes much more real to us during crisis times in our lives. He has all of the resources imaginable...along with an amazing network of children who love to do His bidding. I guarantee that He can make anything happen in your life if you will only get to know Him. Start asking and believe! (Matthew 7:7) On the "flip side", God will expect us to be good stewards of our money. He will not provide money for drugs, alcohol, and promiscuous addictions, but He is faithful to those who love Him and obey His word.

God says in Hebrews 10:16-17 "I will put My laws into their hearts, and in their minds I will write them. Their sins and lawless deeds I will remember no more."

Our Heavenly Father wants us to learn to trust Him. **"<u>Desperation is the indelible ink of our "journey of faith" that will inscribe upon our hearts and minds that our Father will never leave us or forsake us.</u>" – K Land.** He is worthy to be praised and He is to be trusted above all others!

"Father, as I grip your hand tightly through these fiery trials, please do not let go! I do not want to fall back into the pit of despair! I will keep focused on the light of Your face and Your promises. I am desperate for You! I can't do this day without You. Amen"

Can Crisis bring us to God?

The answer is "Absolutely!" Have you ever become really good friends with someone who may have helped you through a difficult time in your life? It almost seems that many times during these stormy crisis situations (The ones that we really never signed up for)...we are left with no choice except to trust Jesus. He is always in close proximity and is available and willing to help us. It does make one feel rather vulnerable when trusting someone that we don't know very well. However, the Bible talks about this too! This is called faith. When we believe that Jesus will do what He says He will do...without proof beforehand,...this is the definition of true faith. God wants to earn our trust by proving that He can answer our prayers, however, sometimes we will have to take a baby step forward in faith first.

Psalm 37:5 "Commit your way unto The Lord, trust also in Him, and He will bring it to pass." Proverbs 3:5-6 says, "Trust in The Lord with all your heart, and lean not on your own understanding; in all your ways acknowledge Him, and He shall direct your paths."

Our creator and Father wants desperately to have a relationship with us. Are we desperate enough...and is the pain bad enough that you are willing to try God? Don't reject His whispers to your heart! Are you willing to sacrifice everything to have a relationship with your savior? Are you willing to sacrifice your favorite TV show, Monday night football or some other hobby to just "sit in His presence and listen for His voice?" As the trials keep coming...you and I will have ample opportunity to get to know Jesus. Being this broken has truly has humbled my heart and made me realize that I never want to lose Jesus again! He has saved me from myself and loves me with all of His heart. He gave his life on the cross so we could live!

"Dear Jesus, I fall on my face before You! I thank You so much for always loving me as Your own Child. Please surround me with Your presence and help me to have unwaivering faith in You! I know that I am loved more than I am able to comprehend! Please continue to heal my heart so that it can hold all of the love and blessings that You have for me. Amen"

Have you heard the Phrase "No Pain–No Gain?"

How do we get over the pain of life? Yep, I know all too well about the part of our human nature that does not want to endure painful things, memories or circumstances.... I was around one family member that didn't like to be reminded of pain. When I was searching for answers, she would say, "Every time you come over... you are constantly bringing up the trash...or airing out the family laundry." This person didn't realize that I wanted to get to the bottom of my family dysfunction so that I could break the cycle of pain and sin. So God intervened and has shown me the Generational sin, my parent's sins and pain and other things that I would need to know in order to "Break the Cycle"!

-Most of us don't like to hear criticism or re-live things that make us see where we have been.

-We don't like to re- live painful events in our lives because it causes tears, pain, anger, regrets, and sometimes depression.

-Sometimes there are situations of physical, emotional or sexual abuse that cause so much trauma and pain that our brains actually can block up to 10 years or more from our memory, until we are strong enough to deal with things. (This is a defense mechanism that is built in to each one of us.)

Years ago I worked with a great nurse who had been sexually molested by her father. As we sat and talked one day at our lunch break, she shared that her father would have his way with her and then say, "If you talk to anyone about this, I will kill you." The nurse said that she was most likely between the ages of four to six years of old. As we talked during our lunch break one day, she shared that one morning when she woke up and opened her window shade to let the sun in, her beloved, favorite cat hung, strangled at the end of a rope in front of her window. Her father had done this to her cat to reinforce what he would do to her if she talked.

This wonderful woman started to cry and then told me about the incredible fear this caused. She explained that this fear actually took her voice away for several years and she was physically unable to utter a sound. Fear and belief in her father's threats had taken its toll on her life and had enough power to shut down the speech center of her brain. She went on to say that her church family had taken her in and that she was trying to get as much help as possible to heal.

"Dear Father, I know that there is no way around the pain. I understand that my only hope at being whole and free is to face the truth and be set free with Your love and Your strength. Please hold my hand as I start taking baby steps towards You. Father, I am on my knees begging You to heal my broken heart, mind and body. Please hear my cries for help because You are my only Hope! Please send someone to help heal the brokenness and show me what Your love looks like. Amen"

Did you know that all "sin" is trying to fill a legitimate need in an illegitimate way?

Jesus is the ultimate healer of broken hearts, addictions and abusive pasts. His greatest desire is to help us fill the longings, the voids and deep wounds of our past. He has closed the door on all of our sin and dysfunction...and offers us a fresh new start each day! Are you up for the challenge? Are you going to change your life forever? This means no artificial ingredients are needed.

The antidote for our lives will read: None of the following are needed with Jesus at the wheel of my life! He is always enough. I will not permit any of the following things to take over the temple of my heart. I will abstain from the following things and put Jesus first in my life where He should be!

Alcohol
Food
Drugs

Sex

Work

Possessions

Pornography

Self-Centeredness

Other Gods

...Whatever might be a temptation that controls your life!

Just as Tozer said in his book, "In Pursuit of God", Pg 25. **"It's alright Abraham, I never intended that you should actually slay the lad. I only wanted to remove him from the temple of your heart that I might reign unchallenged there. I wanted to correct the perversion that existed in your love. Now you may have the boy, sound and well. Take him and go back to your tent. Now I know that you fearest God, seeing that thou hast not withheld thy son, thine only son, from Me."** Jesus wants to re-define our love for these things.

"Dear God help me to live out the values, integrity and purpose that You have for me so that my life is an authentic representation of You and Your Amazing Love and Grace. Please help me to not try to fix my own life with alcohol, drugs, sex, work or any other form of addiction. Please Father, help me to fill my life with You! Please guide and direct my steps. Help me to see evil coming and remind me how horrible it is without You in my life! Amen"

Did you know that pain and hurt in our lives can destroy us and wound others?

1 Peter 5:8-9 "Be sober, be vigilant; because your adversary the devil walks about like a roaring lion, seeking whom he may devour."

How strategic of the Devil! He doesn't even have to destroy us, because with enough woundedness and pain, we destroy ourselves and any potential that we might have had ...unless we can stop being prideful, self-sufficient, or in some cases we begin to feel unlovable, unwanted, unworthy or not good enough.

Most of mankind has been wounded in some way by relationships that are not fulfilling or are abusive. The result of this wounded-ness can lead us to build walls of protection around ourselves. The walls then will keep intruders and abusers out, however, these walls also keep us stifled and prevent us from growing the way God wants us to grow. The walls that we place around ourselves can prevent God from using us. Sometimes it can even derail us from the plans that God has for us. Essentially, it is important that we begin to uncover the pain and deal with it. This way, the healing can happen in our hearts and we can begin to start living life the way that He has always wanted us to. Gradually as our healing takes place, the light of Jesus will begin to shine through the cracks of our broken-ness and give others hope to keep living. Healing happens by living in vulnerability and the light of tuth.

If we can start facing our fears, get some professional, God-centered counseling, and address the pain that has happened in our lives, we may begin to stop the dysfunction that has held us hostage. This may be the opportunity of a lifetime-, for God to help us rewrite our life story! Only when we rely on Him can we begin to experience victory! Jesus Christ alone is our Protector, our Counselor, our Healer and our Best Friend! I truly believe that if we all stopped pretending to be perfect and dared to throw ourselves at Jesus' feet and beg Him to heal us... there would be a whole lot of rejoicing and singing in heaven! There is no man, woman or child on this planet that does not need Jesus. What have we got to lose?

Matthew 7:7 "Ask and it will be given to you; seek and you will find; knock and the door will be opened unto you."

"Jesus, I claim this promise over my wounded life and ask that You heal me! I am kneeling at Your feet- begging for Your Healing Hand on my life! Please start working on my Life of woundedness so that I won't wound or harm others! I can't do this on my own! Please send Your Holy Spirit and other people into my life to heal my wounded heart and soul! Please give me a total "re-do"! I want to be the kind of person that You want me to be! Amen"

Did you know that God never wastes a "test"?

There is always a reason for God allowing hardship and trials to enter our lives. We may not fully realize what lessons we are to learn from each situation until years later, however, **Romans 8:35 says, "Who shall separate us from the love of Christ? Shall tribulation,**

distress, or persecution, or famine, or nakedness, or peril or sword?" Nothing can separate us from the love of God!

"Blessed are the trials that drive us to our knees in prayer!"- EM Bounds

We all face trials and tests of all different magnitudes. Scripture tells us to welcome these tests and persecution,... for it is during these times that we learn to trust and rely on our Father in Heaven. Trials and afflictions can only work to grow us if we take each one to our Father in prayer.

"We rejoice in our sufferings, because we know that suffering produces perseverance; perseverance, character, and character, hope. And hope does not disappoint us, because God has poured out His love into our hearts by the Holy Spirit, whom He has given us." Romans 5:3-5

There was a time in my life where I thought that God was mad at me. I felt that I had a big bulls-eye target on my back! I had moments when I felt demons literally clawing into my back and tearing at my body. There was not one thing that was going right!

I remember back to when David and I were dating. There was one evening, as we were sitting outside on the deck by the fire, I looked over at him and said," I don't know if you want to hitch your wagon to mine just yet." I went on to explain that I had felt that "The devil had been on my tail." I shared with him several stories of persecution, trials and narrow misses where I knew that God had protected me from harm and even death.

I started explaining about my own family...and how they had abandon me when going through a divorce. I told him about having many different jobs over a period of 2-3 years before moving to Arizona. I explained that I was beginning to feel like "damaged goods", because I was rejected by everyone that mattered in my life, and I was also being moved from one job to another. I explained that it almost seemed that with each job, I was having to stand before my bosses and represent "truth" to them. In most of the situations they knew that they were being dishonest and didn't want to hear the truth. Then repeatedly, my boss would fire me and I would start looking for another job. I explained that I have a pretty good work ethic and believe that I did my best to honor my employers. However, as I knelt before my Heavenly Father and begged Him to show me what was wrong with me, and why I couldn't hold a job, He began to open my eyes to see that it wasn't my fault. It was the mere fact that He was using my life in some small way to try to reach my employers. He was trying to wake them up to the fact that they were ultimately accountable to Him for their unethical practices. And one day, God revealed to me, that when He calls them before His judgement throne...He will ask them, "Do you remember how you treated Karen Land (Karen Sharon at the time)?",..." I placed her in your office to remind you that I am still on the throne. How did you treat her when she worked for you?" I am convinced after experiencing these tests,... that God sometimes allows trials in our lives not only to grow us, but also to impact others around us.

As the conversation continued into the night, we sat under the stars and laughed and cried about the stories of God's providence in our lives, David turned to me and said, "I think you should know that if this works out between us, I am in this relationship for life, and I am not afraid to weather the storms with you." I remember bursting into tears and being so astonished at David's love and support for me. I had not experienced this kind of commitment of love and support ever before in my life! I don't know that I ever knew what true commitment and loving support looked like before. Thank God... David seemed to be unruffled and not even close to running away from me and the crazy trials and persecution that I had endured. This is what true Godly love is made of.

"All things Grow with Love"-Unknown

"It is while we are passing through deep waters that God shows how close He can come to His praying , believing saints."–E.M.Bounds

"Dear Father, I know that You test us to better understand the conditions of our hearts. You tried Abraham's heart and asked Him to sacrifice his only son, Jacob, in order to determine his priorities and obedience. Lord, please help me to always be in prayer through these trials of

of life. You have told us that Prayer is the only way to successfully make it through in one piece. Teach me to pray without ceasing! Amen."

What is it that you are pretending "isn't a problem" in your life?

Are there some deep, dark secrets in your life, or things that you do not want anyone else around you to know? Did you know that the longer you keep them hidden...the more power they have over your life? *"The mind grows by what it feeds on."- Josiah G. Holland*

The raw and honest truth is, whatever "we can't talk about" is most likely already way out of control in our lives already. Problems such as finances, marriage, children, secret habits, sexual addictions, abuse, negative thoughts and stress seem to grow into giant obstacles and turn into monsters. How do we deal with stress and feelings of hopelessness that this world imposes upon us? We can rebuild our lives on the Solid Rock, Jesus Christ... all other ground is like quick sand!!

James 5:16 says, "Confess your trespasses to one another and pray for one another, that you may be healed. The effective fervent prayer of a righteous man avails much."

Did you know that, *"Satan wants you to think that your temptations and sin are so unique that you must keep them a secret?" Rick Warren, "What on Earth am I Here For?"* **Pg 213**.

God has impressed upon my heart all week long...that there is a huge need to start talking about everything that is on our hearts!!! The most secure and well-grounded people in this life are usually the ones that are the most transparent! They are also the ones that read God's Holy Word. True godly people are full of the fruits of the Spirit. They are kind, gentle, humble and willing to take advice, direction, or even apologize when prompted to do so by the Holy Spirt. God wants us to be honest and open about our feelings and our lives! Do you talk about your feelings, your hopes, your fears, and your purpose? It is important that you talk with God about these things and that you have at least one person that you can talk to and who will hold you accountable.

We all have read about horrific suicidal events in the paper, we hear about these things in the news, and may even have had a close friend who has taken their own life. These acts are ones of desperation–and are irreversible. Most of the time they involve feelings of unworthiness, shame and self-hate, "I'm not good enough", and most likely, they have never come to know or accept God's true and unconditional love. It seems that there are growing numbers of individuals who are taking their own lives. Taking your life is NOT God's plan for you! God so wants us to come to the full realization of His amazing and non-judgmental love for us. **Our lives are not our own to take.** We were created in the image of God- and were given life for a reason. We were all made with the need for God. Sometimes our hearts yearn for Him and we do not realize what it is. The following are suggestions as to how to "de-stress" your life and bring back the joy and the balance that God intended for us to have:

1. *Slow down!* Take some of the stress out of your life! Start with all of the unnecessary activities or obligations. Pray about which ones to eliminate. Eliminate debt. Pay off bills and other obligations such as your car, house, etc.... It is difficult for all of us to

slow down to the place that we are able to sit in peaceful silence with our Creator. This can be an intentional act of spending quiet time in a designated spot in your home. It can also be taking a walk outside and talking with Your Father in Heaven as you walk. It can be doing your favorite hobby- like fishing or hiking or camping! Whatever your preferred choice is,...it is so very important that we learn to cultivate this attribute so that we can hear from our Heavenly Father anywhere we go! "Be still and know that I am God." Psalm 46:10

2. **Start paying attention to what you think about.** If it is negative, trashy or pure lies of low self-esteem, get rid of it! Tell the devil where to go! Tell him to stop and leave in the name of Jesus Christ! Start reprogramming your thoughts by memorizing scriptural promises that deal with whatever it is that you are facing. If you are dealing with fear, then memorize scripture that talks about fear! Our thoughts ultimately control our bodies. Philippians 4:6-9, 13.

3. **Don't pay attention to what others think.** Ultimately, the only opinion that matters is God's opinion. Start reading Gods word so that you will know what His opinion is. (God's word is His will.)

4. **Spend more time in prayer, talking to God about your feelings and thoughts.** Surround yourself with Godly friends that will pray with you and hold you accountable. **Don't live your life in isolation... Live it in community with your church family, friends and neighbors! Know that you are loved!**

We live in a world that has lost its way! All of us...men, women, children & teens alike are shown indirectly that if we aren't perfect and don't do all the right things, say the right things, live in the perfect house, get perfect grades, etc., that we aren't valuable and aren't worthy of love. This is so wrong!! We are valuable because Jesus died for you and me because He loves us so much!! God doesn't make junk!!

Consequently we have bought into all of these subliminal messages from our society that create huge amounts of stress and pressure that ultimately we were not made or equipped to handle on our own.

"Dear Father, I am so thankful to be Your Child! I continue to bask in Your amazing Love and Grace in my life! I pray that You shower me with Your Love for me, that I will live my life for Your Purpose! May I make a small difference in the lives of those around me today! Amen"

You can't "make it" if you "Fake it"!

Are you aware that God's Ultimate Goal for you on this earth is not your "Comfort", but for your "Character Development"?

The Bible says that we were all created in the image of God.

The scary facts are that our character equals the sum of our habits!! Wow!! Sanctification is actually the process of allowing God's Holy Spirit to change us and our daily habits to be more like Him. Rick Warren talks about this process of reprogramming, cleansing and reshaping our bodies and habits. *He says in his book, "What on Earth am I Here For?", "Becoming like Christ cannot be done on our own strength, but only by the power of the Holy Spirit as we take one baby step forward at a time in obedience. There is no way that we can "Fake it till you make it!"* Many Christians today, try to 'Fake it'! *Rick Warren states, "Christlikeness is not produced by imitation, but by inhabitation!"*

How can you start this process to become like Christ?

1. Ask Jesus into Your heart to stay. Tell Him that you want a brand new life!
2. Make the right choices. Choose to do the right things in **all** situations. If you don't know what is right, open God's word and find out. (God's Word is His will!)
3. Take one step forward in faith and obedience. God will wait for you to act first. Do not wait to feel perfect, strong or courageous. Don't just sit around and wait for it to happen.
   - let go of the old way of life!

   change your way of thinking. (Be transformed by the renewing of your mind)
   - put in the character (habits) of Christ.

I recently had a church member come up to me on the praise team. This person said, "You always look so joy-filled and happy when you sing!" My reply to her was, "My God has done so much for me! I had AIDS and He healed me, I was homeless and He provided for me, I was abandoned by my parents and He brought spiritual mentors into my life. I should be dead, but I am alive, and now I owe God EVERYTHING!" After the astonished look on her face, I said, "I know that was a lot of information in a very short space, however, I will praise Him until the day I die!" A huge smile spread across her face as I gave her a hug. There is nothing imitation about God's sacrifice for you and me on the cross!

"Father, I pray for this fire of Your Holy Spirit to be lit within me! I am asking that You come inside of my heart to live on a permanent basis. I know that change is hard, and there will be days when I want to turn and run. Please carry me through the storms! Help me to rely on Your strength and not my own. Please change my character to reflect Yours! Amen"

Did you know that physical suffering and scars produced during our journey in life can actually become beautiful blessings?

... Pain has the ability to transform and change our hearts and minds forever!!

Pain isn't pretty when you're in the middle of it. The scars that remain with us after the fact can either make us "bitter people" or "better people". Pain can produce hope, kindness, compassion and non-judgmental love if we allow ourselves to learn from these situations and circumstances.

There is no greater privilege that we have on this earth than to enter into someone's pain or crisis and help them. Through the painful situations or circumstances, if we are called to enter into someone's pain, God can pour out His powerfully activated ingredients of love, compassion, and healing! When the fruits of the Holy Spirit are poured out through our love and obedience, they have the capacity to heal other's hearts and lives...even our own!

1 Peter 4:12-14. "Beloved, do not think it strange concerning the fiery trial which is to try you, as though some strange thing has happened to you; but rejoice to the extent that you partake of Christ's sufferings. That when His glory is revealed, you may also be glad with exceeding joy! If you are reproached for the name of Christ, blessed are you, for the Spirit of glory and of God rests upon you."

I understand that no one in their "right mind" would "sign up" for painful things to happen in their lives. However, the pain, trials, inconvenience and suffering that we go through are the preparatory sandpaper that smooth out the rough edges of our character and personality. We actually can choose to have the privilege of being transformed into someone kinder, more compassionate, and more filled with God's Holy Spirit...or we can choose to not grow at all and become a negative, bitter and miserable person.

The beauty of when you start asking God to help you... is that you will find that He can do anything! He can transform you into a well-balanced, spiritually grounded person that He can use in any situation or circumstance! He may ask you to journey with others and rescue their tired and weary souls from the pit of despair and hopelessness. God uses your pain and suffering to witness to others and bring them closer to Him...all the while He is transforming you and me into more compassionate and loving people. God has great plans for your life!

Inevitably, we have several different ways to deal with the pain in our lives. Most of us stay too busy to think about the emotional hurt in our lives. Some of us run from our pain. And then there are others that have buried their emotional pain so deep that they are in denial that anything painful ever happened. Some individuals just "stick their heads in the sand" so they don't have to deal with their emotional pain or past abuse. Our incredible brains are capable of blocking out years of our lives to protect us emotionally and help us function until we are ready to face the pain.

God wants us to be able to look directly at the pain that comes into our lives, talk about it, ask Him what we are supposed to learn from it, cry about it... be vulnerable and willing to lean on others through it. And ultimately we may have to also get professional help to get over it. Pain comes into our lives for a reason and a season. If we don't learn the lessons the first time, the painful teacher will come back over and over again until we realize that God is in charge, we are not... and we are finally willing to learn the lessons and face the pain once and for all!

Laura Story, a Christian songwriter wrote a wonderful song entitled, "Blessings". This song speaks of how our darkest moments and greatest disappointments in this life may be disguised as our greatest blessings ever! Why? ...Because they will change who we are and how we treat others forever!

Our culture and society has misled many into thinking that we can somehow avoid pain, suffering and hard work by taking a "pill", buying the latest quick fix remedy, or anesthetizing ourselves with alcohol, drugs, sex, food, gambling, or other things that make us feel good about ourselves for only a short time. However, most of us develop our integrity and values through our own pain-filled experiences and scars. Here is a heartwarming story to explain how beautiful the scars of pain really are!

Junior was around the age of seven. He got home early and was helping his mother wash dishes. As she put her hands into the soapy water to wash another dish, he said, "Mom, what is that ugly scar from?" She rinsed off her hands and said, "Junior, how about if you and I sit down and have a glass of milk and some fresh home-made cookies while I tell you the story?"

Junior sat down at the table as his mother began the story.... "Well, at least seven years ago, there was this young mother who decided that she would leave the house for just a few minutes and run down to the local country store for some groceries. This mother recently had delivered a precious baby boy at the hospital. She and her husband brought this sweet baby boy home and loved him and took the best care of him. One afternoon when the baby was in his crib for a nap, mom thought she would make a quick grocery run. Mom had peeked in on him before leaving, and he was sleeping very soundly. She proceeded to drive to the store...and arrived there in about five minutes. As she was checking out and paying the cashier, she heard the fire alarm and the truck sirens. Upon exiting the local store, she noticed smoke in the direction of her house. She quickly got into her car and raced towards home. As she pulled up in front of the house, she could see flames from the attic. All she could think about was her baby boy.

There were fire trucks and fireman already starting to put out a blaze that had started. She raced up and told the fireman that her baby boy was in there. The fireman told her to not enter the house, however, she darted around his outstretched arms and demanded that she was going to get her baby if it was the last thing she did! She raced up the stairs and noticed the crib starting to catch fire. She grabbed her baby boy, turned around and reached the door just as the ceiling gave way and caved in behind her. Racing down the stairs, she stumbled against the front door, coughing and sputtering as firemen pulled her out of the house to safety. "

The young boy looked at his mother and said, "Mom, you got the ugly scar trying to save me?" The mother smiled and said, "Yes, Junior, you were the baby boy in the story." As he hugged his mother tightly and brushed his hand across her scar, he said, "Mom that is the most beautiful scar I've ever seen!" Jesus, our Father in Heaven has been through much pain. He carried the sins of the world and is no stranger to suffering. When we see Him, we will have opportunity to see His nail scarred hands and thank Him for enduring the pain and suffering of Calvary.

"Dear Father, sometimes the pain in this life can be excruciating and almost unbearable. Lord, I pray that You are able to prepare and strengthen me to deal with my own pain so that I can be useful in helping others who may need encouragement and guidance. Lord, equip me with the wisdom of Your Holy Word and the power of Your Holy Spirit! Remind me Lord, when I forget, that I am nothing without You! Lord please heal my heart and mind so that I can

Love others like You do. Please bless me with a double portion of Your Holy Spirit! Amen"

Were you aware that your darkest days of suffering may be your most profound moments of growth and worship?

Don't give up! We learn things about our Savior through suffering- that we cannot learn any other way!

Psalm 147:3 says, "He heals the broke hearted and binds up their wounds."

It is the fire of persecution and suffering that brings forth the gold of Godliness. When we have reached the end of our rope, when our spirit is broken, when we have been abandoned, rejected, and when there are no options left, this is when we truly have a chance to call on our Savior! This is when we start to learn to trust Jesus Christ! God did not prevent Daniel from being thrown into the lion's den and he did not keep Joseph from being sold into slavery. He knows that in order for us to trust Him unquestioningly, and to grow and build a faith that moves mountains, we will need to go through some trials and tribulation.

Have you ever heard the phrase, "trust is earned"? Our Heavenly Father wants to earn our trust...and build our faith in Him! He may not ask you to bungee jump off the Golden Gate Bridge or para- chute out of a 747, however, he may require you to hold onto Him through some pretty life-threatening, faith producing, depressing times! Growth usually does not take place on the mountaintops. It is the valleys where our growth happens**. Romans 8:31 says: "If God is for us, who can be against us?"**

Paul in Romans 5:3-6 says," And not only that, but we also glory in tribulations, knowing that tribulation produces perseverance; and perseverance, character; and character, hope. Now hope does not disappoint, because the love of God has been poured out in our hearts by the Holy Spirit who was given to us."

In the first year that David and I were married, he took me out 'road-biking'. I remember it being a very windy day and I was riding a loaner bike. I was a new road biker...and as I rode alongside him, it seemed that the first six or seven miles were effortless, however as we turned our bikes around and headed towards home, I felt the wind pushing my road bike backwards with each attempt to pedal forward. The wind would then come from the side, howling and making me feel as if I might suddenly veer off the road and crash. Finally, after battling the wind for several miles, I stopped my bike on the edge of the road and burst into tears. David had no idea what was going on inside of me. I then blurted out, "I feel that I have been swimming upstream all my life! I feel that the wind has never been at my back... and that I have never had 'smooth-sailing'!!!" David hugged me and I asked him to pray with me. Then he said, "Let's get you home, but you ride behind me and I will try to block the wind." We got back on our bikes again and started to pedal. It made a huge difference to have David riding ahead of me so that I could "draft" off of him. The pedaling then became effortless. I have am continually reminded of how valuable it is to have Godly family support, people, and friends to lean on through the stormy winds and trials of life! There will be times when God allows difficulty to come upon us...but it is so that we run to Him for safety, comfort, instruction and even discipline! These are the times when He begins to form our character and build the foundation of our lives on things that will last and stand the test of time. Then when the strong winds blow and howl around us and threaten to blow us off the path...we can talk with our heavenly father about it. He wants us to trust Him and follow Him one step at a time!

"Dear Father thanks so much for holding me and comforting me through the howling winds of trials and strife! Help me to continually look to You for my strength! It is You, oh Lord, who is my refuge and strength in time of trouble. (Psalm 46) Please continue to walk beside me and carry me through the storms if I get discouraged and cannot take one more step! Amen"

Chapter 4

"About... Fear and Anxiety"

*F*ear is something that we all face at one time or another. Many of us deny that it has any leverage or affect upon our lives. However, Franklin D. Roosevelt, in his Inaugural Address stated, "We have nothing to fear but fear itself!" Source: Franklin D. Roosevelt, Inaugural Address, March 4, 1933, as published in Samuel Rosenman, ed., *The Public Papers of Franklin D. Roosevelt, Volume Two: The Year of Crisis, 1933* (New York: Random House, 1938), 11–16.

Fear is usually a very human reaction to the 'unknown'. It is something that crosses our minds when facing big decisions or change; getting married, a new job, divorce, losing a family member or friend, being diagnosed with cancer or possibly going through financial upheaval and homelessness.

A.W. Tozer speaks of how, "A spiritual kingdom lies all about us, enclosing us, embracing us, altogether within reach of our inner selves, waiting for us to recognize it. God, Himself is here waiting for our response to His presence. This eternal world will come alive

to us the moment we begin to reckon upon its reality." **The Pursuit of God; pgs. 50 & 51.**

Tozer discusses the fact that the idealist and the relavists are not mentally ill, however, they are living their lives according to their limited brain theories and by what they believe is not there. However, it is true, that when you and I live and bask in the knowledge and faith of our Heavenly Father's infinite wisdom and power...all other theories are quite dim and unsound.

Fear has been discussed by many public speakers as truly, (FEAR) False Evidence Appearing Real! Fear is the biggest tool in the belt of the evil one today. There are many people who feel that they don't want to try to become a 'follower of Christ' because it is too hard and they might fail. Really???? When you become a Child of God's... you don't have to be perfect! You get to lay down your fears at Jesus feet,...along with every other burden that you have been trying to carry around for your entire life!

"Perfect Love casts out fear." 1John 4:18

"For God has not given us a spirit of fear, but of power, and of love, and of a sound mind." 2Timothy 1:7

We are not to live our lives in fear of what could happen tomorrow! It would paralyze us and keep us from growing into the loving people that God wants us to be!

Did you know that there was a battle going on for your mind?

Have you read the book, "Battlefield of the Mind" by Joyce Meyer? This is a great read!   The mind is obviously the favorite strategic battlefield for the evil one. (Because the mind controls the body.) The Devil has studied each one of us since birth...and knows our weaknesses.   He tries to keep our minds so preoccupied with the things of this world that we have no time left for God. He also tries to whisper lies in our ears like, "You aren't good enough", "You aren't going to amount to anything.", "No one will ever love you"... and the list goes on and on. The devil is constantly trying to get us to give up! He will never give up trying to derail our lives. God, on the other hand is also battling for our lives, however, he is a gentleman and will not force himself upon us. He died for you and me and He knows that we will need some armor and strength for these temptations and battles that we will encounter. God has left us many wonderful, healing words and instructions to live our lives a certain way. These words are in the Holy Bible- and contain powerful tools with which to battle the negativity of the devil.

We were never meant to live our lives in fear, rejection, anxiety, mistrust, depression or having "no purpose in this life". Our brains are unable to handle the stress of these things.

"Let your gentleness be known to all men. The Lord is at hand. Be anxious for nothing, but in everything by prayer and supplication, with thanksgiving, let your requests be known to God; and the peace of God, which surpasses all understanding, will guard your

hearts and minds through Christ Jesus. Finally Brethren, whatever things are true, whatever things are noble, whatever things are just, whatever things are pure, whatever things are lovely, whatever things are of good report, if there is any virtue and if there is anything praiseworthy—meditate on these things." Philippians 4:5-8

In the past seven years, I have become familiar with the work of Dr. Daniel Amen, Clinical Neuroscientist and Psychiatrist. He has produced many books on conditions of the brain and done incredible research. Dr. Amen has posted "SPECT Scans" on his web site that show an actual brain and how it starts to literally shrink and get craters in it when faced with: Depression, Anxiety and Fear. Dr. Amen has SPECT Scans of the brain posted on his website that show the following disorders: Substance abuse, Bipolar disorder, TBI, ADD/ADHD, Fear, Anxiety, Dementia, and Violence. All of these SPECT Scans are posted on his web-site. (You can Google Dr. Amen to view these amazing findings on your own.) Interestingly enough, our Creator knew that we would not be able to withstand the hard knocks and pressure of this sinful life. And Our Father keeps telling us in scripture ...don't worry, don't be fearful, don't have anxiety, run to Me with all of your problems. Don't turn to alcohol or drugs, food or sex to find relief...it will hurt you. Your body and brain are the temple of God. Our brains are simply unable to handle the stress of this life without our Heavenly Father.

Jesus promises ..."I will never leave you or forsake you." Matthew 11:29-30 "Take My yoke upon you and learn of Me, for I am gentle and humble in heart, you will find rest for your souls. For My yoke is easy and My burden is light."

"Dear Father, I pray for motivation today that You would help me carve out time with You. Lord, I don't know how to start hanging out with You, but I am in desperate need of Your love, grace, mercy and patience with me. Help me to give You all of my fears and anxiety so that it won't stunt my growth... or wound anyone else. Please replace these things with Your unconditional love so that I can grow and blossom into the person that You created me to be. Amen"

Have you been afraid to set out and face your fears?

Have you wondered what failures would look like ~ knowing that on the other side could be huge successes?

1 John 4:18 ...Perfect Love casts out fear."

This was one of the first scripture that I memorized as I was going through a divorce several years ago. I could see that not only my own life, but the life of my biological parents was greatly affected by fear. I so wanted, and continue to desire, to live my life without this "dreaded fear" a work in progress, He continues to:

1. Help me realize that it is okay if others reject me as long as I know that I am in God's will because...He has promised in His word that He will never leave me or forsake me!

Hebrews 13:5, 6 "Let your conduct be without covetousness; be content with such things as you have. For He Himself has said, 'I

will never leave you nor forsake you.' So we may boldly say, "The Lord is my helper; I will not fear; what can man do to me?"

2. Show me that I don't need to be "Perfect" all of the time- because I am His Child ...and He loves me just as I am. The problem with many of us today is that we put on "airs" of perfectionism and forget to show that we are human and make mistakes. We fail to see the value in humanity. We are so caught up in striving to be "perfect"... that our lives get way out of balance. Our goal is to be in relationship with Jesus Christ. If this relationship with Jesus starts to grow...then with time, all other things in our lives will fall into their rightful place.

Many corporate leaders have fallen on their faces due to the fact that they expect perfection and super-human outcomes. If they would only admit they are human, own their mistakes and show a little mercy, grace and love to their employees, their companies would thrive. Their reputations will become solid if their values were based on integrity and goodness. Their workplaces will become coveted places of employment where applicants are valued and respected.

Hebrews 13:16 "But do not forsake to do good and to share, for with such sacrifices God is well pleased."

3. Gently remind me that I am human...and am prone to making mistakes. God has shown me that I can't break some of the strongholds of pride and addiction without His help, and only when I can "admit" my mistakes, "own them" and ask God and others for help and accountability will they have no power over me!

"Dear Jesus, I will continue to take "Baby Steps" if you will only hold onto me! Dear Father, protect me from strife, stress and the demands of perfection that I may find true peace in the shelter of your love! Remind me that I cannot get through the day without You taking my hand and guiding me all the way! Amen"

Do you have a fear of being "Imperfect" or "Not Good Enough"?

Have you heard the phrase "Do as I say...Not as I do?" This phrase is truly is the model of "hypocrisy"!

Have we become a world that makes us feel we cannot be vulnerable or imperfect? We truly live in a world that has lost its way and the longer that I live, the more apparent it has become that we should all have an "S" engraved upon our chests for 'Superman', 'Superwoman' , 'Superkid' or 'SuperTeenager'! This was the downfall of Hitler. He wanted to create the perfect race. He wanted everyone to be "perfect"! What a tragedy! Might I add that there are some churches that still continue to operate in this manner and they are not safe places of healing, restoration, agape love or true worship.

I grew up in a Christian home where there was an expectation of "perfection". It seemed that there was no room for mistakes. I definitely learned an "impeccable" work ethic. However, I have spent a fair amount of time and energy learning how to find balance and have finally realized that my identity was and is not wrapped up in my work or my accomplishments! I still struggle with these things and continually have to give these 'burdens of perfection' back to my Father in Heaven to deal with!

In John Maxwell's book, "How Successful People Lead", He tells a story of how Productive Leaders set an example for the people they lead. He said, "President Abraham Lincoln recognized this during the American Civil War, and relieved General John C. Fremont of his command. He said it was for this reason: ***"His cardinal mistake is that he isolates himself and allows no one to see his example of leadership ...or his vulnerability."*** How often do we do the same as parents and leaders? We expect "perfection" at all cost..., even the cost of relationships. Wow! How tragic! How often have I not invited guests over for fear of what they would think of my messy house?

If we want dedicated, thoughtful and productive children, families, people or employees on our team, we must embody and live out leadership with love, integrity, compassion and vulnerability. Instead of leaving our employees buried in a sea of unending work, and demands of perfection... why not roll up our sleeves and work side-by-side with them until they are caught up? Are we so proud that we are afraid to put on our work clothes or sense of humor and be a true leader? God desires that all leaders use their experiences to help motivate others. We are placed on this earth to build each other up and encourage one another in their giftedness and strengths. God's ultimate plan was that true leaders would be willing to make many sacrifices and become "servants" to mankind. The mentality of true leadership should be, "How can I help you get to where you want to go?" When we help others reach their potential and goals, inevitably we will also reach our God-given potential and the goals and purpose that He has for our own lives.

How often do we require the same as parents and leaders? We expect "perfection" at all cost! This MYTH will have to be thrown out the window if we want to have dedicated, thoughtful and productive people on our team. We must embody and live out leadership with integrity, compassion and vulnerability. Leaders should not in any way require anything from their employee that they would not be willing to do themselves.

Several years ago, I was employed by a "Corporately Owned" home health company. I was offered a nice salary and was told that I would be the "clinical supervisor" for all of the staff there. I met with the director of the local branch and interviewed a couple of times and was soon hired on as "Clinical Director". There was very little orientation and I was pretty much "thrown to the wolves" so to speak. I continued to fight for answers and learned the computer as I went. My husband watched as I burned the candle at both ends to keep up with the corporate expectations. I was so exhausted and discouraged that I wanted to quit. I was putting in 60-70 hours per week doing clinical schedules, seeing patients, charting and taking calls. I would chart well into the night to finish everything before the next day. I remember feeling that I was "just a number" to this corporation. They worked me day and night. I had very little rest and lived on caffeinated drinks and a whole lot of prayer. Thank God that after about three months they decided to relieve me of my duties. I have never been so glad to be "fired" in all my life! The company eventually folded and closed their doors. I learned some amazing lessons that I will not forget! God made a few things very clear to me! As long as I live I will not treat my employees like possessions or slaves. I will not require anything of them that I am not willing to do, and most of all... I will not run people into the ground or around the clock while destroying their health and paying them a measly salary. *"Because ... nobody cares how much you know until they know how much you care!"*

1 Peter 4: 8-10: "And above all things have fervent love for one another, for love will cover a multitude of sins. Be hospitable to one another without grumbling. As each one has received a gift, minister it to one another, as good stewards of the manifold grace of God."

If you can trust God with your family and/or your employees and learn to journey with them towards personal growth and healing, then you can bank on their loyalty and dedication to help you attain your goals of success and take care of business! This is God's way of loving all of us where we are at. He makes children out of orphans, he clothes the naked, feeds the hungry and loves people back to where they have always needed to be! If you have always wondered what true leadership means, you are on the right path my friend! I have found that the most amazing leadership that I have ever seen is what My Heavenly Father has shown to me. He has changed my heart to realize that if I can make the lives of those around me a little more bearable and pleasant, and if I can somehow help others reach their goals, then I will also reach my own!

"Dear Father, Open my heart today and help me to understand and learn the necessity and beauty of vulnerability and integrity as I interact with others. Take my fear away and help me to realize that nothing I do will separate me from Your Love! I ask that You be in charge of this day! I can't do it without You Father! I revel and bask in Your constant love, compassion and grace! Thank You for hearing my cries for help! Amen"

Chapter 5

"About...The Power of Prayer"

"Prayer does not fit us for the greater work;
Prayer IS the greater work."
~Oswald Chambers

My journey may be somewhat different than your journey, however, I have been blessed to have Godly people cross my path in order for me to learn from them and their experiences! One such woman was my adopted black praying mom. She was definitely an intercessory prayer warrior. She would spend all day in prayer- and put a "Do Not Disturb" sign on her door. She was meant to cross my path for a "reason" and a "season". She definitely did have an effect on my life and taught me that praying is truly a conversation that you have with your best friend, and the almighty creator, God. **Matthew 21:22 says, "And whatever things that you ask for in prayer, believing, you will receive."**

I didn't realize that Jesus was all I needed until...Jesus was all I had. I was literally living in crisis for a few years. And during those times, I learned that Jesus does not sleep. He hears our prayers and He cares about every aspect of our lives. He wants us to ask Him for help with every problem that we have…and there is nothing too small or too big for Him to fix.

Currently there is a "special place" in my home that I have dedicated to quiet time and prayer to God. There is nothing wrong with this, however, God began to show me that He truly wants us to take Him to work, school, the gym, and everywhere we go. It has only been in the past few years that I have realized that our entire lives and waking moments can become a prayer offering to Him! At church I began to realize that the music that I was singing…was actually an act of praise and prayer to God. (Prayer put to music is Praise.) Somehow, we need to take Jesus out of the box that we have put Him in and remember to take Him with us everywhere we go!

"Private Prayer = Public Power"- Charles Stanley

This equation is quite profound because it truly is God who gives us the power to function from day to day. He alone sits on the throne and rules the world and the universe. It makes so much sense that He does not give power to those who are hungry for it…but rather gives power to those who have surrendered their lives to Him…and don't care who gets the credit. Yes, it is true, **"The effective, fervent prayer of a righteous man avails much. Elijah was a man with a nature like ours, and he prayed earnestly that it would not rain; and it did not rain in the land for three years and six months. And he prayed again, and the heaven gave rain, and the earth produced its fruit." James 5:16-18**

It is true that God listens and pays attention to those children who spend time with Him and thirst after His truth and obedience. I believe that God hears all prayers and that He pours His power,(the gas)strategically on the fires that are already lit in our hearts by His Holy Spirit. This enables us, (His children), to accomplish the work that He has for us to do as we are awakened to action. He gives us only what we need, when we ask for it in faith...and only as we take one baby step forward to do His bidding. I pray that through prayer and communion with God, that we all become vessels of transforming power with a love for others and God that will be unstoppable!

Dear Father, I ask that You show me how to pray for others throughout the day! I ask that you open my eyes to the importance of "Praying without Ceasing". I know that You will guide me in the way that I need to travel...and in the way that You would have me pray. As I see pestilence, deaths, murders and harmful things happening to others around me, please help me to help others by loving them enough to pray for them and their families. Amen"

Did you know that your prayers can actually bring healing to someone or keep them from certain death?

Believe that your prayers will be answered when you pray!

James 5:15-16 "And the prayer of faith will save the sick, and The Lord will raise him up. And if he has committed sins, he will be forgiven. Confess your trespasses to one another and pray for one

another that you may be healed. The effectual fervent prayer of a righteous man avails much."

There have been many times that I have stepped out from beneath God's umbrella of protection. I was determined to do things **my way**! I know of at least three times when the Devil wanted me dead.... However, my adopted prayer warrior mother was praying protection and safety over me! This woman knew how to PRAY! Our precious Savior saw fit to spare my life and to this day I continue to know that the Power of Prayer is absolutely untouchable! Our Father wants us to "tap into" His strength and begin to rely on Him for everything!

There was one such occasion that I remember well. I know that God has communicated very important things to me in dreams at times. And I do not have many dreams, however, when they come...I take notice. On one particular night I had experienced a recurring dream that somehow I was driving my SUV into the mountains on my way to Flagstaff. As I rounded a corner, there was a semi-truck and trailer stopped in the road. I startled and woke up from this dream as my car crashed into the back of the semi. I was upset enough by this dream that I ended up picking up the phone and calling my adopted mother about it. She shared with me that I needed to be alert and well rested when I traveled up the mountain. She said that God was showing me the danger that lurked ahead. We prayed together about this very dream and asked God to intervene in my life and keep me safe from harm as I traveled up the mountain to see my future husband. She prayed that God would spare my life and that His mightiest warrior angels would escort me in my travels. She named two angels in particular, Gabrielle and Raphael. As we ended the conversation, my adopted mother said, "Do not be afraid or fearful. I will pray this off of you." My adopted prayer warrior mother knew that there was and is great power in prayer...and that it can change EVERYTHING...including the direction and the outcomes of your life. The day approached for me to travel up the hill and spend some time with David. We had been dating long-distance, and tried to block out long weekends and planned intentionally to spend extra time together because we really missed each other's company.

At the time I was working at Phoenix Indian Medical Center on the night shift. I had just finished my fourth 12-hour shift in a row. After giving report, I remember going to the locker room to get my things. I was stopped by three concerned co-workers expressing their concern about me driving up to Flagstaff. I had mentioned to them that I was headed up the I-17 to see my fiancé for several days. In fact, I remember one co-worker going to his locker and getting me an energy drink to keep me from falling asleep at the wheel.

I do remember praying with David before getting into my car... this helped calm my nerves and I asked God for His protection. I was very aware of my state of exhaustion- and as I got about half-way up the mountain, I felt that it would be smart to pull over at a rest area to sleep for an hour or two. I remember David phoning me to see where I was as he also was praying and understood that this trip was a battle between good and evil. I made it safely up the mountain...and after hugging David, I immediately went to bed, sleeping until the next morning. This was a very emotional trip because I knew that there was a battle going on for my life and safety that day. God was warning me of this well in advance. I am constantly reminded that God does try to warn his children of imminent danger... and that He also hears the prayers of our friends, family and others who intercede in our lives and keep us from harm. Our Heavenly Father is all about preventing the evil one from swooping in and taking advantage of our weaknesses. He just needs us to ASK for His help. (Matthew 7:7)

"Dear Father, please teach me to pray for my friends, family, church, and everyone I come in contact with! Help me to pass on the Grace that others have shown me! Teach me to love others so much that I would also pray for their safety and well-being even when no one is watching and when there is no reward. Lord, pour Your Holy Spirit out upon me this day that I can honor and glorify You! Amen"

Have you heard the saying, "Life is not about "What" you know...it is about "Who" you know"?

Did you know that **if** you and I are to accomplish anything of significance...it will only happen on our knees...praying? After all, praying and reading the Holy Bible is about knowing Jesus Christ.

How is your prayer life? What is the purpose of prayer? Charles Stanley is one-hundred percent accurate when he said, *"The purpose of prayer is to build an intimate relationship with our Heavenly Father."* As I listened to Stanley being interviewed by his son on one of his radio broadcasts, he said something quite profound...,*"- Those who know God the most intimately will have the most active prayer life, and will see Gods hand actively at work in their lives."*

James 5:16 "Confess your trespasses to one another, and pray for one another, that you may be healed. The effective, fervent prayer of a righteous man avails much."

I guess this is much like working out. If you are consistent with your work outs, you will start seeing results! The same with prayer and being in God's word. Start talking to Him. Carve out a place and a time to read His Word. Once you have disciplined yourself to meet Him, talk with Him and hear His voice from this one place of worship, you will be more comfortable to take Him with you everywhere you go! You can develop the mindset of "Practicing Gods Presence" and realizing that He is with you everywhere you go.

I have tried convincing my husband that if I didn't have to work, that I would definitely be covering a lot more people in prayer, and could accomplish more for Gods kingdom! I could bake bread or pies... and even keep the house a little cleaner. David's response to this was, "Well, maybe there will be a time when God will make provision for that to happen!" However, in the meantime, while I'm waiting, God has shown me many productive ways to pray all day long in the settings that I am in. I am beginning to witness many miracles and blessings that could only come from Him! I am learning that talking to God and listening for His voice can happen at work, in the car, in the shower, in the kitchen, hiking around the neighborhood, and during the entire day! We can pray for people all day long! We don't always need to close our eyes; we can walk and talk with God everywhere. **"Pray without ceasing" 1 Thess. 5:17.** Our lives can actually become a prayer offering to our Lord! The following is a very important equation – and it will not fail you.

"PRIVATE PRAYER = PUBLIC POWER"–Charles Stanley

"Dear Father, this day is Yours. I can't do anything without You! I pray for obedience, wisdom, protection and endurance to run the race that is set before me. Lord, I pray for all those people that I come in contact with today. Show me Your will for my life today. Help me to obediently carry out Your will, Father. Keep me on the right path and help me to realize that this life is about You and... NOT about me! Dear Father, increase my awareness of you in my everyday life. Amen"

Did you know that your "life" can be a prayer?

"Prayer does not fit us for the greater work; Prayer IS the greater work." ~Oswald Chambers

This is actually not such a "far-fetched" idea when you start breaking it down. Prayer is defined as "Communication with God." Enoch was a prayer warrior who lived to be 365 years old. **Genesis 5:21-24** tells a little bit about Enoch. Verse 24 says, **"And Enoch walked with God; and he was not, for God took him."** This phrase does not mean that Enoch ceased to exist; instead it means that he was taken into God's presence, for God took him up to heaven to live with Him! I can only imagine that Enoch spent a lot of quiet time with God while he walked from place to place and was being productive at the same time. "Being Quiet", is definitely something that does not come easily, and it truly is a discipline that is necessary in order to hear from God.

Philippians 4:6-7 "Be anxious for nothing, but in everything by prayer and supplication, with thanksgiving, let your requests be made known to God. And the Peace of God, which surpasses all understanding, will guard your hearts and minds through Jesus Christ."

Our Pastor Bob recently told a joke at the beginning of the service that went something like this, "Why is it that when we Christians try to talk with God, things are fine up until we start hearing His voice and then people usually label us as SCHIZOPHRENIC?"

There was a very lonely time in my life where I had just moved to the state of Arizona and had accepted a traveling nurse assignment in Phoenix. I had moved with very few possessions. I was sleeping on an air mattress and brought out only what I would need for a short time, as I was not sure how long the assignment would last. Most weeks I would work 3-4 days and then would have 3-4 days off. It was during my days off in the solitude of my own home that Jesus became much more than just a name! I began to "Practice His Presence" with everything, and would talk with Him everywhere that I went. I soon began to realize that it was difficult to hear God's voice when I had too many distractions or if I was way too busy. I had a very difficult time disciplining myself to spend quiet time with God. The following are some suggestions that might help you find and create the right environment for God to speak to you:

1. First, build quiet time into your life where you are able to reflect, read and listen. I was starting each morning by memorizing God's promises that ministered to my loneliness, my vulnerability, my fears, and the list goes on. I sat on the floor

beside my air mattress reading God's Promises and then would turn Christian radio music on and sing with the praise songs as I was getting ready for work. I somehow knew that I would need to memorize God's Promises that dealt with some of the issues in my life; because they brought amazing comfort to my soul as God would bring them back to my memory during times of trial. There is no "perfect or acceptable" way to spend time with Jesus...you just have to start and find out what works best for you. Many times I hear his voice consistently talking to me while in the shower or out on the road cycling with my husband. Sometimes I will talk with Jesus while sitting in our spa out under the stars. I have had friends that also get up early in the morning and spend time in their "prayer room" and deliberately have quiet one-on-one time with our Father and Creator. This is the first step in tuning our ears to "hear God's voice!"

2. Secondly, after you have built some quiet time into your life and you have started to hear God speak to you, then take another bold step and ask Him to show you how to hear Him during your busy day. Ask Him for wisdom and discernment to show you how He would like you to help those around you. He will give you discernment and wisdom that you need to determine what your assignment should be. Many times it will be a gentle whisper in your mind. Sometimes it will seem that God will tell you to do something that might seem a little strange...like even walking up to a complete stranger and giving them some money or food. On occasion, I would walk into a patient's room and see a Bible on their bed. Usually then, I knew it was safe to ask them if they were a Christian.

3. Thirdly, take Jesus out of the box that you have put Him in and start taking Him with you! He really does care about everything in your life, not just church. He is a "dynamic" God! He would much rather get out of the box then sit at home and get 'cabin fever'. I mean...really! He gets excited when we start to understand His amazing love and His ability to lead us through each day! God wants you to start asking for His unfailing wisdom, guidance and protection! He will show up! Start praising His name for what He is about to do! Jesus loves You so very much!

Psalm 46:10, "Be still and know that I am God."

"Dear Father, this busy world that we live in does not seem to promote our quiet time with You! I pray that You show me how to guard my quiet time with diligence. However, if I happen to miss a day here or there, Lord, help me to remember that You love me just the same, and that I can just pick up right where we left off and never fall from Your Grace. Teach me to be still and know that You are with me everywhere I go! Amen"

When God speaks to you...Do you know how to listen?

Our Heavenly Father loves us so much and wants us to hear His voice. In 1 Kings 19:11-13 talks about God revealing himself to Elijah. It said that God was not in the wind, the earthquake or the fire. It does say that after all this was past "a still small voice came to him." Many have heard God's voice that sounds much like our conscience.

Some have actually heard the audible voice of God talking to them. There are many other instances of God speaking to His children in the bible. Samuel heard God speak to him when he was just a child. It seems that usually He will speak with a "still small voice" much like our conscience...and then there have been a few times where I audibly heard God's voice speaking to me.

Back in 2007, I moved to Phoenix as a traveling nurse. I had spent most of the Holidays alone. Christmas had become very difficult ...and I found myself very "alone" once again, in the big City of Phoenix. I remember telling God how lonely I was, only to hear Him whisper, "But I love you!" On one of my days off I was swimming in the pool in the back yard. I had my Boom box outside with Christian radio playing and my Bible was sitting on a little table beside the lawn chair. I stopped reading and started swimming laps in the beautiful morning sun. As I slowly swam, I started talking to God. I told Him the desires of my heart. I asked Him questions about His Love, Mercy and Grace... and I began to hear His gentle replies. My "Aloneness" drove me to search for the wonderful love and companionship of Jesus Christ! It was during these dark and lonely days that I came to know Jesus and was thrilled to actually hear His voice talking to me.

So, remember that The One who created you, numbered the hairs of your head and calls you by name..., He loves You more than anything in this world!

"Father, help me to make quiet time to spend with You! I want to hear your voice. Please tune my ears and open my heart to hear your calling. Amen"

Chapter 6

"About...The Light of Truth"

*D*id you know that it has been said that, "The truth will set you free?" This is so true on many different levels. A.W. Tozer speaks of removing the veil that kept us from communicating directly with God. Tozer speaks of the Veil that was torn from the top to the bottom in the tabernacle when Christ was crucified and died on the cross -in the following words:

"In human experience that veil was made of living spiritual tissue; it is composed of the sentient, quivering stuff of which our whole beings consist, and to touch it is to touch us where we feel pain. To tear it away is to injure us, to hurt us and make us bleed. To say otherwise is to make the cross no cross and the death no death at all. It is not fun to die. To rip through the dear and tender stuff of which life is made can never be anything but deeply painful. Yet that is what the cross did to Jesus and it is what the cross would do to every man to set him free.

The cross is rough and it is deadly, but it is effective. It does not keep its victim hanging there forever. There comes a moment

when its work is finished and the suffering victim dies. After that is resurrection, glory and power, and the pain is forgotten for the sheer joy that the veil is taken away and we have entered into an actual spiritual experience of the presence of the living God. A.W. Tozer, In Pursuit of God; Pgs 44 & 45.

Wow, that was very deep and profound- and I am here to tell you that Tozer is talking about dying to the sins of the flesh, and to our selfish motives. This dying to self is painful and we have to be vulnerable, admitting our wrongs, and then giving them up to our Creator. It is what we all must do in order to be new creatures and resurrected from our painful pasts. In all matters speaking, the cross represents truth.

Along with the Cross is also God's Holy Word...which also represents truth. **2 Timothy 3:16 says, " All scripture is given by inspiration of God, and is profitable for doctrine, for reproof, for correction, for instruction in righteousness, that the man of God may be complete, thoroughly equipped for every good work."**

How come it is so difficult for us to read the Holy Bible? God's word says that the Word "discovers our condition." **Hebrews 4:12 says "For the Word of God is living and powerful, and is sharper than any two-edged sword, piercing even to the division of soul and spirit, and of joints and marrow, and is a discerner of the thoughts and intents of the heart."** It is not always pleasant to have constructive criticism, however, this is one of the Truths of God's Holy Word. It seems that many individuals have had so-called Christians 'beat them over the head' with truth instead of praying that God's

Holy Spirit would open their hearts and minds to God's truth. Unfortunately, the bible has been viewed as a weapon of abuse instead of a wonderful source of truth, wisdom and guidance. This act of being a 'bible thumper' has turned many away from the light and truth of the world. Wow... no wonder this world does not like to open their bibles. It is an instrument used to convict you and me of our sinful condition...and to lead us to a wonderful light of truth!

John 3:19-21 says, "And this is the condemnation, that the light has come into the world, and men loved darkness rather than light, because their deeds were evil. For everyone practicing evil hates the light and does not come to the light, lest his deeds should be exposed. But he who does the truth comes to the light, that his deeds may be clearly seen, that they have been done in God."

A.W. Tozer states, "The bible will never be a living Book to us until we are convinced that God is articulate in His universe. To jump from a dead, impersonal world to a dogmatic Bible is too much for most people. They admit that they should accept the bible as the Word of God, and they try to think of it as such, but they find it impossible to believe that the words on the page are actually meant for them. The facts are that God is not silent, has never been silent. It is the nature of God to speak. The second Person of the Holy Trinity, God the Son, is called the Word. The Bible is the inevitable outcome of God's continuous speech. It is the infallible declaration of His mind for us put into our familiar human words." A.W. Tozer, In Pursuit of God, Pgs 76 & 77.

"The truth will set you free!" -Jewish Carpenter

Did you know that you are called to be a "child of light"?

I have heard some people say that Jesus is both darkness and light. And to this I respond with what is in scripture. Light represents truth, transparency and vulnerability. Jesus is not darkness.

1 John 1:5-7 "This message which we have heard from Him, and declare to you, that God is light and in Him is no darkness at all. If we say that we have fellowship with Him, and walk in darkness, we lie and do not practice the truth. But if we walk in the light as He is in the light, we have fellowship with one another, and the blood of Jesus Christ, His son will cleanse us from all sin." *(To have fellowship with someone, each party must be vulnerable and share from the innermost chambers of the heart.)*

Matthew 5:14-16 "You are the light of the world. A city that is set on a hill cannot be hidden. Nor do they light a lamp and put it under a basket, but on a lamp stand, and it gives light to all who are in the house. Let your light so shine before men that they may see your good works and glorify your Father in heaven."

Our Heavenly Father wants us to live in His light! He wants us to shine our light on others so that they will find their way! I was working as a traveling nurse at an I.H.S.,(Indian Health System) hospital. Our ward clerk this day was a woman in her 50's who was suffering from depression and some bipolar disorder. She was in one of her moods and later told me that she had run out of her medications. I was in the locked medication room getting my patient's medications for the morning. This woman came in to put some new orders on a patient's medication sheets. She came up beside me and started leafing through the med sheets. All of the sudden, out of the blue, she shivered and said, "Boy, there are some kinda' vibes that are coming off of you!" I smiled at her and said, "Really, what kind of vibes are you talking about?" With that she turned and fled the med room, saying, "I'm outta here"...and the door slammed shut. I was somewhat taken back, and felt rejected at first, however, God showed me that this was actually the light of the Holy Spirit that she was not liking. It is somewhat humorous to this day to remember that brief encounter with her. I am convinced that darkness cannot stand the light! Jesus suffered much worse things while He was on this earth. There are worse things than rejection. We are not to conform to the ways of man, but to be transformed by spending time with our Heavenly Father. Remember, you are a child of the King... and that is the most amazing honor and privilege in our world!!

I continued to run into daily situations while working at this hospital. I felt a darkness that I seemed to have to fight off every day. This ward clerk eventually accepted a devotional book as a gift from me. I often wonder how she is and where she is at in her life journey on this earth.

John 3:20 talks of how evil hates the light. You and I, my friend, have been called to be filled with light, truth, integrity and every good thing from our Father in Heaven. We are asked to turn over every dark corner and dark secret to our Savior. He wants to change us from the inside out...and He is able to if we are willing!

"Dear Father, I thank you for your steadfast Love and guidance. May this day be filled with Your light, wisdom and truth! Please come into my heart and soul. I ask that You get rid of the darkness that would enslave me to this world. I want to live my life for You and walk worthy! Thank You for the victory that You have already won over this present darkness! Help me to claim Your promises against evil and the prince of darkness. Amen"

Did you know that God wants us to be "Candid" (Truthful) with Him?

Vulnerability and Candor are very important to our Heavenly Father. (Candor means that you say things straightforward and truthful.) He can handle us being angry at Him, yelling at Him and even telling Him how we feel. Bitterness, anger and self-sufficiency keep us from having an authentic and real relationship with God, and also from experiencing blessings and healing! The pain and trials of this life can either make us "Bitter or Better" people.

In Rick Warrens' book, "What on earth am I here for?" He states,"... everything that happens to you or me has spiritual significance." He goes on to say, "real fellowship happens when people get honest about who they are and what is happening in their lives!" Only when we are real, authentic and transparent and vulnerable, can the Holy Spirit work. There have been times in my life when I was afraid to say exactly what I thought. I felt that I would be rejected if I was straight forward with others. I was not raised to "Say what you mean" or to "mean what you say". I became very candid and very angry with God for a while. I begged Him to show me why I was going through all of the pain and trials. I was shown that God was using this pain to mold my heart and life into something much more useful and beautiful than I ever imagined!

David, Job, Moses and Abraham all had times of anger, doubt and questioning of God. Expressing doubt and anger is many times the first step towards healing ...and the next level of intimacy with God. The more that we become a candid and authentic friend of God's, the more we will begin to care about the things that He cares about most! The faster our hearts will heal!

The truth is that we are as "close to God as we choose to be." – K Land God has always been there and is waiting to hear from you!

"Draw close to God, and He will draw close to you!" James 4:8

"Dear Father, I confess my anger and frustration with the pain and trials that have made my life hard! I lay this anger and pain at Your feet. As I kneel and look into Your face, I pray that You have mercy on me! Please trade these horrible feelings and events for Peace and Blessings, Grace and Mercy that I do not even deserve. Show me what I am supposed to learn from this pain and tribulation! I am so grateful to be Your Child. Lord, I so want to be a child of Your light and truth. Amen"

Chapter 7

"About…Peace and Rest"

*T*he Bible talks about the Hebrew word, "Shalom"… which means "To rest in Him"… or to "Enter His Rest". In Hebrew, the root of the word (usually in a three or occasionally four letter format), and depending on the vowels that are used, has several meanings (that are relevant to the general meaning of the word Shalom); as for example: One meaning is "Whole", another could be the actual verb "Pay" usually in command form. The conjugated verb has other spins that are worth noting, such as: "Hishtalem" meaning "it was worth it" or "Shulam" as "it was paid for" or "Meshulam" as in "paid in advance" Hence one can jokingly say that, "when it's paid-for then there is peace."

The Hebrew term *shalom* is roughly translated to other languages as *peace* [En.] (i.e. *paz* [Sp. and Pr.], *paix* [Fr.], *pace* [It.]), from the Latin *pax*. Pax, in Latin, means peace, but it was also used to mean truce or treaty. So, deriving from the definition and use in Latin, most Romance terms simply use the word peace to mean such, and also provides a relational application (be it personal, social or political) – a state of mind and affairs. Peace is an important word in the Christian sacred scriptures and liturgy. *Eirene*, the Greek term translated to peace, also means quietness and rest.

As I have weathered through my own personal valleys of fire, torment and persecution, "Shalom" has come to mean a whole lot of things. It means that I can **chose** to have "Peace" and "Rest" in my mind and soul when my entire world has been turned upside-down and I would rather worry, cry ...and curl up in the fetal position and suck my thumb. This also means that no matter where I am,... when I receive bad news such as health issues, loss of home, loss of job, or losses of friends or loved ones... that I won't have to weather through these difficult times alone. *During these times, if I possibly can get on my knees wherever I am, I like to do so- because it puts things into perspective. It places God back on the throne- in charge of the universe, in charge of everything, right where He should be. Then, as I am on my knees in prayer...my state of humility takes the scepter out of my hand and puts it back into His where it belongs.*

These times of prayer are where, in the quietness of my inner heart and soul, I proceed to be angry, to cry, to yell, to say I am sorry, to ask for forgiveness, to recite God's own words that He has left for me in scripture- reminding Him of His promises to me... as I work through the pain grief and anger, asking God to heal my heart and show me what He wants me to learn from this... or what direction He wants me to go from here? After I have laid my burdens down at Jesus' feet, I feel the "Rest" and "Peace" flooding my weary soul. Only then can I allow my body to sleep without worry or concern about events and situations of the present and the future. After weathering through the difficult times with Jesus, facing homelessness, depression, abandonment, scorn, financial upheaval, and job loss, I have come to know that I can trust Him with all of my heart, soul, mind, and body. There is no-one like our Jesus! Without Him you and I will never find rest and peace!

Interestingly enough, the Children of Israel also went through wandering in the dessert for forty years to learn how to trust God. ***They failed the tests of their lifetime because they did not believe in God's promises to them. They never knew peace and rest before they died off while wandering around in the wilderness. They never were able to collect their inheritance and blessings of "Peace of Mind" while "Resting in Him"!*** (You can find this story in Hebrews Chapters 3, 4.)

The bible refers to us as sheep for a reason... Sheep can be very stupid animals. They follow their feelings, they follow each other into very dangerous situations and they follow the leader of the pack without asking questions. Just like the "sheep" in scripture and just like the Children of Israel, we try to fix our own feelings and problems instead of running to Jesus and throwing ourselves at His feet. We choose to carry our problems around with us like trophies in back-packs of our own making. We get so burdened down by the weight of them that we begin to have health problems, we may even cave in to drugs, alcohol, and other addictions that will allow us to forget how heavy these burdens have become. Jesus is our only hope for peace and rest! He is waiting to take those burdens you have been carrying. His outstretched arms can handle anything! What is weighing on your heart and mind today?

Don't miss out on what God has for you! Don't let the following things keep you from "Shalom", "Rest" and "Peace"!

- Pride
- Busyness
- Control
- Distractions (TV, movies, facebook, computer, I-phones, etc....)
- Friends
- Fear of quiet time
- Shame
- Lack of boundaries- inability to say "No"
- Work

Matthew 11: 28-30 "Come to Me all you who labor and are heavy laden, and I will give you rest. Take My yoke (of freedom) upon you and learn from Me, for I am gentle and lowly in heart, and you will find rest for your souls. For My yoke is easy and My burden is light."

Have you ever wondered what it meant to "Rest in God"?

Have you heard the phrase, "There ain't no rest for the wicked." I always have pondered this phrase and have felt that somehow there was no rest for God's children at times. Through the years I have continued to ask God to show me "**HIS REST**"... and He has kept His word.

Matthew 11:28-30 says," Come to me all you who labor and are heavy laden, and I will give you rest. Take My yoke upon you and

learn from Me, for I am gentle and lowly in heart, and you will find rest for your souls. For My yoke is easy and my burden is light."

No one ever mentioned that as I started into the adventure of "putting Christianity into action", that I would suffer such severe trials and persecution. However, when Jesus calls our name and we start to walk with Him through our lives...everything changes for the better. As events started to unfold, I felt that I had a "bulls-eye" target on my back! One weekend I shared with a trusted, godly couple about the current events in my life, I vividly remember Greg saying, "Well, you have got to be doing something right, otherwise the Devil wouldn't be on your tail!" Greg went on to explain to me that when God has a purpose for us to carry out in this world, that the Devil comes along and does everything that he can to keep it from happening. He and Ane prayed with me and encouraged me to continue on the path that God had for me. They directed me back to read God's word for wisdom, guidance and comfort. These following passages began to mean a lot to me.

1 Peter 4:12-14 "Beloved do not think it strange concerning the fiery trial which is to try you, as though some strange thing happened to you; but rejoice to the extent that you partake of Christ's sufferings, that when His glory is revealed, you may also be glad with exceeding joy. If you are reproached for the name of Christ, blessed are you, for the Spirit of glory and of God rests upon you."

1 Peter 5:7-9 "Casting all your care upon Him, for He cares for you. Be sober, be vigilant; because your adversary the devil walks about like a roaring lion, seeking whom he may devour, resist him,

steadfast in faith; knowing that the same sufferings are experienced by your brotherhood in the world."

God talks about trials in James 1:2-4 He says, "My brethren, count it all joy when you fall into various trials, knowing that the testing of your faith produces patience. But let patience have its perfect work, that you may be perfect and complete, lacking nothing."

Hebrews chapter four talks about rest. I encourage you to read what the bible has to say here. The author of Hebrews mentions that the children of Israel could not enter God's rest because of **"unbelief"**! What a tragedy! God wanted all of the Children of Israel to enter His Promised Land, but instead...they had to wander around in the wilderness for forty years until they died or actually started to listen to Him. Unfortunately, the majority of them never learned to trust God with every aspect of their lives- and died before seeing the Promised Land. God wants us to get "immediate rest" and sleep at night so we are refreshed the next day. But He also wants us to understand how to access His "**Learned Rest**", which involves journeying with Him–and learning to trust Him. It involves handing over every trial, problem, finances, your future, relationships, your house, car and job...and even the most difficult people in your life! This will produce a "total rest" in Jesus! You will have a calm peace about you...and will know how to choose to "rest in Him"...no matter what is going on in your life!

"Dear Father, help me to continue to come to You with everything that bothers me! I don't want to be learning these lessons of trust for the next forty years! Lord I pray that You bless me with wisdom. Nudge me when I need to hand over my trials, fear,

worries, finances and difficult people to You! Give me the Godly wisdom and love that only come from You! Help me to make time to listen to those around me and speak words that will help support and encourage people around me." Amen"

Chapter 8

"About... Spiritual Warfare"

I was once told by a very wise friend that, **"Every earthly battle is won in the spiritual realm"**! It took this profound statement awhile to really 'sink in'. As I began to ponder this concept...I also began praying to God to open my eyes to the spiritual battle going on around me.

I am writing about this very thing because of the importance of its nature. Every time there is a battle on this earth or in a movie, someone wins and the other loses. This is even a more serious concept in the spiritual realm, due to the fact that the winning of a spiritual battle usually results in life- and the losing of this spiritual battle results in death.

You and I are here playing in this game called "Life" on this experimental soil called "Earth". My journey has taken me to many places on earth...but it has also taken me to many places in my heart and soul. My eyes have been opened to the fact that, *"Situations are rarely what they seem to be, people are rarely who they say they are"*, and for the most part, when things happen at work, at school, at church or anywhere, it usually is something of a spiritual nature that involves a spiritual battle. Now, my immediate reaction is to pray about it. I ask for His protection and guidance...and to show me how I should proceed. I ask Him to fill the room that I am in with His presence. I pray for the person that appears to be in a foul mood, or attacking me. I ask God to intervene in their lives and also in mine. Usually these prayers are a powerful and can stop evil in its tracks!

The devil is bound and determined to use other people's wounded hearts, addictions, and desires to try to derail you and me from the path and wonderful plans that our Father has for us. Don't be surprised...just expect it! The devil has been studying you and I since we were in our mother's womb. You and I have a great and huge work to carry out on this earth! Our Heavenly Father has given us tools and instruction in His Holy Bible on how to prepare for spiritual warfare, if necessary!

Ephesians 6:12 & 13 "For we do not wrestle against flesh and blood, but against principalities, against posers, against the rulers of the darkness of this age, against spiritual hosts of wickedness in the heavenly places. Therefore take up the whole armor of God, that you may be able to withstand in the evil day, and having done all, to stand."

Have you heard the saying, "Don't swing at a pitch in the dirt?"

Proverbs 16:32"He who is slow to anger is better than the mighty, and he who rules his spirit than he who takes a city."

Let us constantly be aware that there will always be those times where others may take **cheap shots** at you and me to get us all wound up and ready to fight. The evil one takes great joy in watching us fall prey to our adversary's level of stinkin' thinkin'! I remember one great friend who said, *"If you are being attacked for some unknown reason...or things just don't add up or make sense and you have done nothing to provoke this person, just know that it is most likely Spiritual Warfare- and a test."* I have found that I do not have to "mirror" anyone else's attitude. I am convicted that I need to be the one that is calm, kind and collected.

These are the steps that God has asked me to use when my buttons are being pushed:

1. **Take a time out!** I try not to talk with the person who is pushing my buttons for at least 30 minutes to 1 hour, or as long as it takes me to unwind. I need to look at the situation and ask myself why I am so upset. Then I must take the situation to God in prayer and asked Him to forgive me for getting angry and show me how I should handle this person and the situation at hand.
2. **I ask my spouse or a close friend to pray with me.** I specifically request patience and the ability to understand this person a lot better. I ask for discernment and wisdom when dealing with these matters. (Matthew 7:7)
3. **I take a "time out"...at least thirty minutes to one hour.** I don't talk with this person that is pushing my buttons until I feel calm

and composed and I have an idea of how to approach the situation with respect and kindness. ***Thomas Jefferson once said, "When angry, count to ten before you speak; if very angry, then count to one hundred!"***

4. Now I am also asking myself and God why I am getting so upset with the situation- so that I can examine my own hurts, feelings and motives to through the situation in a healthy way. Maybe my heart has been wounded in the past and it brings up issues inside of me that I need to deal with...maybe with a counsel, with God or by talking them through with my husband.

Proverbs 16:16 "How much better to get wisdom than gold! And to get understanding is to be chosen rather than silver."

"Dear Father, I pray that you turn my heart towards you when I get angry with others! You have said, "Father, forgive them for they know not what they do!" As they crucified You and spit on You, beat You and nailed You to the cross! Help me to always remember- that for every battle I have each day- the victory will come as I kneel in prayer! Every physical battle is won in the spiritual realm! You have won the victory on the cross, thank-You Father! Amen."

Did you know that Jesus warns of "wolves in sheep's clothing"?

Matthew 7:15. "Beware of false prophets, who come to you in sheep's clothing, but inwardly they are ravenous wolves."

I recently gave the following advice to a friend who was being tempted: ***"Remember that situations are rarely what they seem to be, people are rarely who they say they are, and...You will know the good people by their fruits."***

In this life there are so many **counterfeits**! I am here to proclaim that there are counterfeits in every church, business, and school and everywhere we go! Early on in my journey I know that there was a target on my back. It seemed that the evil one kept sending almost irresistible temptation in the areas that I was weakest. I look back and now realize that I was so "starved for affection and love" that I fell prey to some individuals that were very handsome, smooth (told me exactly what I was craving to hear), and deceitful. I realized in one of these situations that this handsome and attractive individual had been stalking me to lure me into temptation and derail me from the path that God had in store for me. I was faced with some hard decisions and broke up with this man at least 7 or 8 times before finally succeeding. Towards the end of this relationship, a Godly friend said to me, **"It seems as though this person has been assigned to you to take you off the path that God has for you!"** Sure enough, it was truly happening that way! Today, if you are wondering if you have allowed the right people into your life, it may help to ask yourself these questions:

1. ***Are the people and friendships that you have developed edifying or helping you reach your God-given potential?*** (Do they pray with you and bring you back to God when you have strayed...do they genuinely care about your welfare ...even if it may bring a personal cost to them?)

2. **Are you able to accurately discern what type of Spirit is living inside of each individual that you come into contact with?** (Words cannot always be trusted. "Believe Behavior".... watch the person's behavior over a period of time.)

3. **Are you so lonely and love-starved that you are allowing "anyone" into your life and personal space?** (Remember that most temptation is very appealing and can be very pleasant to our senses.)

If you are finding it difficult to see whether or not you are surrounding yourself with the right people or friends, I encourage you to begin reading God's word and seek the counsel of a "Godly" friend. It is ABSOLUTELY OKAY...and God wants us to pray and ask for wisdom and discernment... You are His child and He gave His life for You! He wants to pour out His blessings upon you today!

"Dear Father, I am grateful for your involvement in my life! I am so glad that You are my Father and my protector. Lord, I humbly ask for the gift of discernment. Show me which people You want me to have in my personal life. I pray that You would take the ones out of my life that have false motives for being my friend. I pray that You would open my spiritual eyes and show me which spirit they have allowed to take over their hearts. Please grow my ability to identify what type of spirit lives inside of those that I come in contact with. Lord, I pray that You would protect me and help me to guard my heart. Fill the loneliness that I am feeling in my heart, and give me peace, strength, wisdom and endurance to run this race for You. Help me Lord to be patient and wait on You for the right soul-mate or friends. Help me to realize that if they don't love

You, then they could never love me unconditionally and the way that I was created to be loved. Amen"

Did you know that you have armor?

Ephesians 6:10-13 "Finally brethren, be strong in the Lord and in the power of His might. Put on the whole armor of God that you may be able to stand against the wiles of the devil. For we do not wrestle against flesh and blood, but against principalities, against powers, against the rulers of the darkness of this age, against spiritual hosts of wickedness in the heavenly places. Therefore take up the whole armor of God that you may be able to withstand in the evil day, and having done all, to stand." So, how does your armor become strong and "bullet proof"?

James 1:2-4 " My brethren, count it all joy when you fall into various trials, knowing that the testing of your faith produces patience. But let patience have its perfect work, that you may be perfect and complete—lacking nothing."

Looking back at some of the more desperate trials that I encountered, I remember talking to a Godly friend and prayer warrior that helped me so much. She and her husband both made the comment, *"You must be on the right path, because the Devil wouldn't be on your tail unless you were a threat to him."*

I remember how difficult it was to laugh and praise God through the humiliating and devaluing trials—because I had virtually lost everything that ever meant anything to me and I found myself homeless. There were only a few people that could see through the unfortunate circumstances to the spiritual battle going on around me. There were only a few that didn't label me or shun me when I was around them. Something about this journey of Fire and Faith has made some of the spiritual attacks more readily identifiable. These are a list of things that will start to happen when you have already been through a few rounds of these attacks:

1. When you have faith and "believe" in your Father God's abilities, you begin to call on Him and His promises sooner. (He has angels and abilities that are far beyond the horsepower of the US army, navy and air force combined!)

2. You will find and learn that eventually the things that would have paralyzed you in fear —soon lose their power over you as you fall at His feet and give it all to Him to handle.

3. You will not hesitate to call on your Godly friends for support. You will begin to pray sooner than later. It is a privilege to have prayer warriors praying with you. The bible says, **"Where there are two or three gathered together in My name, I am there in the midst of them." Matthew 18:20**

4. You will see God's hand at work—and the arrows of attack and trials will eventually start bouncing off of your armor! Your armor is made up of Faith, Truth, Trust, God's Word, Prayer and Praise...interwoven with real life application of obedience, integrity and memorization of God's promises. **See Ephesians Chapter 6**

Remember that you are Gods child! You have the authority and privilege of rejecting any hurtful negative messages that may come flying into your thoughts. **"Put on the whole armor of God that you will be able to stand against the wiles of the Devil. For we do not wrestle against flesh and blood, but against principalities, against rulers of the darkness of this age, against spiritual hosts of wickedness in heavenly places." Ephesians 6: 11-12**. I pray today, for discernment, wisdom, peace and boldness for you...and a double portion of his Holy Spirit in your life! May your day be victorious! **Proverbs 17:3 "The refining pot is for silver and the furnace for gold, but The Lord tests the heart."**

"Dear Father God, please help us to "Go for the Gold!", finish the race, and face the pain and trials of this life so that we will honor You and glorify You! Father, I claim my room in Your mansion and my inheritance as Your child. I can't wait to see You and ask You questions about my life on this earth. Mold my life so that I am fit to be used to further Your Kingdom. Amen"

Invisible Enemies: How do you wage war on something that you can't see?

The bible tells us in Hebrews 11:1 & 3 "Now faith is the substance of things hoped for, the evidence of things not seen... By faith we understand that the worlds were framed by the word of God, so that the things which are seen were not made of things which are visible."

2 Cor. 4:18 says,"...while we do not look at things which are seen, but at the things which are not seen. For the things which are seen are temporary, but the things which are not seen are eternal."

Have you ever watched the movie "Batman Begins"? In this movie, batman struggles with his past and guilt over the death of his parents. He discovers in the movie that many of his battles were with fears that he had as a child...things that were not tangible or seen. The vulnerability and helplessness that he felt as he watched his parents being shot, along with his ongoing fear of bats all disappeared when he found the inner confidence and strength to fight for the people of Gotham that his father had loved so much. There are some amazing lessons depicted in this Hollywood production.

As children of God, we are to be certain of things that we see and things that are unseen. We are to know that a spiritual battle exists... and that we can expect to wage war with the prince of darkness on any given day or any moment of the day. Many times these attacks will come through the woundedness of others. The devil will use the areas of weakness and lack of discipline in others to wage war against us.

Just this Sunday my husband and I had a conversation with a public school teacher who is male. He described several instances where he had other teachers and female students come and talk with him about their marriages or how horrible their sex lives were. He stated that he was constantly barraged with potential temptation in the form of sexual desire, intimacy and lust. He mentioned that he is ever aware of his boundaries and directs them to get professional help. He mentioned that he goes home at night and tells his wife of each instance–to keep him accountable to their marriage and to God. This man stated that one woman, who was very attractive, had come to him with impure motives at least four different times in one day. As we ended our discussion I said, "I believe that you have been encountering spiritual warfare. Can we pray for you?"

The devil will use other people's wounded hearts, addictions, and desires to try to derail you and me from the path and wonderful plans that our Father has for us. Don't be surprised...just expect it!

Our Heavenly Father has given us tools and instruction in His Holy Bible on how to prepare for spiritual warfare, if necessary!

2 Cor. 5:7 "For we walk by faith, not by sight" ... Because things are not always what they seem to be, and most people are not who they say they are.

"Dear Father, I pray that You open my spiritual eyes that I might be more discerning of situations throughout the day. I ask for Your protection and wisdom to see danger and run to You in prayer. Make me a spiritual warrior for Your kingdom–that I may protect myself, my family and those around me from harm. Amen"

Do you believe that demons exist? Have you read about them in scripture? Do you know how to protect yourself and your loved ones from demonic activity?

141

For the last 10 years, God has placed me in the practical "School of Training". I have had some personal experiences involving demons and also have been exposed to individuals who have been afflicted by them. At first, in my quest to find books and resources, it was all that I could do to read about some of the real-life exorcisms and casting out of demons.... It scared me to death. I was somewhat fearful and would start to read, then I would put the book down and pray for courage. I would then pick up the book and read another chapter...and this would happen over and over. I felt that God was leading me to become more educated on this topic of demons. However, it has taken some time to work through the mystic mentality and fear of the dark side of the spirit realm associated with demons.

Corrie Ten Boom said of demons, "The fear of demons is from the demons themselves."

God has since strengthened me and helped me to realize that these books are not, "Scary Novels"...and I definitely am not to be fearful.... These books are real-life situations that are many times situations that we may all face. Recently I came into possession of another such book that was given to me by a wonderful friend. The title of this book is, "THEY SHALL EXPEL DEMONS", by Derek Prince. This book is biblically sound and gives very practical and understandable advice and instruction.

Derek Prince states in the first chapter of this book that it became very clear to him that; ***"Satan had developed a special opposition to this ministry of healing. He is by choice a creature of darkness*** and prefers to keep the true nature of his activities concealed. If he can keep humanity unaware of his tactics–or even of his very existence. He can use the twin tools of <u>ignorance</u> and <u>fear</u> to open the door for his destructive purposes."*

In my first years in Arizona, I had the privilege of observing how addictions can actually turn into "demonic possession." When turning to scripture and reading stories of how Jesus healed multitudes of people, there were those situations where He had to cast demons out of people in order to restore and heal their broken lives.

If you have been given the gifts of healing and restoration and you feel that God is asking you to take the next step to understand how be able to cast out demons in the name of Jesus Christ,... then I encourage you to purchase the above mentioned book by Derek Prince. I pray that God will lead you in your quest to set others free from bondage in Jesus' name. The days in which we live are evil- and may require that we know how to command these demonic beings out of hiding so that people can get on with their lives. The God that we serve is more powerful than any evil spirit or demon ever was. **Matthew 17; 14-21**

"Dear Father, open my eyes to see the spiritual battle that is waging all around me. I pray that You would guide me as I continue to walk and journey with You in faith. Lord, help me to understand that I am just an "instrument" to be used by You. Help me to continually realize that I am nothing without You, and help me to be obedient to Your promptings and to pray over the sick and anoint and pray over the afflicted in the precious name of Jesus Christ. Amen"

Have you ever felt an evil presence surrounding you? You can just say, "Jesus"! His very name has the power to dispel all evil and darkness!

Twice in the past two weeks I had felt an evil presence visit our bedroom. On both occasions, it seemed to happen in the same way... and at approximately 2:30 in the morning. David and our two golden retrievers were fast asleep. I don't know why I was awake on these occasions; however, it was as if this evil presence was so strong- that it was trying to pull information from my mind. My head felt as though it was ready to burst! I sat bolt-upright in bed and started praying. I can remember saying under my breath, "My God Jehovah lives here...and You are not welcome!" I remember telling the devil to leave our house in the name of Jesus Christ!

I hadn't wanted to waken anyone; however, I reached over and turned the light on. David and the dogs both were making unusual jerky movements and were very restless. David had started talking "gibberish" and the dogs were each starting to whine. I reached over and placed my hand gently on David's shoulder and prayed for his protection. Then in a loud voice, I raised my hands to the heavens and said, "In the name of Jesus Christ I command you to leave!" Immediately this ominous presence left. David woke up startled. He immediately said that he could feel an eerie dark presence lingering in our bedroom. We prayed over each other and demanded once again that this presence leave us in the "Name of Jesus Christ"! We both noticed that the dogs had stopped whining and were resting peacefully. As we talked and prayed about this, Ephesians 6:11-13 popped into my head. It says, **"For we do not wrestle against flesh** and blood, but against principalities, against powers, against the rulers of darkness of this age, against spiritual hosts of wickedness in heavenly places. ...therefore take up the whole armor of God that you may be able to withstand in the evil day!"

Praise God that we can call on Him anytime of the day or night... and He will hear our cries for help! When our friend and pastor, Mel, heard of this encounter, he and his son, Ben came over and brought 'blessed oil'. After sharing the specific events of the encounters, we walked through our home praying over and anointing the window sills, doorways and everything in our home, claiming it all as God's territory! When we had finished, Mel anointed David and I, saying, "Whenever the evil one pays someone a visit, it is a sure indicator that God is going to do something great in and through your lives!"

"Dear Father, thank You so very much for being my protector. I know that in Your Holy Word You tell us that even the demons tremble when they hear the name, "Jesus". I thank You for loving me enough to come to my assistance when I have cried out for help! Lord, it is such a privilege to be Your Child! Please send out Your mightiest warriors from the North, South, East and West to my home to fight off the enemy. I ask that You guard my home, my family and my heart with Your Holy Spirit and Your Presence, in the precious name of Jesus! Amen"

Did you know that "Obedience" is what the devil fears the most?

What are those things that separate us from God and keep us from being obedient?

- Sin
- Worldliness
- Pride
- Self Focus

These things listed above can accompany each other. However, *HUMILITY can bring all of them to a screeching halt!*

James 4:7 says," Therefore submit to God. Resist the devil and he will flee from you."

When we "submit" to God it means that we obey without questioning...He is our Commander in Chief! Last year, my prayer warrior friend had experienced a physical spiritual attack. She was telling me that she had been sitting outside on the porch of her home relaxing and looking at her plants when she felt the Holy Spirit telling her to go inside and get some water out of the refrigerator. She immediately obeyed and got up and went inside to get some water. As she stood beside the refrigerator and opened the bottle of water, there was a tremendous crash and her whole condo shook. A woman had driven her car right through the wall of her condo. If she had delayed or not listened to that still small voice, she would have been a statistic!

God can and will do the same for you and me! My prayer is that He uses YOU and me in this crazy battle between good and evil. So, take some baby steps today. Pray out loud and let Him know that you want Him in your life. Then start reading His word (the Holy Bible) and walking with Him daily... (This means take Him to work with you, talk with Him in the car, He is with you everywhere you go!)... He will show you how to be an obedient and unstoppable spiritual warrior for Him.

"Dear Father, I pray strength, wisdom, obedience and protection over my brothers and sisters in Christ this day. Father please help me to listen to Your still, small voice. I am Your child and want You in my life forever! Please help my ears to begin to hear Your voice above the noise of this crazy life. I want to be obedient in all that I do. I know that Obedience is a requirement when wanting to follow You. Amen"

Did you know that our Heavenly Father commanded us to use our armor?

He didn't mean for it to sit in the closet and collect dust! The greatest weapon of warfare is God's Holy Bible. Scripture can be used as a weapon when we use God's promises and hurl them at the negative things and attacks that come at us.

Ephesians 6:11-13 says, "Put on the whole armor of God that you will be able to stand against the wiles of the devil. For we do not wrestle against flesh and blood, but against principalities, against

powers, against the rulers of the darkness of this age, against spiritual hosts of wickedness in heavenly places. Therefore take up the whole armor of God that you may be able to withstand in the evil day, and having done all, to stand."

David and I didn't get to see Iron Man III when it came out, however, bought the video when it came out. As we were watching certain scenes, it struck us how very vulnerable Robert Downey Junior was without his iron suit on. We are just as vulnerable, without our "armor", as Robert Downey Junior was without his iron suit. God tells us in Ephesians, that we can use the promises from His word as a sword. We are to hold up the shield of faith and prayer against any attacks of the devil. As children of God, if we are unwilling or unable to put on our armor,(as discussed in Ephesians 6: 14-18) and start to apply what we are learning to our daily lives, we will certainly fall without our heavenly Father's protection! This means that when we have negative messages running through our minds that are causing discouragement and depression, we are to tell the devil to leave in the name of Jesus Christ! Then we are to replace those evil thoughts with God's promises that relate to fear, discouragement and unworthiness until we have memorized them and eventually our mind will go to these texts as a habit when we come under attack!

I have prayed for years that God would increase my discernment, Godly wisdom and insights. He has shown me this very important fact... "EVERY EARTHLY BATTLE IS WON IN THE SPIRITUAL REALM!"

Our battles are not with the human cultists, false religions, atheists, agnostics, Obama, pseudo Christians, people at work, etc... Our battles are with the demonic beings working through these people, of which many times even the flesh and blood components are themselves unaware that they are being used by demons. Spiritual warfare is ramping up! Many of us struggle with negative thoughts and depression that tries to take over our mind. The only way to win over these things is to be in prayer and reading God's word. The word of God discovers our condition and exposes all that is dark, false and bad for our lives.

Hebrews 4:12-13 says, "For the word of God is living and powerful, and sharper than any two-edged sword, piercing even to the division of soul and spirit, and of joints and marrow, and is a discerner of the thoughts and intents of the heart. And there is no creature hidden from His sight, but all things are naked and open to the eyes of Him to whom we must give an account."

"Dear Father, help us to work the kinks out of our armor before the battle is upon us! Open our eyes to the spiritual warfare around us. Show us how to put our armor on and use it every day! Thank you for the victory that You already won! Amen"

Did you know that there are ways to "spiritually weatherize" your home?

Our homes are our refuge and sanctuary from the insanity of this world. James 5:14 talks of anointing people who are sick in the name of The Lord..., however, we can also claim physical territory and draw "boundaries" in the name of Jesus Christ that the Devil cannot cross!

The practice of anointing is highly underutilized. Some Christians feel that it should only be used as a last resort and don't entirely understand its significance. I have learned through the years that God wants us all to be Children of Faith! He wants us to believe in His abilities and to act on what He has told us in scripture. Anointing people and our homes is actually "claiming" this territory for God! It says that we expect God to 'show-up'!

Joyce Meyer in her book, "The Confident Woman" Pgs 175 & 176, talks about anointing in this way! She says, "When I think of the word, 'Anointed', I think of something being rubbed all over. We are anointed and rubbed all over with God's power. He has anointed us with the presence and power of the Holy Spirit to help us live life in a supernatural way!"

Before I ever met my sweet husband, David, I was living in Phoenix in a house that I had rented. There were some "frightening times" where I would hear the doorbell ring at 2:00am. On another occasion, I heard something in the back yard by the pool—only to turn the lights on and see a couple of young men in stocking caps jumping back over the fence. When telling my prayer warrior friend about these instances, she said, "Get some olive oil from your kitchen, bless and pray over this oil and anoint the windows and doorways of your home. Pray Psalm 91 through your house." I obeyed, and immediately I knew that God's spirit was alive and well in my home!

Even now, my husband and I have gotten into the practice of using simple olive oil from our kitchen. We pour olive oil into a small clean container or cup and then pray over it. We ask that God would fill this oil with The Father, The Son and Holy Spirit and every good and blessed thing from Him. Then we carry it through the house, dipping our fingers into it and gently brushing it across the door-ways, windows and every entrance into our home while praying to our Father in heaven- and reclaiming it as His territory. There are times when we go through and re-anointed our home. We all have the capability of allowing the wrong spirit into our homes because of our own poor choices of TV watching or we had groups of individuals over to our home that may be harboring a wrong spirit. We can allow evil into our homes in the following ways; through TV programs, by listening certain types of music, looking at addictive things, such as pornography, on the computer... or even by allowing ungodly individuals into our personal dwellings. Evil is much like a computer virus. It can seem very innocent and harmless until it grows into a monster and takes over. We can allow demons into our bodies through our senses; our eyes, ears, mouths, noses, through our rectum and our vagina. These are all entrances that we need to be the "gatekeeper" of!

Anointing with oil is an ACTIVE expression of our inward Faith! It shows our Father that we BELIEVE that ...He will "show up!" He dispels evil and darkness when we show Him that we aren't afraid to step forward in Faith.

"Dear Father, please help me to "weatherize" not only my home for you this day, but also my heart! Keep me from evil and renew my

heart and mind in You! Lord, increase my awareness of the battle that is waging for my life! Help me to show my children and grandchildren the importance of knowing You! Amen"

Are you aware that the Evil one loves to create "smoke" in our lives to cause us to get fearful and distracted?

Let me explain. "Smoke" is a term that I use to describe what happens when the devil tries to throw things or stuff in your face so that you get fearful, distracted or want to give up!

One weekend, David and I decided that we needed some exercise. Despite our better judgment, we hopped on our road bikes. About one mile out, we ran into horrible smoke from the wildfire burning up the canyon. We rode about 12 miles, however, the last 6 miles it became very difficult for me to breathe. I was tempted to accept David's offer to go get our truck and come back and pick me up. But then I began to remember all of the "symbolic smoke" the devil had thrown at me in the last 10 years. I emphatically turned to my husband and said, "Honey, I am going to keep on going!! This is just 'smoke'! Determined beyond belief, I wrapped David's bandana around my nose and mouth and pedaled methodically, taking slow, deep breaths, as I kept my eyes on the goal and my thoughts grounded in scripture! We finally ended up back at the truck exhausted and smelling of smoke.

The big test for us is: How will we react to the "Smoke" that comes into our lives? Do we crumble and cave in and get discouraged at the first sign of "smoke"? Are we immediately defined by the bad news, or do we reject the bad news and immediately turn to our Father in a Heaven and ask Him to turn it around or that His will be done?

The year David and I were married was full of "smoke". The realtor who had rented me a house in the valley that I had been living in, had been great to work with... until I gave notice that I was moving out.   I had a gut feeling that somehow she was up to something underhanded. So, I asked David, my fiancé, and another friend who had been with me when I rented the house, come to the exit walk-through to support me. This realtor showed up and was testing each of the shades to make sure they worked, flushing the toilets, looking in cupboards and examining the refrigerator and oven to make sure that they were clean.   I had left the place spotless. The yard was well-kept and groomed, the bushes and shrubs were trimmed and everything was in tip top shape. I had even replanted and up-righted a barrel cactus that had been on its side when I had moved in.

Several months after this exit walk through, I received a very offi-cial letter in the mail. As I opened it, I was shocked to find that it was a legal notice in the mail from this realtor stating that we owed them $5,000.00 due to the horrible condition that I left the rental home. I looked at David and said, "This is just "smoke"! I tore the letter up and burned it, praying that God would prevail.   (After all, we had 3 witnesses and pictures of the house from the exit walk-through indicating that I had left the home and yard in very good shape). God did prevail and there was never anything that came of this pseudo-legal pursuit!

There may be a day when you are rejected by your own, end up homeless, lose your job, get in an accident, lose your best friend, or your husband tells you that he no longer loves you... Do not give in to the "smoke"!   Don't accept the devil's wishes for your life! Remember, you are God's child! You are valuable! You are worthy of better!   You have someone to help you!   You can pass it all through your Father in Heaven!!   He will love you and help mold your character through it all!   He will turn things around and make blessings out of every situation!   ...And best of all, "**He will never leave you or forsake you!" Hebrews 13:5**

"Dear Father!   Please continue to carry me through the storms of this life!   Remind me that I don't have to react or take in the ugliness of this life. Help me to come to You with Everything!   Please turn my sorrows into Joy!   Give me hope, strength and endurance to run the race set before me!   In Jesus Name, Amen"

Chapter 9

"About... God's Love"

I want to spend a little more time on God's Love...because it has **POWERFUL**, *Healing Qualities*! I want YOU to know how IMPORTANT it is for us to ACCEPT God's love! The HUGENESS of this cannot be comprehended*!*

Joyce Meyers says this so eloquently in her book, "The Confident Woman." Pg. 40, "Without acceptance of God's Love...we are unable to love and accept ourselves. We cannot love ourselves unless we realize how much God loves us, and if we don't love ourselves, we cannot love other people. We cannot maintain good, healthy relationships without this foundation of love in our lives. Many people fail at marriage because they simply don't love them-selves, and therefore they have nothing to give in the relationship. They spend most of their time trying to get from their spouses what only God can give them, which is a sense of their own worth and value."

How can anyone describe it? God's true and unconditional Agape' love is something that we all can experience. Everyone desires and needs to be unconditionally loved and accepted by God and others around us. Although not everyone will love and accept us, some will. I encourage you to focus your energy and time on those people who do love you …and forget about those who don't. God certainly does love us, and He is able and ready to provide other people to support us who do as well. I encourage you to look to Him and stop making bad choices about who we bring into our intimate circle of friends! I do believe that we need to pray about our circle of friends…and even family sometimes. Trust me…you don't want anyone in your life unless God wants them there!

I have been one of those women that felt so bad about myself that I got involved with men who used me, hurt me and then would leave. Somewhere in the back of my mind…I believed that these types of relationships were what I deserved. In the reality of today's world, there are times when our hearts are hurt very badly…(many times by our own choices), and we are not able or ready to accept God's love because of our fear of abuse, lack of trust or inability to feel our own emotions. It is, however, entirely possible to experience God's unconditional love through others that God has brought us in contact with! This amazing and unconditional love can channel through us… directly from our Father in Heaven Himself…and into the person that He is trying to reach!

The Bible describes Love as the "Greatest Gift" that we can give or receive from each other. The bible describes love in this way, **1Cor 13:1-13 " Though I speak with the tongues of men and of angels, but have not love, I have become a sounding brass or a clanging cymbal. And though I have the gift of prophecy and understand all** mysteries and all knowledge, and though I have all faith, so that I could move mountains, but have not love, I am mothing. And though I bestow all my goods to feed the poor and though I give my body to be burned, but have not love, it profits me nothing. Love suffers long and is kind; love does not envy; love does not parade itself, is not puffed up; does not behave rudely, does not seek its own, is not provoked, thinks no evil; does not rejoice in iniquity, but rejoices in the truth; bears all things, believes all things, hopes all things, endures all things. Love never fails. But whether there are prophecies, they will fail; whether there are tongues, they will cease; whether there is knowledge, it will vanish away. For we know in part and we prophesy in part. But when that which is perfect has come, then that which is in part with be done away...Now abide faith, hope, love, these three; but the greatest of these is love."

My perception of God's Love is an irrefutable and wonderful warmth that floods your heart as it leaps within you. It then invades your soul and spreads through your entire body. When this happens, you know that God is looking down on you with such compassion, kindness and great love! He is smiling down upon you! I describe it as a wave of energy and warmth that captivates you in a big hug that continues spread through your entire body- leaving you with an awareness of energy and power from the Holy Spirit... sometime producing a pounding heart and goose-bumps as you become aware that you have had an encounter with God's Agape' love that very moment! What we all tend to forget is that we all can have God inside of us, beside us and all around us!

A.W. Tozer states, "As a sailor locates his position on the sea by shooting the sun, so we may get our moral bearings by looking at God. Much of our difficulty as seeking Christians stems from our unwillingness to take God as He is and adjust our lives accordingly. We insist on trying to modify Him and to bring Him nearer to our own image." A.W. Tozer, In Pursuit of God, Chapter 8, Pg 95.

It would seem that the pain, abuse or mistreatment that we have endured ...may have had a profound impact upon our minds, blocking us from the ability to feel our Father's love. I know beyond the shadow of a doubt, that God's amazing love exists. I have experienced it within my very being! He tells us of this amazing love in **John 3:16 says, "For God so loved the world that He gave His only begotten Son, that whosoever believes in Him should not perish but have everlasting life."** Are you willing to be the vessel that God will use to show others how profound His love is?

The Beach Boys sang the song, *"All You Need is Love."* And yes, I do agree with them, however, it is not the sexual love that we need... but the *agape* and *unconditional love*! I understand very well how difficult it is to accept God's love. It has taken me a long time to feel "loveable" and "worthy" of God's Love. However, He loves you even though you are not perfect and never will be as long as you are on this earth! He knew that many would struggle with the "Acceptance" of this free gift! **Joyce Meyer's said, in her book, "The Confident Woman, Pgs. 40, 41, "There is only one thing that you can do with a free gift...and that is to receive it and be grateful!" And now is the time to say out loud, *"GOD LOVES ME UNCONDITIONALLY, AND I RECEIVE HIS LOVE!"*** You may have to repeat this over and over to yourself maybe one-hundred times a day for several months before it sinks in, however, keep asking God to show you His Amazing Love! He will pour it out upon your heart in a way that you will not be able to comprehend it or refuse it! He loves you so very much!

Have you heard the saying, "All things grow with Love"?

It is amazing how true this really is! The catch is... Our love has to be **UNCONDITIONAL**! I was brought up in a good home where I thought that I was loved. However, much later, after leaving home, I have realized that there are certain types of love that are very "conditional". When this happens, the conditions placed on us, actually instill a fear inside of us that we aren't good enough or perfect enough and eventually these false concepts of love stifle our growth. My parents did the best they could with what they had, however, the love in our home was very conditional and was based on "performance". This was transferred into my adult life and all of the relationships that I tried to make succeed. It is amazingly true that, "we become products of how we were raised and what was 'role-modeled' to us." But we have a special "privilege" and "hope" as God's child! Just as surely as I am typing these words on paper, I am here to say that I have witnessed that our God is stronger than any generational sins or patterns! He has and will show mercy and love to us and stop the cycle of dysfunction if we only come to Him and ask Him for help!! If you will pray and ask Him to stop the generational pain and patterns in your life and your family...He will!

1 Corinthians 13:4-8 "Love suffers long and is kind; love does not envy; love does not parade itself, is not puffed up; does not behave rudely, does not seek its own, is not provoked, thinks no evil; does not rejoice in iniquity, but rejoices in truth; bears all things, believes all things, hopes all things and endures all things. Love never fails."

As I reflect back on and celebrate several years of marriage with my husband, David, I thank God every day that He has placed him in my life. It has been David's unconditional love and acceptance, along with the Holy Spirit taking up residence in my heart that has helped me become the woman that God wants me to be! My prayer is that I reflect his love and nurturing back to him in a way that his needs are also met! Thank you God for hearing my cries for help and sending me the most amazing soul mate and friend ever! He truly is the "Love of my life!" David's unconditional and constant love for me has provided a solid and sturdy basis from which God has produced a great passion and love in my heart for others. It is difficult to explain, in this world that we live in, the very precious ingredients that have helped me to love and accept myself the way that I am. However, God has shown me that I needed to see what His love was truly like. My husband, David's integrity, commitment, loyalty and love speaks volumes! I know that I don't have to be the "Perfect Stepford Wife" that so many women feel they have to be. Because true beauty comes from within and is from God. This is what God intended a true marriage to look like! He didn't intend us to be pointing out each other's imperfections, injecting one another with Botox, or keeping lists of what He didn't do or what she didn't do. God intended us to jump in with both feet, make a commitment and love, pray for and encourage one another through the storms of life. It is the hard and darkest times in the valleys of life where our love can grow into something beautiful and unconditional... only if we stick with God and let Him do the work!

Psalm 121:1-2. I lift up my eyes to the hills—from whence comes my help? My help comes from The Lord, who made the heavens and the earth."

Love covers a multitude of sins. It is the most important fruit of the spirit ...and we need its stability in order to grow! You and I are unable to grow into the confident, Godly people that we are supposed to be without the unconditional love and support of true friends and family! I will never take this for granted again! God wants you to be all that you can be!

I thank God for you! I pray immense blessing upon you with victory over low self-esteem and self-worth! My prayer is that you begin to realize your immeasurable value to God and to others around you! You are God's child! You are royalty! He knows your name! He died for You! He created you after His own image...and **God doesn't make junk**! God loves you so very much and wants you to accept His invitation to live with Him in heaven when He comes. His desire is to scoop you up in His arms and love you for the rest of your life.

"Dear Father, thank you for this amazing opportunity to be your child. I know that I have prioritized everything else "EXCEPT" You. Please forgive me, dear Father for sinning against You, and for not recognizing the fact that my relationship with You is the most important relationship that I will ever have. Lord, I am on my face

before You. I want to be Your child! Please prepare me a room in Your kingdom. Help me to learn to walk with You "one step-at-a-time". Thank You for never leaving me or forsaking me. Please come and make Your home in my heart. Help me to be a child that honors You. Amen"

Did you know that God has designed us to help each other, and bear one another's burdens?

"Bear one another's burdens, and so fulfill the law of Christ." Galatians 6:2

We live in a world that has lost its way. How tragic that it has become "all about me" in many households and hearts! Why don't people bear each other's burdens as Christ called us to?

Galatians 6:1: "... Brethren, if a man is overtaken in any trespass, you who are spiritual restore such a one in a spirit of gentleness, considering yourself lest you also be tempted."

Let us walk in the Spirit and pray for each other, thus lightening each other's load of burdens. As we confess our sins to each other...may the Truth set us free! I pray that God uses your Spirit led life today to help lighten somebody's load. Sometimes the smallest smile and act of kindness will make the biggest difference ever!

David and I recently were privileged to officially join our church as members. As we sat in our membership class, Pastor Bob painted the vision of what it means to be a member. He went on to say that we all are "ministers in Christ". He mentioned that "membership" was a dynamic word of action which didn't involve sitting in a pew. He said membership is all about "Love One-Anothering". Pastor Bob went on to explain that when we see someone that is down and depressed, we need to come along side of them and take them food, go out for coffee or ask them what we can do to help them. It is coming alongside someone to help them.

We are called to love others and do good,… even when we are tired and maybe even grumpy!

Because our God can turn our weary, grumpy hearts into grateful and thankful hearts of compassion and love for those that we reach out to! When we take the baby steps forward, it is like a transformation takes place in our hearts and also in the hearts of those that we are ministering to!

"Dear God, help me not to grow weary while doing good, for in due season I will see Your love at work. Dear Father, please use me today to make life a little more bearable for someone else. Lord, fill me up with a double portion of your Holy Spirit! Help me to love others the way that you do! Amen." (Galatians 6:9)

Did you know that there is no greater privilege in life than to make life a little more bearable for another human being?

The all-encompassing question is, how do I help lighten someone's load of burdens without being an "enabler"?

Galatians 6:1-2. "Brethren, if a man is overtaken by a trespass, you who are spiritual restore such a one in a spirit of gentleness, considering yourself lest you also be tempted. Bear one another's burdens, and so fulfill the law."

When you see people with burdens, they can be emotional, physical, spiritual or financial...or all of the above. I had burdens that I didn't realize were weighing me down. I had spiritual strongholds and generational pain that was very oppressive. I was also being hunted down by the prince of darkness. His intent was to take me out early on, so I wouldn't be a threat to the dark side!

I was at Church one weekend with my ex-husband and children—just a matter of months before going through with our divorce. I was approached by a woman who said, "I would really love to go out to lunch sometime. I really didn't know her very well; however, she seemed very kind. I mentioned that I thought it would be really great to meet for lunch, so we set a date for the following week to meet at this little Greek restaurant. I didn't realize how very wounded I was until we began to talk. I remember apologizing because I felt that I was unloading all of my baggage on her. As I sat in this restaurant booth pouring my heart out to this lady I tried desperately not to cry. I held the tears back for a while and then the dam broke loose. I began to mop up streams of tears and mascara that were running down my face, as she said, "Karen, I am so privileged to sit here and listen to what you have been through!" She then grabbed my hands and prayed with me. She told me that she had noticed my sadness from across the room and wanted to help me if she could. I also shared with her that I had been praying for God to send someone to help me. This woman was sent by God to help get me out of the pit! We met several more times and she was very instrumental in helping me during one of the darkest times in my life. I remember her repeatedly saying, "I'm so sorry that you had to go through the pain... that isn't normal." Through the course of our meetings, she shared that her husband was a clinical counselor and she had experienced depression in her own family. She said that she had been able to identify my sad demeanor and countenance and was impressed that she needed to intervene.

On another occasion, after my divorce, I remember a certain woman with an amazing heart who owned some apartment complexes. This woman was such a guardian angel in my life! I remember her wonderful caring spirit. She helped me get into an apartment when I was in crisis and shared her spare room with me until I could get on my feet and into a safe situation. She gave me a safe place to be when I was in danger and someone was stalking me. This woman prayed and believed in me when no one else would. I was definitely "labeled" and ostracized by many in the community where I was living and eventually became homeless.

Things were drying up for me in Lincoln, NE. I had lost my job, my apartment, and was destitute. I was invited to live in the basement room in the home of an amazing family in Lincoln. God again was looking out for me. Their wonderful hearts of compassion saved me from the streets and offered me shelter! I was so grateful and blessed by their generosity. I pitched in to help with the cooking, cleaning and other duties around the house while I was there. They were so loving and accepting, that I soon felt like part of their family. During my afternoons of job-hunting I found a traveling nurse position in Phoenix, AZ and accepted a traveling nurse position in Phoenix, AZ, where I have lived ever since. God has restored the years that the locusts have eaten.

I thank God every day for the people that He placed in my life to help protect, guide and mentor me. Somehow they weren't the judgmental type and didn't label me as a product of my own poor choices. They came along side me and helped me battle the devil and waged Spiritual Warfare on my behalf. Little did they know at the time, that their unselfish kindness had a miraculous part in pointing me towards a life of God's blessings!

"Dear Father, You are my protector and provider. You heard my cries for help...and knew that I would need someone to help bear my burdens at one of my weakest points. Lord, I pray that You show me when others are needing strength to bear their burdens. Prepare my heart and mind that I will know when to act to help someone in need. Give me the insight, strength, courage and endurance to do Your Will. Help me not to label people, but to

love and accept them just as You did! Help me to be obedient to your callings. Amen"

Galatians 5:14 "You shall love your neighbor as yourself."

Did you know that Jesus is in the "heart repair business"?

Psalm 139:23 "Search me, oh God, and know my heart; Try me, and know my anxieties; and see if there be any wicked way in me, and lead me into the way everlasting."

For years I knew that I was very wounded. Before I finally stopped trying to fix my own heart, I was literally "looking for LOVE in all the wrong places." All of my searching ended up empty and in very twisted relationships and circumstances. I kept falling deeper into the pit of despair. I remember, after changing the locks on my door and kicking my boyfriend to the curb, I collapsed on my couch and cried out to The Lord for healing, restoration and protection. My prayer out loud to God was, "Dear God, please heal my broken heart!" I prayed that God would heal me so that I could love others again–and so that I would attract the kind of person that He wanted me to be with!

As I laid down on the couch and dozed off, God sent me this amazing answer in a dream.

Jesus was standing in front of me in my dream. He tenderly placed his hand over my heart. Then He reached into my chest cavity and removed my heart and gently held it in His cupped hands. He then surprised me and threw it around and started juggling with my heart over His head! Then He forcefully threw it to the ground–where it shattered on the cement where we stood. He then scooped it up and re-shaped it...oh so carefully, in His cupped hands. I watched as He gently placed this re-formed heart back in my chest cavity... ever so lovingly. He then placed His hand over my heart to heal and reseal the opening that He had created. To this day I have never for-gotten this dream. Because as I woke up, I began to realize that "I" was the one that was constantly making choices that were wounding my heart over and over again. Jesus showed me that He would heal my heart and repair all of my woundedness if I would only turn my life over to Him to manage!

In the days and months that followed I shed many tears and had unbelievable moments and conversation with God.... Finally I said one day, "Dear Jesus, I don't want anyone in my life, unless You want them there!" "It is up to You from here on out!" "And if I am sup-posed to be single for the rest of my days, help me to be okay with that decision. Please give me peace about whatever You decide!" God heard this prayer and must have decided that I had passed the test. It was as though there was a switch that flipped and God said, "Okay, now she is putting the Kingdom of God first!" My husband and I started talking on E-Harmony seven days later. Today, I am married to the "Love of My Life!" God matched us up with close to 100% compatibility and an incredible growing love for the Lord!

Whatever is on your heart today, I urge you to start trusting Your Heavenly Father with it! He is the "Only One" that has the power to move mountains! He can turn your life into something more beautiful than you ever imagined!

Matthew 6:33 "Seek ye first the kingdom of God and His righteousness, and all of these things shall be added unto you."

"Dear Father, You are love! Thank You for loving me through my woundedness and for not giving up on me! Please give me a heart like Yours... And a double portion of Your Holy Spirit to fill me up so that I can minister to others for Your glory! Bring me to the place in my life where my heart is healed and repaired enough that I won't wound others. Teach me to love others as You do! Amen"

Did you know that God wants our lives to flourish? He doesn't want us to settle for just "mediocre"!

Jeremiah 17: 7-8. Says, "Blessed is the man who trusts in The Lord, and whose hope is in The Lord, for he shall be like a tree planted by the waters, which spreads out its roots by the river, and will not fear when the heat comes; But its leaf will be green, and will not be anxious in the year of drought, nor will cease from yielding fruit."

As my husband, David and I had ended the week, we discussed how it seemed that every possible form of tribulation had come knocking on our front door to try our hearts, distract us...and tempt our exhausted minds. That night as I knelt before my Heavenly Father in prayer to dump my burdens at His feet, I became very emotional. I started weeping and calling out to God with intensity and desperation. I begged Him to walk beside us through these trials and tribulations. I asked God to show me what David and I were to learn from these situations. I immediately felt a peace come over me as He impressed upon my heart that it would all be okay...and that it would be for His Glory. I am continually reminded that our Heavenly Father brings testing and trials to keep us close to His heart. He never tires of hearing from us!

Just as the great tight rope walker, Wallenda, was talking to his Father in Heaven, with every step that he took while crossing the biggest test of his lifetime—The Grand Canyon, so our Father in Heaven wants us to draw near to Him when our tests and trials come. He yearns to wrap His arms around us, comfort us with His loving promises, and wrap our tired bodies in the warmth of His peace, safety and love. He continually whispers in our ears that He loves us so immensely, and that He gladly gave His life so that we could live abundantly! Why is it that we don't run to Him in our spare moments to tell him what is going on throughout the day? Why do we keep turning to other things? Is it because we think He doesn't really love us... Or do we get distracted with life?

Our Heavenly Father's love is truly important! There are some of our earthly fathers that never were shown how to love their children. Over the July 4th weekend, David and I were in the car and turned the radio on. A song started to play that was sung and introduced by Reba McEntire. It was entitled, "The Greatest Man I Never Knew." As the song went on, it basically said that all of her father's energy went into making life possible for her, however, she regretfully never got close to her father..., and he never told her the "Greatest words that she had never heard,"...and longed to hear," I love you." As the song came to a close, I couldn't help but weep because the story rang all too true in my own life and in the lives of others that I know. My heart is very saddened at the growing number of fathers who have not learned how to love their children or themselves.

Our Heavenly Father, He has all the time and energy in the world to get to know you!   He isn't held captive by time or the inability to connect with His Children.   He knows you by name! He knows how many hairs are on your head, He knows where your heart is or if your heart is breaking and what is bothering you. He can be in more than one place at a time...and he always clears His schedule to talk with you! Especially when the trials of this life become unbearable, our Heavenly Father wants to hear from you and me! He so loves us!

"Dear Father, even though I can't see your face through the black clouds that try to hover over me, please continue to show me Your will for my life! I may have utterly disappointed You at times,... But Lord, please continue to journey with me and always remind me and tell me that You love me and will never leave me or forsake me. Amen"

Did you ever think that your "heart" and "bubblegum" may have in common?

Let me explain. Years ago when my daughter was in the eighth or ninth grade, I remember that we really started to butt heads.   I recall that she felt my expectations of her were unrealistic. (You

171

must know that I was quite a perfectionist at this time and expected perfection from everyone around me.)

I felt she should have her room perfectly spotless each day before she left for school. Britanny was involved in sports, drama team and had a lot of homework to do. It seemed that we really weren't getting along at all. One night I had a dream that was so very real. I awoke sobbing and crying. The dream went something like this:

I remember watching my daughter and her friends pile aboard this train. They were going to travel across the United States and Europe and experience all the different cultures. In the dream, my ex-husband, myself and my son, Nick, were watching the train pull away from the station as we waved at their smiling faces.

As the train pulled out with Britanny and her friends on it, we piled into the car and drove alongside the train for a few miles. Suddenly, the train unexpectedly veered off the tracks and crashed into a wooded ravine. As we watched in disbelief, I screamed and started to cry. We pulled over to the edge of the road and ran over to the ravine to see if there were any survivors. There were none found alive. My son, Nick came up shaking and carrying a big "wad of bubblegum" the size of his fist. "I can't believe it," he said, "This huge wad of hardened bubblegum derailed this train!" I was so struck with grief and all I could remember was my son sitting there on the tracks, shaking his fist and comparing it to the size of the "wad of bubblegum" in his hands. I was sobbing over my daughter's lifeless body inside the wreckage.

As I wakened and fully realized that this had been a dream, I knew that God had sent this dream for a reason. I tiptoed out to the living room so that I wouldn't waken anyone and began to pray for God to show me what this was about. He showed me that the train Britanny was on, represented her journey through life. The "bubblegum", ironically, being the size of a fist, represented my heart. My hardened, prideful, perfectionistic heart had hardened to the point that I had derailed my daughter off the path that God wanted her to be on. The following week as I reflected, I realized that my daughter was trying to meet the demands of her teachers, volleyball coach, drama teacher, and a whole lot of other people that were wanting a piece of her. She was so stressed out this semester that she actually developed "shingles". We ended up compromising on the cleanliness of her room and a few other things.

"Most people need one area in their life where they can just breathe and not have to be perfect." –unknown

I needed to allow my daughter to have her room as her place of escape and relaxation. I just asked her to keep the door shut. Sometimes, we parents, may win the battle and loose the war... unless we can expect a little less perfection at times...and just love our kids when they are around. Through the years I have been learning that: **<u>Rules and Expectations without prioritizing Relationships can end in chaos.</u>** I have realized that my heart can either be a soft, pliable and flexible wad of bubblegum, or it can become a very hardened wad of bubblegum that has the potential of derailing those closest to me off of their God-designated path.

"Dear Father, I kneel at your feet today, begging that you will keep me humble and keep my heart soft and useable. Please nudge me when my expectations and agenda become way too important. Help me to consider others ' needs before my own and "Bear others' burdens and love others as You would have me to. Help me to be a useable vessel instead of a stumbling block. Amen."

Who really is the ultimate expert on Love and its effects on the Brain?

Dr. Daniel Amen is known as an expert on the brain. I recently visited Dr. Daniel Amen's website and listened to a presentation of his conclusions after having done thousands of spect scans of the brain. Dr. Amen emphasizes the fact that most violence, anger, ADD, ADHD, depression, anxiety and even dementia can be treated if the person is willing to get professional counseling to help heal their brain! He emphasized, with great excitement, that if you have the opportunity to help someone change their way of thinking, they have a much greater chance of living a productive life! This can be done with professional counseling, behavior modification, diet, and placing the right people around you! **However, Dr. Amen left out the Spiritual aspect of being securely and unconditionally loved by our Heavenly Father!** *THE SINGLE MOST IMPORTANT THING THAT WE NEED TO KNOW ABOUT GOD'S LOVE...is that it has the power to transform us! We can't truly love ourselves without accepting His love for us...and we truly cannot love others unless we accept His love for us!*

Psalm 110:10 and Proverbs 9:10 say, "The fear of The Lord is the beginning of wisdom."

JESUS is actually where all true love and wisdom come from. He created us and has known all the scientific reasons for doing what we do! His instruction book- the Holy Bible has exuded wisdom and secrets for fruitful and productive living for centuries! God's Word is a powerful instruction book for all of us! God basically wishes for all of us to be whole, healed, and happy, well- adjusted human beings. God speaks of loving one another and how it is the most powerful thing we can do! ... The reason behind this, and the reason that unconditional love is said to be the most powerful fruit of the spirit is because it has the power to HEAL people's lives! INCREDIBLE!!! **1 Cor. 13:13 says that "The greatest of these is Love."** Unconditional love, which only comes from knowing Jesus Christ, has the ability to change our brains and lives...and even mend our broken hearts. ....but only if we can accept His wonderful love!

God knew all of this before Daniel Amen ever came across this! Even though Dr. Amen is an expert in his field of neuropsychology ...we, Christians can have healthy brains and lead productive lives if we will only read God's instruction book and carry out and do what God's Holy Spirit tells us to do. The word of God is more powerful than a two-edged sword. (Hebrews 4:12) God will show you what you need to eat, how to live healthfully, get enough rest, and which friends you should hang out with! He knows everything about YOU!

"Dear Father, thank You for your unconditional love! Please show me how to love others the way You live them! Thank You for never

giving up on me when I was rejected, feeling unloved and abandoned. Help me to love others and provide a healing environment so that You can be glorified! Amen."

Do you know that Your Heavenly Father loves you so much that He is preparing a place for you?

John 14:1-4 says, "Let not your heart be troubled; you believe in God, believe also in me. In My Father's house are many mansions; if it were not so, I would have told you. I go to prepare a place for you. And if I go to prepare a place for you, I will come again and receive you to Myself; that where I am, there you may be also. And where I go you know, and the way you know."

As my husband and I were preparing for my son to come see us, I was overcome with a lot of emotion and anticipation! It had been about two years since we had actually been able to hug Nick, talk with him about his life, laugh together and talk of the wonderful things we remember, eat some homemade food together, and do some special things that we all enjoy! It chokes me up to think of my own children- and then to think of our Heavenly Father's anticipation of having us come home to live with Him in heaven for eternity!

Our Heavenly Father loves us so much...He is preparing a special place in heaven for us! He even calls our houses, "mansions"! In fact, He already knows;

-your favorite colors

-your talents

-your favorite foods

-what hobbies and things you like to do!

Psalm 139 talks of how well Jesus knows us all,...after all, He did create us! Isn't it amazing that when we know that someone (Our Father in Heaven) loves and believes in us...we find the courage to put one foot in front of the other?

Wow, Our Father in Heaven knows so much about us- and has taken the time to make us so unique that there is no one else that is like us! Don't you think that it is just as important to read His word and start learning about Him too? One of my Godly friends calls the BIBLE, God's "Basic Instruction before Leaving Earth". Our bibles weren't meant to sit on a shelf somewhere collecting dust! God's Holy Word is meant to teach us all things. What is keeping us from digging into scripture and finding out about this Wonderful Jesus, our Heavenly Father that has adopted us? We can read all about our Father's personality and about our inheritance as His Children!

Jesus said in John 14:21 "He who has My commandments and keeps them it is he who loves Me. And he who loves me will be loved by My Father, and I will love him and manifest Myself to him."

Dear Father, "Thank You for never giving up on me! I can't wait to hug You and ask You a million questions when You get here! I know that You are preparing a place for all of Your children! I am so humbled and excited that You tell of the fact that You are coming back to rescue us from this world. Lord, I pray that as I read Your Word, that You would increase my knowledge, under-standing, and the favor that I have with God and man. May Your Spirit be poured out upon me that I would love others and help them prepare for their mansion and their place in heaven as Your Children." Amen.

Did you know that true love covers a multitude of sins?

"And now abide faith, hope and love, these three; but the greatest of these is love." 1 Corinthians 13:13

Why is love the greatest of these? And what would "true love". Look like? Well I assure you that it is not the erotic, sexual love that most love songs sing about. It is unconditional and has no expectations of you. There is something about true love, that when given uncondi-tionally, it actually heals hearts and relationships! It also Increases our capacity to carry this gift of love around to bestow on others!

1 Corinthians Chptr 13 talks of how love suffers long and is kind. There is something about true love that suffers long, is full of humility and truly puts up with people that it would be easier to give up on. It does not agree with the world's advice and doesn't label others.

If I truly am a Child of God, I will set aside my own plans and agendas and journey with my Christian brothers and sisters. This means that I will drop my plans to help someone in need, provide transporta-tion or a meal for someone who is hungry. I will help someone financially if they have legitimate needs. Because this life is never all about me!

I have found that as I have prayed for God to give me a double and triple portion of His love, unexplainable things start to happen when I begin to take my baby steps forward to help others! This is during these moments when Jesus and His Holy Spirit begin to change our hearts of stone with the most wonderful, soft and loving hearts possible! It truly is a miracle! When we come alongside each other in true Godly love and bear each other's burdens...a true Miracle happens! Our hearts leap within us and it causes such great joy to help others that we never want to stop! There is absolutely no room for the Scrooge heart anymore!

I pray healing over each of our hearts this day! I pray that we all continue to seek God out and ask Him to change our hearts! It truly will be the beginning of the most beautiful You ever!

"Dear Father, I know that my heart and mind are at the core of everything that you want for my life! I need You to heal my heart and mind from past woundedness so that I can live what life I have left with such Joy and Love that I have never known! Please teach me to love others...and to remember that this life is not about me, but it is about Glorifying You! Amen."

Chapter 10

"About... Faith"

"Faith". What is it? How do you get it? And where does it come from? Faith is something that is very high up on the list of "must haves"! The Bible places a weighty importance upon faith. **Hebrews 11:6 says, "Without faith it is impossible to please God."** As a Child of God, faith will get you anything, take you anywhere in the kingdom of God. It seems a bit difficult to understand, however, I will give it a shot! I was working with the youth group and we had a discussion about faith versus trust. "Trust", I explained, is something that is earned. For example, "Faith", on the other hand is when you and I take one "Baby-step" into the unknown. It is much like walking out onto the end of a diving board blindfolded... and diving into something that you cannot see. Faith is when God asks us to believe in something without seeing it. **Hebrews 11:1 states, "Now faith is the substance of things hoped for, the evidence of things not seen."** Faith is an "active" word. It is not something that we can attain by staying in our comfort zone. We cannot attain it by, "Playing it safe" or by getting lost in trying to prove our own theories through scientific or medical research. There are miracles that happen every day as a result of individuals that step forward in faith.

Hebrews is the "Faith Book" ...and I would encourage you to read the entire chapter of Hebrews if you really would like to see what faith is all about. By faith- Noah built the ark in his backyard. He endured taunting and jeering for his blind faith. I am sure that Noah questioned his own sanity at times. He may have even endured harsh criticism from his own family for standing up for his faith in God. Then there was Moses, who led the children of Israel through the Red Sea on dry land by faith. I am most certain that when God told him that he would make a path through the middle of the Red Sea that Moses wasn't sure what to believe either, however, Moses moved forward and started walking into the sea anyway! The walls of Jericho fell because the children of Israel had faith enough to believe that God would give them the victory over this city by just marching around it seven times and being obedient!

"Faith" is the same as "Believing". Do you recall the dramatic story in the book of Numbers 21: 3-9 where faith is seen in action? The Children of Israel became discouraged and were speaking out against God. God then sent fiery serpents among them, and they bit the people; and many of the people of Israel died. The people then came to Moses and admitted that they had sinned against God and also against Moses. They begged Moses to pray to God and ask for forgiveness. Moses began to pray- and God instructed him to make a fiery serpent out of bronze and place it on a pole. **"And it shall be that everyone who is bitten, when he looks at it, shall live." Numbers 21:8** So Moses made a bronze serpent, and put it on a pole; and so it was, if a serpent had bitten anyone, when they looked at the bronze serpent, they lived.

A.W. Tozer states, "Faith is the gaze of a soul upon a saving God." From "The Pursuit of God", Chapter. 7, Pg. 83. It seems to me that if you and I simply acknowledge that there is a God- that in itself is the beginning of our faith journey. It is this "baby step" that God requires in order to save us from sin. With it there would be no approach to God, no forgiveness, no deliverance and no salvation. There would be no conversations with God and no spiritual life at all.

George Muller is a man who was full of faith. It is told that he was no stranger to hard times. His faith was such that one night as his wife and children came to him and were crying out in desperation that there was not a scrap of food in the house, he instructed them to go ahead and set the table and prepare for dinner anyway. They sat down to the table and prayed for the meal that they knew that God would provide. Sure enough, soon after their prayer, the doorbell rang- and some kind friends were at their door with food for dinner!

Faith becomes a way of life...and more importantly, faith happens when we live out our lives in total dependence upon our Savior!

Did you know that, "The Christian faith has not been tried and found wanting... It has been found difficult, and left untried." -G.K. Chesterton

There is great cost to discipleship. The Bible talks of Jesus' discipleship and the selflessness that His followers had. The world that we live in has lost its way. Our world believes, and will tell you, that life is, *"All about you"*...when scripture plainly says that our purpose on this earth is to glorify our creator and to love everyone that we come in contact with.

Matthew 7:13-14 says," Enter by the narrow gate; for wide is the gate and broad is the way that leads to destruction, and there are many who go in by it. Because narrow is the gate and difficult is the way which leads to life, and there are few who find it"

There was a time in my life when I was living in adultery. I was divorced, and was starved for attention and affection. I moved in with a man who had not made any commitments to me. He was saying all the right things and was 20 years older than I was. He had a winning smile with a Boston accent. We had a wonderful time cooking and taking walks, watching movies and spending time together. However, I could not share with him my relationship with God that was beginning to grow. Somehow there was a "darkness" about him that I could not put my finger on. My conservative and strict upbringing had pushed me to find a better way of life that was more loving and rewarding and less judgmental. However, I was pretty much living a life that was contrary to God's desire. I was not reading God's Word consistently...and was living in rebellion. I was desperately searching for a man to love me, hold me, and treat me with love and respect. Somehow I was under the impression that if I physically gave everything that I had, that this man would love me back with everything that he had.

Wrong Answer! I soon felt that this man wanted someone to "control". He got angry if I was at church for too long. He said, "Church is somewhere that you go for an hour and listen to a sermon and then come home. It shouldn't last all day!" He would frequently get upset about my involvement in activities at the church and I would then hear about it when I got home. Soon after I had moved in with him he was diagnosed with non-Hodgkin's lymphoma and started receiving treatments for cancer. As I looked up this diagnosis in my Tabors Medical dictionary, the words hit me in the face like cold water. I read that non-Hodgkin's lymphoma typically hits men in the 50's-70's age group. It then talked about many different factors could cause this lymphoma. I then turned the page and read that, "it can also be caused by auto immune disease". Immediately, the Holy Spirit impressed upon me the discussion that we had about his sexual involved with several hundred women. It was in this moment when God revealed to me that this man whom I thought loved me, had a "sex addiction". I knew at this time that I had also been infected with HIV and eventually, over the course of the next 2 years, I ended up with full blown AIDS. I was in prayer immediately asking for God's healing. Soon the opportunity came to move out one weekend. I knew that God couldn't heal me physically or emotionally if I were to stay with this man and continue to be a part of the darkness and sin in his life! I needed to show God that I was serious!

I was offered an apartment with an attached garage by a wonderful woman from our church. I did not hesitate to act on this opportunity to move out. This man continued to "stalk" me for the next 6 to 12 months. One day I came home from work and he was sitting on my couch. Eventually, God helped me break totally free of this relationship. And soon after, I became homeless and was taken in by a wonderful Christian couple with big hearts. I stayed in their basement room for several months until, with God's guidance and help, I was hired as a "traveling nurse" to move to Phoenix, Arizona. I had already begun to lose weight, and upon moving to Arizona, my daughter, hardly recognized me. I was approximately a size two. Today, however, I am totally healed from AIDS! God has restored my health and filled my life with many blessings—including an amazing husband! I owe everything that I have and everything that I am to My Jesus...and I don't want to ever live my life without His guidance!

So, my friend...when this lost world is telling you to do "this" or "that", don't believe it! Go to God's word for guidance and direction. Our Father has left all of us many promises and instruction. **Only He can do all things!** If you have faith the size of a mustard seed...the bible says that you can move mountains! (Matthew 17:20)

"Dear Father, please help me to never doubt your abilities when I come to you in prayer, but to believe that You, Jesus, can do ALL THINGS! Amen."

Mark 9: 23-24 "If you can believe, all things are possible to him who believes." "...Lord, I believe; help my unbelief!"

Matthew 6:33 "Seek ye first the kingdom of God and His righteousness, and all of these things will be added unto you!"

How are your Faith Muscles...What do you believe that Jesus can do in your life?

Mark 9:23-24. (Jesus is asked to heal a boy who had been plagued with demons since birth.) **"If you can believe, all things are possible to those who believe." Immediately the father of the child cried out and said, "Lord, I believe, help my unbelief!"**

There were many times of desperation in my life as I was becoming reacquainted with Jesus. One such occasion happened as my little car, all of the sudden, lost power in the middle of morning traffic. I had no money to take my car in to get it fixed. I was literally sweating bullets and in the middle of rush hour traffic. At the time I was working as a home health nurse for an agency in Nebraska. In my mind I kept thinking, "If my car doesn't work... then I am out of a job!" As my little Rodeo gradually lost power and all of the lights started flashing on the dashboard, I wrestled it to a side street and turned it off, the tears started to come. I had no idea how to fix my car- and really had no one to phone to help me. Then it struck me to phone a wonderful woman that I had met. She had helped me pray over other things in my life just the week before. The phone started to ring and I prayed that she would pick up. Her familiar sweet voice came over loud and clear. I explained what had just happened to my car and I knew that she sensed the desperation in my voice. She prayed for all of the electrical wiring, the spark plugs, the transmission and every part that existed under the hood of my little car. After her prayer she said, "Okay, now I want you to stay on the phone while you start your car!" I was so fearful that

I could hardly breathe! I slowly turned the key in the ignition...my car started immediately as if nothing had ever been wrong with it!

Our Father in Heaven wants us to start "practicing" our journey of Faith with Him! If we don't start running to Him and testing Him with these smaller things... our faith muscles will not grow larger and we may not have faith or trust Him when are faced with life or death situations. We must have the faith of a little child! I know that our Heavenly Father can do **ANYTHING**! Call on Him! He loves you so much!

Matthew 6:25-34 has a lot to say about faith and worry. Verse 25 starts out by saying, "Therefore I say to you, do not worry about your life, what you will eat or what you will drink; nor about your body, what you will put on...." And then in Verse 30 God says, "Now if God so clothes the grass of the field, which today is, and tomorrow is thrown into the oven, will He not much more clothe you, O you of little faith?"

"Dear Father, I realize that I need to run to You with every need that I have. I now know that You want to help me find my car keys when I have misplaced them, my phone when I can't find it, my dog when she has escaped and is running around the neighborhood! I will come to you when I need help with groceries and finances.. and when I don't know if there will be food on the table tomorrow. You want me to start coming to You with all of my concerns, needs and desperate situations and circumstances! You, Oh Lord are the One that is on the throne. You are my protector, provider, counselor, friend and healer! With You all things are possible! Amen"

Is Trust the same as Faith? How do you "Have Faith in Jesus Christ"?

This is the million dollar question that has caused many people to walk away from Jesus Christ... only later to find themselves desperate to know Him. There is not one Christian alive on this planet today that just woke up and "had" faith! As the old saying goes, **"Trust is Earned"...** but Faith is stepping out into the unknown and believing that God will be there with you! It is something that the world looks at and says is "crazy"! It is something that only your repeated journey can build. Somehow, miraculously,... as we hand our burdens and problems over to God on a daily basis, is He able to show us what He can do in our lives!

"But without Faith it is impossible to please Him, for he who comes to God must believe that He is a rewarder of those who diligently seek Him." Hebrews 11:6

Have you tested God recently? Our Father in Heaven really does want us to lean on Him and trust Him...and even test Him to see if He is trustworthy! I once heard a story that put it this way:

Once there was a young man that was getting ready to purchase a brand new car. He went to this local used car lot and chatted with the owner. He mentioned that he had a certain budget to work within. He said, "I want something dependable and something that will last for a while. I also could use some extra room to carry my friends around and would love something that has a little extra power under the hood, just in case." The owner looked at him and started to show him around. He took him towards a beautiful shiny mustang convertible. The young man loved this car, but when quoted a price his face fell and he said, "Sorry sir, that is out of my budget." The owner, also a mechanic, had suddenly remembered his old faithful Cadillac that was sitting out back. He had owned this car for a very long time and had actually replaced the original engine with a much bigger and faster one when he was in his late 20's. He and his wife had decided they would put it up for sale soon. As he showed the young man his old Cadillac inside and out, the owner said, "I know it doesn't look like much, but you will have to take it out for a test drive!" The owner brought out his keys and handed them to the young man. He said, "I have named this car 'Old Faithful' because it has taught me many things! As the young man started out on his test drive the owner yelled, "Oh, it also has an emergency turbo button left of the steering wheel that might come in handy!" The young man took the car out on the road and began to slowly and diligently stop at the stoplight and then went the speed limit of 25 MPH as he exited the small town. Getting on the freeway, he muttered under his breath he said, "I wonder if this thing has any guts?" As he stomped down on the accelerator, the car leaped forward. The jolt almost took his breath away as he was plastered to his seat. The car surged forward as the pressure of the accelerator took effect. "Wow, he exclaimed, this old car still has some get up and go!" He kind of chuckled to himself and then pushed the Turbo button. His face turned almost white with fear. The car started to whine and whir, then it jolted ahead again as if it had wings. He had gone from 0 to 120 MPH in just minutes or was it seconds?! He muttered to himself, "I think that this one will do!" We never know or understand Gods power until we actually put it to the test. Are you willing to take God out for the test drive of your life?

Jesus has a history of asking the *"unusual"* of people time after time. He asked the rich young ruler to sell everything that he had and give it to the poor...He asked Noah to build a big huge ark in his back yard before the flood. Jesus asked his disciples to start breaking the 5 loaves and 2 fishes into pieces to feed 5,000 people! God is the creator of *"unusual"*!

Matthew 7:7-8 says, "Ask and it will be given to you; seek and you will find; knock, and it will be opened to you. For everyone who asks receives, and he who seeks finds, and to him who knocks it will be opened."

Everything that we are...everything that we have...and everything that we hope to be is His already! What are we waiting for!?

What is God asking of you today? Take the first baby steps...and allow God to show you what He is capable of doing in your life. Learn to trust God with the little things in your life so that when He starts asking you to do the *"unusual"* and *"unexplainable things"* that require faith without knowing what He will do....you will be ready to take that leap!

If you feel that God is asking you to take some leaps of faith today and you are not sure what to do. Take these steps.

1. Pray about it.

2.   Get His word out and make sure it aligns with scripture.
3.   Call a Godly Person and ask their advice.

Every time you step forward in Faith...you will see Gods Hand in your life! *HE WILL SHOW UP!!* Expect a miracle or an amazing manifestation of "God showing up"! He loves to reward His children's faith!

God may ask you to sell your house when the market is at its worst.

- God may ask you to quit your job without having another one.
- God may ask you to set the table and trust Him to bring the food.
- God may ask you to change your lifestyle so that you can become more focused on His agenda rather than your own.
- He may ask you to sell your material possessions and follow Him to the mission field.

Whatever He is asking you to do... know that it will be the most exciting thing you have ever experienced in all of your life! You can rest assured that He has great plans for you!! God knows that building trust in Him will take some time and some testing. <u>He will ask you to trust Him with a whole lot of things and circumstances in your life before you are able to have an "unshakeable faith" in Him.</u> You are His precious child and He wants to be a part of your messy daily life! God asked Noah to build an ark and He told Abraham that he would be the father of many nations. God asked Gideon to march 7 times around Jericho and that the walls would fall and crumble at the sound of the trumpets. These men had all experienced a lot of trials hanging onto God. Most of them had built a history of amazing victories on Jesus Christ before they were asked to step out and have unwavering faith in the face of the impossible!

Matthew 19:26 "...But with God, all things are possible."

"Dear Father, I am so very humbled that You love to watch my faith grow! Thank You for allowing me to test You, and for inviting me to run to You with all of my problems, concerns and feelings! Thank You for loving me right where I am at and for never giving up on me! Please remind me that it is okay to journey with You and talk to You, just as king David did in the Psalms. Dear Father, please help me to run to You each and every day with my burdens. I do not want to carry them around anymore! Please help build my faith in You so that I won't waiver when I am tested and tried. Amen"

Did you know that God loves the Faith of the "Underdog?"

Did you realize that the minute you decide to trust God and take a baby step forward in faith, that is the very moment the Holy Spirit is poured out into your life? God likes to come from "behind the eight ball" and show us that the absolutely impossible is actually very possible with His power.

Romans 5:3-5 says, "...and not only that, but we also glory in tribulations, knowing that tribulation produces perseverance; and perseverance, character; and character, hope. Now hope does not disappoint, because the love of God has been poured out in our hearts by the Holy Spirit who was given to us."

Wow! The Father God that we serve is full of surprises. He is constantly using our horrible predicaments and trying situations to prove that He is there...and has the "power" to back it up!

Don't be surprised if he asks you to make unusual decisions that will glorify Him! God loves to help His oppressed children come out from behind the "eight-ball" and experience victory! Perhaps you are considering selling or buying a house, He may ask you to sell your house during one of the worst economic housing markets ever. This will prove to you that He is in charge...and that it was nothing else! The following are what I call "Underdog Stories":

Before leaving Nebraska, I drove an Isuzu Rodeo, which was in great need of some mechanical work and maintenance. I continued to experience problems with this vehicle and had no money at the time to fix it. My job was in Home Health and without my car, I wouldn't have an income. Suddenly it would lose power, and I would have to wrestle it to the side of the road. I remember crying out to Him in prayer on many occasions and asking Him to keep my little car running. I remember that God was asking me to trust Him time after time. It seemed that my little car acted up quite a bit! Ironically there were times that there was a message that would come up on my dashboard and it said, "REDUCED POWER"! It seemed that this message would show up only if I had not been taking time to spend with my Heavenly Father. It became very apparent to me that when this "REDUCED POWER" message came on- that God was trying to tell me that He wanted me to spend more time with Him. He showed me through these trials with my car- that I would have more power to live my life and help others if I would only spend a little quiet time with Him. Inevitably a day or so would go by and I would have forgotten the little "REDUCED POWER" episode with my little Isuzu. Then that lovely "REDUCED POWER" light would flicker and appear on my dashboard again. When this happened, my little ISUZU would only go about 30 miles per hour top speed. I would then be forced to pull off the road and let traffic go by. I would usually stop my vehicle and then pour my heart out in prayer to the only one that could help my little car function normally. God knew that I could not afford to get my car fixed. He also knew that this would grow my faith in Him. God did reward my faith and the prayers that I prayed were answered every time. I soon realized that He truly wanted me to come to Him with all of my problems. I was constantly amazed at the very fact that He was in control of my car, my finances and everything else in my life!

Another short story that comes to mind about trust and faith, is about a friend who had just purchased a Jiffy Lube car repair business. He was bemoaning the fact that it had not been very busy. I then asked Him, "Have you prayed and asked Your Heavenly Father to bring more business in?" He looked at me like I was from a different planet and said, "No I hadn't thought of that!" So, we bowed our heads and prayed that our God in heaven would bring people from the North, South, East and West sides of the city. We prayed that so many cars would be lined up for service that they would be overflowing with business. We even prayed for a specific amount of revenue that month–so he could keep his shop open! I got a call the next day from a very excited Jiffy Lube owner. He said, "You wouldn't believe what God has done, there were so many cars lined up outside our doors that they were blocking the street!"

Oh yes, believe it! Our Heavenly Father is in charge of EVERY aspect of our lives! Have you been taking your concerns to Him? He is all about empowering His "underdog" children and leading them to do the impossible. So, put your armor on and your cape and face the day!

"With men this is impossible, but with God, all things are possible!" Matthew 19:26

"Dear Father, thank you for never giving up on me...even when it looked hopeless! Lord, I bring this day to You! Remind me to run to You with even the impossible situations. That You will stretch my faith and show your miraculous outcomes. All things will turn out according to Your Will if I have faith in You. Amen"

Do you know that your Faith can make you an 'Overcomer'?

Mandisa's recent song, "Overcomer" is a huge source of encouragement to any child of God. Her album, Overcomer, was nominated for a Grammy award.

1 John 4:4-6. "You are of God, little children, and have overcome them, (them refers to: demonic and false spirits, spirits of the antichrist), **because He who is in you is greater than He who is in the world. They are of the world. Therefore they speak as of the world, and the world hears them. We are of God. He who knows God**

hears us; he who is not of God does not hear us. By this we know the spirit of truth and the spirit of error."

To be an Overcomer means much more than just a bunch of words! It means that we "Believe" that our Heavenly Father can and has already won the victory. I pray that God will open our spiritual eyes so that we eventually come to see that every earthly physical conflict, difficulty, disagreement or battle is actually won in the spiritual realm.

Mark 9:14-29 tells a story of healing and a spiritual battle for a young boy's life. I encourage you to read it. In verse 23, Jesus says, **"If you can believe; all things are possible to Him who believes."** Jesus cast these deaf and dumb spirits out of the boy and he was freed from a life of torment. His disciples asked Jesus why they could not cast these demons out. **Jesus replied and said, "This kind can come out by nothing but prayer and fasting."**

Jesus wanted His Disciples to overcome! He also wants you and me to **overcome**! He has made it very clear that as His children, He has given us the tools and the ability to have victory! It is now up to you and me to spend time with God—reading His word, praying, learning to trust Him, and then applying it to our lives.

I challenge you today to start praying for your co-workers that might be making your life miserable at work. Start praying for those around you that might be finding fault with you. Start asking God to show you His hand in your life every minute of the day! You need to know that things are not always what they seem to be... That there is a

spiritual battle waging for every person on this planet! Every physical battle on this earth is won in the spiritual realm.

"Dear Father, I fall on my face before You today. I am humbled at
Your love for me. Lord, help me to remember that Your presence is
able to conquer and dispel any evil that I will encounter in my day!
Thank You for showing me how to overcome evil! Amen"

Do you have the Faith to actually believe that God is "Who He says He Is?"

We spend our lives telling God what He can't do! He wants us to
ask Him to do the impossible!

Matthew 21: 22 says,"…Whatever things you ask in prayer, believing,
you will receive."

When I taught nursing school, I used to say over and over to my students, *"It is the Application that is the hardest."* I knew that when
they had grasped a concept …that only then would they would be
able to demonstrate it to me and *"show me!"*

It is the same with scripture. There is huge Power in God's Word…but
the power can only truly become a reality as we apply it to our daily
lives. On many occasions I have heard Gods whisper saying, **"You say**
that you trust Me with everything in your life…now "Show Me!"

During some of these times I have wanted to climb back in bed, cover my head and cry like a baby. Ultimately He has required that I hand over my job, my house, my car, my family and children. As I have learned to trust Him, he has protected me through some horrific times and saved me from certain death on more than one occasion! If you are in a place where you are faced with situations that seem hopeless, I encourage you, my friend, to stop being so safe and comfortable where you are at in life! Start taking some baby steps while you lean on Him. He will never leave you or forsake you! (This is the only way we learn to trust Him.)

"Dear Father, there are so many times when I am fearful of letting You take control of my life. I know that everything that I have and everything that I am is Yours! I fall to Your feet—so humbled that You have given me so very much grace and mercy. Jesus please take the wheel of my life. Lord I believe, but help my unbelief! Amen"

Did you know that Jesus wants you to put your Faith into action?

As Jesus and His disciples were in a boat out on the Sea of Galilee, a windstorm came up. His disciples woke Him saying, "Master, we are perishing!"

Luke 8:24-25 says: "...Then He arose and rebuked the wind and the raging water. And they ceased, and were calm. But He said to them, "Where is your faith?"

With all of the tornado tragedies going on, I can't help but remember a time growing up. I was probably in the 3rd or 4th grade. My parents had invited a couple families to our house for lunch after church. We lived in a farmhouse in Northern Minnesota. Being very close to the Canadian border, and having extreme humidity and heat, we always were on the lookout for tornado clouds forming during the summer months.

On this fine afternoon towards the end of our visit with friends, we all walked outside to say goodbye. As we stood there the wind picked up and the clouds started swirling. One gentleman took off in his van hoping to outrun the storm. The other couple said, "let's pray!" As we prayed, and our circle of prayers rose to the heavens, we noticed that the tornado which had been coming straight for our house turned and followed our property line in a totally different direction!

How many times does God talk about faith in His Word? He wants us to grow our faith and use it for His Glory!! We grow our faith by bringing everything to Him in prayer...and watching Him do amazing things because we dared to ask Him! God is not only on the throne, but He has the "horsepower" to do anything! When we, His children, see people battling depression, suicide, divorce, financial difficulty, cancer, diseases and other spiritual attacks, Our Father wants us to "Move forward in Faith!" **Billy Graham said, "The most eloquent prayers are those of action where hands are laid on people for healing, deliverance and blessing."** Let's get off the couch and be a "force to be reckoned with!" Jesus needs you as a mighty spiritual warrior for His kingdom!

Your untiring prayers of faith may save someone's life! Your interest and love for the neighbor's kids down the street might be what shows them what God's love is really like! Speak the word of Faith over the sick so that God can heal them! Don't worry about what anyone thinks!! Just be obedient and do it anyway! He asked Noah to build an ark in his back yard.

"Dear Father, show me when You are asking me to do things for You that will require extreme faith. Help me to press forward and be a bold warrior for you! Please take this fear away and replace it with Your peace. Amen"

Did you know that there is great power in the focus of Faith?

Corrie Ten Boom, who suffered in a Nazi death camp, explained the power of focus! She said, "If you look at the world, you will be distressed. If you look within, you'll be depressed. But if you look at Christ, you'll be at rest!"

Your focus will determine your feelings and your feelings will determine your thoughts. This might seem really easy, however, it isn't easy to re-program our thinking.

It has been determined that it takes approximately 30 days to create a new habit. Here are some tips to help you keep your focus:

1. **Keep your eyes on Jesus.** He is the only One that can help you battle the devil and his evil schemes.

2. **Memorize, Meditate and reflect on God's promises.** Find God's promises in scripture that pertain to whatever is bothering you. **2 Timothy 3:16 says," All scripture is given by inspiration of God, and is profitable for doctrine, for reproof, for correction, for instruction in righteousness, that the man if God may be complete, thoroughly equipped for every good work."**

3. **Fill your mind with good things.** Shut the TV off, listen to Godly music. Surround yourself with Godly people and influences! Philippians 4:8 says, think about good things! Think about whatever things are true, noble, just, and lovely and of Good report!

4. **Forget the pain of the past.** Focus and press on towards the goal. Philippians 3:12-14. God wants us to look to Him during the storms. He wants us to Praise Him through the storms! Focus on the victory!!!

The devil wants nothing more than for us to take our eyes off Jesus! He is battling for our minds, hearts and souls! He wants to derail you and me from God's anointed path for our lives. Don't let Him! Claim your heritage as a child of the King! Rebuke him and tell him to get out of your life...in the name of Jesus Christ!!

Focus on Jesus! He has great plans for you! Don't let this world's material things, relationships, sex, drugs, alcohol, or any other form of ungodliness distract you! You are a child of the King!!! He is welcoming you with open arms right now!!

"Dear Father, I am such a mess! I really don't even know what or how to pray or even talk to You sometimes! I frequently fall off the path that You have for me! I have so screwed my life up and have turned my focus in the wrong direction! I pray that You will forgive me and love me back into your arms! I have been lost, but now You found me again! Please help me to re-focus my life on You! Thank You for never giving up on me! Amen"

Did you know that..."When you have faith in people, they do the impossible?" -Nancy Dornan

Ralph Waldo Emerson said, "Trust men and they will be true to you; treat them greatly and they will show themselves great."

If you become a believer in people, then even the most tentative and inexperienced people can blossom before your eyes*. In John Maxwell's book, "Becoming a Person of Influence", he says, "The reality of life is that difficulties rarely defeat people; lack of faith in themselves usually does it."*

Who was it that dared to believe in you? Our world today has become a community of isolation, and is lacking the strong sense of commitment and vulnerability towards one another. Robert Schuller tells a story of his uncle, Henry who had faith in Him. Robert Schuller remembers his uncle's car driving past the barn and stopping in a cloud of summer dust at our front gate.

He said, "I ran barefoot across our wooden porch and watched my uncle Henry bound out of the car." Schuller went on to explain that his uncle was tall and handsome, and terribly alive with energy. After many years overseas as a missionary in China, he was visiting our Iowa farm. He ran up to the gate and put both of his big hands on my four-year-old shoulders. He smiled widely, ruffled my uncombed hair, and said, "Well Robert, I think you are going to be a preacher someday!" Schuller shared that he prayed to God that very night and asked God to make him a preacher when he grew up! Schuller said," I believe that God made me a "possibility thinker" then and there!"

As you become a person who loves people, remember that your goal is not to get others to think more highly of you, the goal is to get others to think more highly of themselves!

"Faith is more than thinking something is true. Faith is thinking something is true to the extent that we act on it!" -W.T. Purkiser

The bible says, "Faith without works is dead." Hebrews is the faith chapter. Hebrews 11:6 "For without faith, it is impossible to please Him." Who is God calling you to believe in today?

"Dear Father, I pray that You slow me down enough to have an impact on someone's future! Lord, thank you for believing in me and never giving up on me! Lord, hear the cries of my heart and help me to help someone else reach their goals and accomplish great things for You! Amen."

Chapter 11

"About... Loneliness"

*Y*ou and I were not created to live in isolation! Loneliness is not fun...and Jesus knew this when He created Eve as Adam's soul-mate in the Garden of Eden. **In Genesis 2:18 Jesus said, "It is not good that man should be alone; I will make him a helper comparable to him."**

Ecclesiastes 4:9-12, talks about the value of a friend. It says, "Two are better than one, because they have a good reward for their labor. For if they fall, one will lift up his companion. But woe to him who is alone when he falls, for he has no one to help him up. Again if two lie down together, they will keep warm; But how can one be warm alone? Though one may be overpowered by another, two can withstand him. And a threefold cord is not quickly broken."

God did not intend that we live out our lives in isolation on this earth. He did intend for us to live in community with each other. This means that we help each other grow into people that God wants us to be. This happens only in honest, open and vulnerable communication of truth, love and willingness to change.

There are times, however, when God does wants us to "Be still" and hear what He has to say. He has been known to keep individuals in isolation and loneliness until they have come to an acknowledge-ment of "God" in their lives!" Countless times in scripture, God led many humble and common people into isolation and loneliness for "desensitization and leadership training!" These times can be very painful and are not without deep heart and soul searching. I am fully convinced that Moses, David and Joseph could not have been used in their God-ordained leadership roles- had they resisted God's "desensitization and leadership training". They may not have placed God at the center of their lives. I am fully convinced that you and I need to understand "where we stand with Jesus Christ", before our lives will take on true purpose and meaning! We can have all the talent and motivation in the world, however, it can all result in "Nothing" if we don't realize where it comes from...and Who is in charge of our lives!

There are alarmingly few men or women who have the desire or dis-cipline to experience God at this level... so, invariably He uses other ways to cause us to come to Him. (Because we are like sheep and don't always know what we need) Sometimes we encounter illness, financial hardship, loss of family and friendships. All of these things that come into our lives are meant to get us asking, "God, why is this happening in my life...show me what You want me to do!" In scrip-ture, when it came to Joseph, he was sold into slavery- and went through years of trial, testing and heart-rending torture before he became the "Prince of Egypt" and eventually saved the entire nation from starvation and famine! This Loneliness, to you and me, would be like taking several weeks or months off and traveling to a very remote area without TV, Radio, Internet, I-Phones, I-Pads or any other people around us. The whole purpose of this sabbatical would be to "build a relationship with our Creator, Jesus Christ". During this time, we could begin to learn how to talk with Him out loud, how to "listen" and then how to "wait expectantly" for God to speak to us. We may even begin to understand the difference between God's voice and the Devil's whispers. We may also begin to realize that we also have the voice of our own self-talk. God wants us to trust Him to train our ears and hearts to "tune in" to His voice and His heart! This most likely will require some heart and soul work ... that is usually done without distraction in the depths of loneliness, isolation and tribulation. Loneliness and isolation can serve a positive purpose when it comes to "being still" and listening to what God wants us to hear! The "Huge reality" is that we cannot get to where God wants us to be until we are fully aware of "Who" is in charge of our lives and "What" it is that God wants us to do! There are countless leaders like; Moses, Joseph, Elijah, David, and others that God intentionally led into isolation, captivity, the desert, or the wilderness for a reason and a season.

I encourage you to start looking at "who you really are"! Don't be afraid of "Loneliness"! It is the person that you are inside when there is no one around that really matters! It is the person that remains after everyone has gone home and the lights are turned off...that really counts! If you really don't like to "hang out" with yourself, or be alone with yourself, ask God why. He will lead you to the heart and soul work that needs to be done in your life so that you can become the leader and the person that loves God, is able to love themselves...and that can love others in a powerful and

unconditional way! He tells us that even though we may be lonely...
He is always with us!

**Hebrews 13:5 & 6 says, "... I will never leave you nor forsake you."
So we may boldly say, "The Lord is my helper; I will not fear. What
can man do to me?"**

Do you Hate Being "Alone"?

You are not alone in this dreadful state of "Loneliness"! No one that
I know, readily enjoys going out to eat by themselves or going to a
movie by themselves. It is much more enjoyable to be in the company of someone that you enjoy spending time with! Have you ever
said, "I just want to find my soul-mate"?! You are not alone! After all
in **Genesis 2:18 God said, "It is not good that man should be alone."**

I was in this very place several years ago. I was so very lonely that
I was going crazy and feeling very depressed and sorry for myself...I
felt as if I was "defective" in some way. I felt like God was "punishing
me". Now I realize that I didn't feel comfortable being alone with
myself in silence...and I didn't feel comfortable in my own skin. I had
purely been floating along in life—driven by others expectations and
the busyness of life—not knowing what my own values were...or who
I really was. I was only beginning to find out who I was "in Christ".

Even though I was determined that every handsome, eligible, single
man who waltzed into my life..."Had to be the One", I saw that I was
trying to fill my emptiness with all of the wrong priorities...and I still

hadn't placed God in the driver's seat of my life! I really wasn't sure if He was interested in "who I was" ...or "who I was trying to date... or potentially marry!"

I soon realized that God wasn't going to bring the right man into my life until I began to get to know **Him** on a daily, first name basis. He also wanted me to "Be" the kind of person that I was looking for.

Exodus 20:3 says, "You shall have no other Gods before Me."

I began to realize that the better I got to know My Jesus, the better I was getting to know myself. I had no idea who I really was...or where I was headed in life. I knew that I wanted to be loved, held, respected and cherished, but little did I know that GOD DOES CARE ABOUT WHO WE ARE, WHERE WE ARE HEADED, WHO WE MARRY AND THE FRIENDS THAT WE CHOOSE!

In the years that followed, my Jesus became more important than anyone that I had ever known. He went with me everywhere. He greeted me at the end of a long day–and would calm my nerves some nights so that I could sleep. His promises rang out loudly as they chased fear and doubt from my mind. I talked out loud to Him when I was at home all of the time...and soon began to hear His still, small voice answering back.

God brought David, my husband, into my life only after:

1. **I had developed an intimate relationship with Him**...and began to realize that I couldn't live without my beloved Jesus! Psalm 46:10

2. **I had dated enough "good men" to realize that they weren't "Godly men."** (They didn't love God—and had no intention of living a Godly life. They weren't there to pray for me or support me spiritually, emotionally, physically or even financially. They didn't want to live their lives with God at the center of it.)

3. **God had to take me to the end of myself so that I would lean on Him.** I had to give up and cry out to God that I was, "done looking for a soul-mate". I prayed that God would either give me peace about being alone for the rest if my life...or I asked that He would bring someone that was Godly into my life.

4. **I wrote down a list if of 35 attributes that I knew I needed and wanted in my future husband**. (I figured some of these out from past failed relationships and knowing what I absolutely did NOT want in a spouse.). A Godly friend encouraged me to write down what I was looking for in a man because she said, "God can't bring him to you if you don't know what you are looking for!"

5. **I had to get my priorities straight! I needed a Godly man FIRST!** Someone who loved God before anything else! Someone who would pray for me and with me, someone that I could share my heart's desires with—and the purpose and passion of my life, which was to LIVE for Him. Then the physical attraction, emotional compatibility and other preferences would fall into place.

I pray that if you are at this crossroads in your life—you begin to get to know Jesus Christ! I pray that He becomes so important to you, that you will never make a single decision without His approval. If you are dating someone who really loves God not just in word...but in action, he will also love you beyond what words can express! If the person that you are dating is not SOLD OUT on God, I would probably encourage you to stop seeing this person for awhile until you had time to re-evaluate your relationship and priorities.

"Dear God, help me to not just settle! Please give me wisdom, discernment and trust in Your guidance with every aspect of my life... especially my relationships! Lord, help me to always prioritize my relationship with You above all others! Amen"

Did you know that Jesus is in the "heart repair business"? He does not want us to be lonely in this world.

Psalm 139:23 "Search me, oh God, and know my heart; Try me, and know my anxieties; and see if there be any wicked way in me, And lead me into the way everlasting."

For years I knew that I was very wounded. Before I finally stopped trying to fix my own heart, I was literally 'looking for LOVE in all the wrong places.' All of my searching for "love" ended up empty...and in very twisted relationships and circumstances. I kept falling deeper into the pit of despair. I remember, after changing the locks on my door- and kicking my boyfriend to the curb, I collapsing on my couch and cried out to The Lord for healing, restoration and protection.

My prayer out loud to God was **, *"Please heal my broken heart!"*** I prayed that God would heal me so that I could Love others again- and so that I would attract the kind of person that He wanted me to be with! As I laid down on the couch and dozed off, God sent me this amazing answer in a dream.

Jesus was standing in front of me in my dream. He tenderly placed his hand over my heart. Then I saw Him reach into my chest cavity and removed my heart and gently held it in His cupped hands. He then surprised me and started throwing my heart around. Soon He started juggling with my heart over His head, and then all of a sudden, He forcefully threw it to the ground—where it shattered on the cement at our feet. I was shocked beyond belief at this point! Then I watched in disbelief as Jesus scooped my shattered heart off the cement and re-shaped it,... oh so carefully, in His cupped hands. I watched as He gently placed this re-formed heart back in my chest cavity...ever so lovingly. He then placed His hand over my heart to heal the opening that He had created.

To this day, I will never forget this dream. Because as I woke up and realized that "I" was the one that was constantly making horrible choices that ended up wounding my heart over and over again. Jesus showed me that He would heal my heart and repair all of my woundedness if I would only turn my life over to Him to manage! He impressed upon me that very afternoon that I would **not be able to** participate in a healthy relationship **at all,** unless I was able to heal from some of the damage and wounds of my past. He wanted me to learn to **"become"** the type of person that I wanted to attract.

In the days and months that followed- I shed many tears and had unbelievable moments and conversation with God.... One day, I asked a friend to pray with me and for me. My prayer was this, *"Dear Jesus, I don't want anyone in my life, unless You want them there!"* *"It is up to You from here on out!"* *"And if I am supposed to be single for the rest of my days, help me to be okay with that, and please give me peace about whatever You decide!"*

My husband's profile showed up on E-harmony 7 days later. Today, I am married to the "Love of My Life!" God matched us up with close to 100% compatibility. Whatever is on your heart today, I urge you to start trusting Your Heavenly Father with **ALL OF IT!** Only He can make things turn out better and more amazing than your wild dreams!

Matthew 6:33 "Seek ye first the kingdom of God and His righteousness, and all of these things shall be added unto you."

"Dear Father, You are love! Thank you for loving me through my woundedness- and for not giving up on me! Please give me a heart like yours... And a double portion of your Holy Spirit to fill me up so that I can minister to others for your glory! Amen."

Chapter 12

" About... God's Plans for Your Life!"

*D*id you know that God has amazing plans for your life? The catch is...that it is all up to you! Are you willing to listen to Him and be obedient to what He is asking you to do? Most of us like to think of ourselves as "Self-sufficient", " Independent", and the types of people that don't need a lot of assistance with things. The problems arise when we are too stubborn and headstrong to realize that we are only a very small part of the "Big Picture"! God created us to glorify Him,...not to glorify ourselves! So, the answer is, "No, it is NOT ALL ABOUT YOU AND ME!"

Ouch!! This is a blow to the ego! It took me at least forty years to realize that "I" was "NOT IN CHARGE OF MY LIFE"...God was and is! I truly thought that I could forge my way through life with my brains, talent, looks and maybe a little bit of luck tossed in here and there! I don't really know that I even knew what God could really do in my life. So, here are some tough questions...Where are you at in your life? Who is the most important person in your life right now? I hope that it is Jesus Christ! If He hasn't become your B.F.F. or your

"Go-to-Person", I suggest that you start talking to Him and ask Him to come into your life! He can change EVERYTHING for the better!

Jeremiah 29:11-14 says, " For I know the plans that I have for you, says the Lord, plans of peace and not of evil, to give you a future and a hope. Then you will call upon Me and go and pray to Me, and I will listen to you. And you will seek Me and find Me, when you have searched for Me with all of your heart. I will be found by you, says the Lord, and I will bring you back from your captivity; I will gather you from all nations and from all the places where I have driven you, says the Lord, and I will bring you to the place from which I caused you to be carried away captive."

John 3:16 says, "For God so loved the world that He gave His only begotten Son, that whoever believes in Him should not perish but have everlasting life."

Did you know that we have the choice of living in God's "Permissive will"...or in His "Perfect will?"

So you ask, ***"What is God's perfect will for my life?"*** Charles Stanley has on several occasions said, "God's Word is His Will."

Let me explain.... You and I have our own free will and the power to make choices. However, if we are not constantly in God's word and in communication with our Heavenly Father... We then run the risk of never knowing what His "Perfect Will" is for our lives. Day after day we get up and go through our routines without ever consulting the ***wisest*** and ***most powerful*** person in the universe! We fail to ask Him for advice and for what we need each day! How tragic that we would chose to live powerless lives on a daily basis, instead of living the life of abundance and blessings that God had planned for us!

I must admit to kind of... floating through life without giving God a chance to have any sort of input into my life decisions. It has actually taken me years to realize that I am horrible at making choices about relationships, moving decisions, job changes... or anything else important, for that matter! I had to fall upon very hard times before fully realizing that Jesus was ALL that I needed! My Heavenly Father, I have found, is so much better at helping me make those difficult decisions than I am. He promises that His plans for us are to prosper us and not harm us! He wants us to have hope and a future! (Jeremiah 29:11)

So, why do many of us end up in God's ***"Permissive Will"*** and not His ***"Perfect Will?"***

There are several reasons that we end up out of our Father's "Perfect Will" and in less than perfect circumstances.

1. We are selfish and not wanting to give up total control of our lives to Our Heavenly Father. **Proverbs 16:9. "A man's heart plans his way, but The Lord directs his steps."** We have become a very self-centered, self-sufficient world! In our quest to have total control over our lives, we have forgotten Who really is in charge!! **Prov. 3:7 says, "Do not be wise in your own eyes; fear The Lord and turn away from evil."**

2. We want things NOW!! **Isaiah. 40:31 "But those who wait upon The Lord shall renew their strength; they shall mount up with wings like eagles, they shall run and not be weary, they shall walk and not faint."**

3. Sometimes we are afraid to Trust in God and His will! **"Trust in The Lord with all your heart, and lean not upon your own understanding; in all your ways acknowledge Him, and He will direct your paths." Proverbs 3:5-6**

We all have the choice to start our journey of faith with God! Start somewhere! Start with the small things! Pray to Him if you have lost your keys or phone. Pray to God about your worries and concerns. Ask Him to show you His Will for your life! He will!

Be prepared! Start asking God to show you and lead you to His perfect will! You will begin to see that God cares about EVERY ASPECT of your life. He especially cares about who you are as a person and what motivates you! He cares about the individuals that you surround yourself with! He knows that they will have a HUGE impact on your life!

Don't just settle for "mediocre"! Pray and continually ask God to show you and lead you into His "Perfect Will" for your life! *A.W. Tozer said, "The reason why many are still troubled, still seeking, still making very little forward progress is because they haven't yet come to the end of themselves. We are still trying to give orders, and interfering with God's work within us."*

"Dear Father, please forgive me for being so narrow-minded and stubborn! Lord please show me what Your Perfect Will is for my life! Please help me to trust You totally with my life, my family, my job and all of my possessions. They are all Yours anyway! Take the Fear, the pride, confusion and anything that is not of You! I surrender my will to You and am waiting in obedience to do Your bidding. Amen"

Did you know that God actually wants you and me to have a purpose for our lives and a testimony?

Revelation 12:11 says, "And they overcame him (the accuser) by the blood of the Lamb and by the word of their testimony, and they did not love their lives to the death."

It really hit me one evening a couple of weeks ago as I was listening to Charles Stanley. He was talking about how he prayed for his children. There were several things that he wanted for their lives:

1. That his legacy of obedience and usefulness would be passed down.
2. That they would find what Gods purpose was for their life early on in their lives.
3. That they would have God's protection and blessings over them.
4. He said, "And I have prayed that God would give them a testimony."

You and I will have more authority to speak into someone's life and help mentor them, if we have already weathered the path of pain that they are headed down...and come out victorious!

In one chapter of his book, "The Forgotten God", Francis Chan addresses two main things that keep people from developing a relationship with Jesus Christ:

1. We are way too comfortable. We don't want to be inconvenienced, we don't want to have to change. We truly aren't desperate enough to even think that we might need a savior. We are a culture of people that are too self-reliant! We don't want to put God in charge of our lives.
2. Secondly, we are too fearful. We don't like to be thrown into new situations or environments. The "what-ifs" paralyze us with fear and we are unable to move forward in faith and trust.

- "What will people think?" (The only opinion that counts is God's opinion.)

- "What if I lose my house and car?" (Your Father can eventually restore all of this and more after He has walked with you through some pain and restores your right priorities) Matthew 6:33.

- "What if I am rejected by my family and lose my support system?" (God is the ultimate counselor and He can bring individuals into your life that have greater means, knowledge, and love for Him than your past support system. They will have the God-given tools to help you and restore you!)

I encourage you to plunge into the waters of faith. Sell yourself out to Jesus Christ! He is ready to take you on the journey of a lifetime of faith if you will only begin to trust Him.

"Dear Father, I know that You have never given up on me. Even when I was in the pit of despair—You were there. Thank You for showing me that there is nothing that I can do that is of any value without You in the middle of it! Father, help me to stop clinging to my comfort zone and get beyond my fears so that You can create a wonderful testimony and purpose for my life! I want to be an unstoppable force for Your Kingdom! Amen"

How do I find and develop God's Purpose and Testimony for my life?

It seems to happen when we dare enough to wade through the pain in our lives. One of my Christian friends would encourage me saying, **"You must be doing something right! The Devil usually doesn't mess with people that aren't a threat to Him!"** If you are finding that you are going through a lot of angst, misery and hardship at work, at school, or even at church, just know that you are probably doing just what God wants you to do! If you want to make sure that you are on target and in His will, turn to scripture for guidance. God will use these difficult times of trial and persecution to show you where your purpose is in this life. He will give you a testimony that no one else will have but you! Being a disciple of Christ is not the easy way out... but it is worth every step taken and every burden that you bear in His name!

These are some of the things that I have chosen to do in order for God to "heal my heart". He did require that I wade through the pain, one step-at-a-time. I didn't realize that each step full of pain would lead me towards the purpose and testimony that He had waiting for me. The great thing was that Jesus was there every step of the way!

1. I pray and asked God every day to heal my heart of the woundedness of my past.

2. I continue to acknowledge my need of His grace. I had and continue to admit that I am nothing without Him and that I cannot do anything worthwhile unless He is beside me holding onto my hand.

3. I started by going to counseling—and had a Christian counselor do EMDR therapy (Eye Movement, Desensitization and Reprogramming) on me. (We may need help processing the pain so God can use us even more.) I encourage you to "google" this on your computer and go get help to deal with the pain of your past so that you can live in the present.

4. I ask for forgiveness where I have wronged others. We cannot heal or help anyone else heal unless we can be vulnerable and humble ourselves before God and others. We need to repent to God for our ways of error and then will have a clean conscience and a right spirit.

5. It helped to read numerous self- help books that have assisted my healing and have provided me with a better sense of what "normal" is. (Many of us do not know what "normal" is because we have been brought up with emotional abuse, physical abuse, sexual abuse, alcoholic households, work-a-holic parents or many other situations.)

When we have been wounded deeply, as each of us have at one time or another, it is important to realize that it is okay to talk about our feelings and that we need be vulnerable in order to heal. Our emotions may start feeling kind of "raw" and we may not enjoy the pain and the tears. As you allow God and His Holy Spirit in your heart to work…there will be a lot of tears. Crying is very cleansing–and is actually an indication that the Holy Spirit is at work in our heart. God's intentions are to change our "hearts of stone" and turn them into loving "hearts of flesh".

Ezekiel 36:25-28 "Then I will sprinkle clean water on you, and you shall be clean; I will cleanse you from all your filthiness and from all your idols. I will give you a new heart and put a new spirit within you; I will take the heart of stone out of your flesh and give you a heart of flesh. I will put My Spirit within you and cause you to walk in My statutes, and you will keep My judgments and do them. Then you shall dwell in the land that I gave to your fathers; you shall be My people, and I will be your God."

You and I so desperately need to start talking about what Jesus has brought us through. Don't be hard on yourself. I guarantee that there will be times when you feel that all you do is cry. There will be times where God will ask you to be alone with Him so that He can show you things and talk with you. You will begin to discern His voice and identify Him speaking to your heart. It will be a wonderful and crazy ride of trials and victories! However, our relationship with God is something that can be robbed from us if we choose distractions and busyness over Him. You will need to make an intentional choice to sit at His feet.

221

I must confess that there have been times in my life where I felt like I was living the most boring Christian life ever! There was never anything amazing, exciting or unusual happening in my life. It was always the same old grind. I was WAY too comfortable! I hadn't yet *sold out* for Jesus Christ. The bible has a term for this. It is called *"Laodicea".*

Revelation 3:16 says, "So then, because you are lukewarm and neither hot nor cold, I will vomit you out of My mouth."

(This scripture is saying that God rejects the half-hearted efforts of self-satisfied Christians.)

I was living a life that was LUKEWARM !! My life was way too comfortable. Living in a 4,000 square foot home that my ex-husband and I had built. I had a great job, I was driving a Chevy Tahoe, and my kids were in a Christian school. From the outside it looked like we had it all together and had the perfect little family.   I was utterly depressed and truly wanted to end the pain. I realized that if my marriage and my life was at the place that I wanted to end my life– well then, I needed to file for a divorce and change what I was doing. I know that God does not condone divorce; however, there are times when certain personalities absolutely should not be together. I then filed for a divorce and we sold our home.

In the months that followed, I experienced horrific losses. I lost my job, ended my marriage and my children went to live with my ex. My parents and friends rejected me. I also became homeless and destitute while still living in Nebraska. Only when things looked impossible, did I become fully aware that Jesus is really alive and all powerful! He was the only thing that I had left in this world to hang on to! I was "forced to wade through the pain" hanging onto Jesus. It wasn't until Jesus was all I had,...that I realized that Jesus was all that I needed!

Our testimony of what Jesus has done in our lives will come to pass only if we agree to start taking some risks, not caring about what anyone else thinks and begin to trust God with every aspect of our lives. This concept of trusting God doesn't happen without a whole lot of pain and profuse sweating! I pray that Jesus brings you to the bottom of the pit of despair so that you can see His face.

Philippians 4:13 "I can do all things through Christ who strengthens me."

"Dear Father, I beg You to never leave me nor forsake me! I pray for a powerful testimony in my life–so that I can talk to anyone about You and what You have done! Please strengthen me so that I can bear the fiery trials that I will need to endure. Lord, mold me in this fire so that I come out as pure gold! I am nothing without You. Amen"

Were you aware that God has given you many talents and spiritual gifts...and they may also lead you to finding your purpose?

"Well done good and faithful servant; you were faithful over a few things, I will make you ruler over many things." Matthew 25:23

I was on a praise team at a church in The Midwest. Each service was approximately 2,000 people. I loved to sing, however, before each performance my heart would race, my mouth would dry up and I felt sick to my stomach. I know that I looked really scared and uncomfortable up front. One weekend after our team had performed, one of the pastors came up to me and said, "I wanted to tell you that your performance looked rather painful and you may possibly want to pursue a different spiritual gift." I was crushed. But from that day forward I was determined, with Jesus' help, to overcome this fearfulness no matter what! Jesus has rewarded me in many ways. I am no longer afraid.

"The gifts and callings of God are irrevocable" Romans 11:29. (I wish that I could have shared this with that certain pastor.)

What are your spiritual gifts? Do you have some "hunches" as to what they are? Start asking God to show you! I believe that He loves us so much and I have watched Him merge many of my own spiritual gifts with other talents and hobbies that I have worked on to develop.

Are you...
-an encourager?
-do you love to help people?
-do you have the gift of exhortation?
-are you a motivator?
-are you a leader?
-do you have the gift of faith?
-wisdom and knowledge?

-instruction and teaching?

- do you have the gift of healing?

- do you have the gift of discernment?

- do you sing?

-do you play the piano?

-do you garden?

-do you love people?

-do you entertain and love to cook?

- are you a prayer warrior?

- are you a carpenter?

- are you an artist?

- do you have the gift of prophecy?

- are you someone who loves children?

- are you good with money?

1 Corinthians chapter 12 talks about Spiritual gifts. It seems that they all come from one place. The Holy Spirit is the giver of these gifts. When the one who has bestowed these gifts upon you sees that you are developing and using your talents to help others, don't be surprised if you receive more spiritual gifts in the process!

We are a part of God's wonderful family. His desire for us is to use our gifts and talents to bring wholeness, healing and joy to His church family, to other believers, and to our world. We are to minister to each other in order to bring healing, wholeness and restoration to this world of woundedness and pain. These simple acts of kindness and compassion will glorify God and honor our creator who ultimately is the Greatest Physician and Healer this world has ever known.

Of all the gifts that God could bestow upon us the greatest gift is Love. If we do not have love, then we are nothing. (1Cor. 13: 1-13)

I remember about a year ago as I was praying to God, asking Him how I could be a better boss and co-worker to those that I worked with. His whisper to me kept coming back the same. Sweetly and softly, He whispered, "Just love them, just love them!"

"True love puts up with people that would be easier to give up on." -Unknown

You are an amazing child of God with many talents, gifts and abilities! Begin by asking God to show you what He would like you to do. If you aren't getting clear answers, move forward in faith. Start your piano lessons or your voice lessons ... Or whatever your interests are! He will grow you!

"Dear Father, I thank You for the opportunity to grow and be a vessel that is useful for Your Kingdom! What a privilege to serve others and honor and glorify You! Help me to see people the way that You do! Lord, help me not to give up on others...but to journey with them and love them where they are at! Amen"

Do you know what things you may need in order to grow into the person that God wants you to be?

Romans 8:26-28 says, "Likewise the Spirit also helps in our weakness. For we do not know what we should pray for as we ought,

but the spirit makes intercession for us with groaning that cannot be uttered. Now He who searches the hearts knows what the mind of the Spirit is, because He makes intercession for the saints according to the will of God. And we know that all things work together for those who love God, to those who are the called according to His purpose."

To be real honest, we don't always know what we need in order to grow emotionally, spiritually and in every other way! God is the one who knows what we need! He is the only one that can turn our lives into something beautiful!

"Take Rest; a field that has rested gives a beautiful crop." -Ovid

As a child, I sensed that there were times that weren't always easy for our family. There were also those times where I felt that I could not talk about things that I was feeling. I found myself not wanting to ask for things that I needed. I remembering feeling very unworthy and ashamed and many times...not loved or valued. I remember my family not talking about situations of conflict. I vividly remember my mother sewing most of my clothes when I was in grade school. My father worked two jobs at times to support our family. We all worked hard in our huge acre-sized garden, in the field- putting up hay, feeding the cattle, and at the health food store that my parents owned. I was brought up with the saying and mindset that I was to be, "seen and not heard". Our heavenly Father, however, has a much different mindset and set of rules! He wants to see our smiling faces and hear from us all day long. He wants us to tell Him how we are feeling and ask Him for help when we need it!

Don't just settle for meaningless conversation with your heavenly father… or anyone else for that matter! He loves us and wants us to come to Him with everything! He can handle it all! God, our Heavenly Father, wants to be a part of our lives! He wants to journey through life with us! He wants us to come to Him…even the small everyday things like when we lose our keys, when we are sad, when our car has run out of gas, when we have lost our dearest friend, when we have negative tapes playing in our heads, when we are tired and overwhelmed, when we have problems at work , when we need to feel love and peace, when we have failed an exam, when we have started a new job, when we have just been diagnosed with cancer. Our God wants to be a part of ALL aspects of our lives!! He tells us to "Pray without ceasing" and talk to Him as we would to our best friend! He is never tired of hearing from His children.

In a little book that was given to me called, "Courage to Change"; written by Al-Anon Family Groups, Page 7 caught my eye. *It says, "Just for today I will have a quiet half hour all by myself to relax." How simple that sounded until I tried to do it. I found it difficult to spend even a little time alone—thirty quiet minutes out of my busy schedule were far too many! So I started with five minutes. In time I was able to find ten, and then twenty, and then thirty minutes for myself." "Amazingly, these quiet half hours are restoring me to sanity. It is through these times with my-self, much of which is spent in prayer and meditation, that I find the peace and power of my God. As a result, I have learned to tolerate and even enjoy my own company. Now, no matter what is going on, I need this half hour every day to get a perspective on my life. By sitting quietly in the midst of turmoil, I find that I am not alone. If I take the time, my Higher Power, God, sends the message."*

Matthew 21:22 says" And whatever you ask in prayer believing, you will receive."

Matthew 7:7 ..."ask and you will receive."

King David says in Psalm 63, "Oh God, You are my God; Early I will seek You; My soul thirsts for You; My flesh longs for You in a dry and thirsty land where there is no water. So I have looked for you in the sanctuary, to see Your power and Your glory. Because your loving kindness is better than life."

"Oh Father God, may I continually live my life in communion with You! Please open my eyes to see Your constant presence in my life and in the world around me. Please Lord, I ask for blessings, protection and for Your Holy Spirit and presence to live inside of me! Lord, use me as a vessel to bring others to love You! Amen"

Were you aware that the majority of people on this earth do not understand the concept or importance of their Spiritual DNA?

It is very tragic NOT to know about our Father in Heaven that created us. It is Worse Yet to forfeit all of the benefits that come with having a relationship with our Heavenly Father. Daniel Henderson, in his book, 'The Seven Most Important Questions You'll Ever Answer', gives a great example of a Twentieth-Century Fox version of the mysterious and famous story of Anastasia, the exiled daughter of the Czar of Russia. This woman was of Royal heritage and notoriety, yet, throughout most of her life, this woman did not know that she was the King's daughter, nor did anyone else. This woman lived out most of her life, never understanding or experiencing her true identity of Royalty! This woman was not able to live as though she was a child of the King. This is exactly why our Father in Heaven left us His Holy Bible to read and find out how to have a heart like His! God wants us to live vibrant, successful lives that will Glorify Him!

Matthew 6:33 "Seek ye first the Kingdom of a Heaven, and all of these things will be added unto you."

When you have found Jesus and are starting to journey with Him, He will show you many things you may not have otherwise known about yourself. He will begin to show you the spiritual DNA that you may already possess. He will also begin to grow you in other areas and give you with certain talents and gifts to use for His glory. He will bring to light areas of ministry where you are excited to serve- because they may resonate with important events or healing in your life.

1. Ask Him, and He will reveal to you what your spiritual gifts are. Spiritual gifts encompass your desires, natural talents, aptitudes and abilities. These gifts involve your ability to minister with a supernatural ability in these areas- to serve others and glorify God. It might be service, teaching, exhortation, singing, leadership, prayer or many other areas.

2. 2. God can help you use your desires, or the areas of 'passion' in your life to help others find their way to Christ. (Many a person's passions were discovered going through the most trying and difficult times of their lives.)

3. 3. Most of us were born with a measure of natural talent. Whether it be mechanical, cooking, computers, sports or mathematics. God uses these areas also, and will help us mold our lives into the most beautiful success story anyone could ever hear! Our Father believes in "Re-do's and second chances!"

"Dear Father, I pray that You show me Your Face and all of the amazing things that You have wanted for my life! I so want to get to know You and love You with all of my heart! I pray that you come into my heart and change me. Please forgive me for not allowing You to have full control of my life! I am not very good at being in charge of my life, Lord, I beg You to take over, clean my heart of anything that is not of You! Please create in me a clean heart and turn me into the person that You want me be! Amen."

Did you know that it is only when we have discovered who God is, that we are truly able to discover who we are?

A French writer in the 1600's coined this phrase, "A man who cannot find tranquility within himself, will search for it in vain elsewhere."
-Francois- Duc de La Rochefoucauld (1613-1680)

There are many people that say, "You will discover who you are when you look deep within." The issue at hand is that our Father who created us does have the capacity to come and live within our hearts and minds in the form of His Holy Spirit. And this, my friend, is the only way that we will discover who we are... by looking to our Savior, Jesus Christ to provide us with answers of our identity and purpose.

"We cannot climb up a rope that is attached only to our own belt."– William Ernest Hocking

interestingly enough, we all at one time or another set out on a mission, to define who we are. Many times these missions are ones where we seek to be the most successful, educated, accomplished, popular or respected. In any case, Charles Stanley says, ***"There is nothing worthwhile that we will ever accomplish in this world today unless we are on our knees praying to God about it."***

So, how do we start our relationship with God? I hear many people say that they pray, however, don't feel like God is listening or that their prayers "don't get past the ceiling!"

I understand this comment- and have also experienced the very same feelings. I have realized since that time that usually, God had not moved away ...I had moved away from Him and stopped spending time with Him. I have heard people say that if they go to church once a week and send up an occasional prayer before a meal that they are "covered"! However, we are tragically mistaken if we think that we will grow spiritually, get nourished, and have a fulfilling and intimate relationship with Jesus Christ while attending church one hour per week! It is much like developing other friendships! Our relationship with Jesus can grow if we are willing to sacrifice the time and energy to get to know this beloved Savior who died for us.

Jeremiah 29:13. "..And you will seek Me and find Me, when you search for Me with all your heart."

The following are proven ways to help you get to know Jesus better and will help you establish your own personal friendship with Jesus Christ. I will warn you that it will not be an easy thing to discipline yourself to sit in quietness and meditation as you talk to God. You may find that there will be constant distractions that will try to over-power you and will compete for your attention. The evil one will con-stantly try to distract you and take over your quiet time. Do not let this discourage you... or persuade you to stop. The peaceful serenity and calmness that you will feel and understand as you begin to talk with God and listen to Him will be worth it all! The road to Jesus is very narrow...and few will discipline themselves enough to find Him.

1. Reading God's Word Daily is able to:

-transform your mind.

-renew your spirit.

-convict us of sinful choices

-lead us to a better path

-keep us in God's perfect will for our lives.

-give us hope and dispel depression

-strengthen us

-help us live lives of integrity

-give us sound advice for major decisions in our lives.

-gives us joy

2. Pray without ceasing: (Prayer is a "state of mind", where we are acutely aware of God's Presence) During this time, where our minds are focused on Him, we are not only able to hear His voice much better, but our minds are better able to grasp what He is saying to us!   The following items are benefits of Prayer:

-Private Prayer = Public Power

-prayer is the only way to access our Father in Heaven along with His Power.

-prayer is communication with God!

-prayer can also be a mindset where you acknowledge Gods Presence throughout the day–taking Him with you in everything that you do.

-prayers set to music are called praise!

-prayer is actively worshiping our creator.

-prayer can be dancing, joy, praise, cries for His Help, asking for His guidance, thankfulness for His Blessings and much more!

- Prayer is a lifestyle where we learn to pray to our creator and depend upon His strength and not our own strength.

-Prayer is the greatest life- insurance policy you will ever have!

-prayer can be you venting and telling God how mad you are.

-prayer can be you running to Him with fears and problems, along with Joys, sorrows and praises.

-prayer us the greatest thing you will ever do for anyone!

-prayer is to be shared ,treasured and offered as an intercessory sac-rifice for those around us- as we hold others up in prayer and pray for God to bless them.

*** By not praying, we are declaring to God that we can handle our
    lives without Him.

3. By surrounding yourself with Godly people.

-A Godly friend is more precious than gold.

-Godly friends will enter into spiritual warfare with you and lift you
 up in prayer and help meet your physical needs.

-True Godly friends will support you and encourage you- and won't
 tear you down.

4. Listen to music that will point you to God and grow your relation-
    ship with Him. There are great Christian radio stations that play
    uplifting music and give encouragement throughout the day.

5. Watch movies and TV programs that will strengthen your integrity
    and strengthen your relationship with God.

"Dear Father, I am begging You to come into my heart! I humble
myself before you, Oh Lord, please fill me with Your Holy Spirit
and everything good that only comes from You! Most of the time
I don't even know what to ask for, or what I even need. I am ter-
rible at asking for Your help and guidance. Please teach me to run
to You with all of my problems and fears! I know that I cannot live
this life or do this day without You in charge." Amen.

Were you aware of the incredible power of the tongue...It can take you off of the path that God would have for you!

The bible talks about the power that our words have in **Proverbs 18:21 "Death and life are in the power of the tongue."** My adopted mother has told me over and over again that I should not say bad things about myself. She is very discerning, and one day I had shared the fact that I had done something and felt that "I had lost my mind." And then I said, "I feel so stupid."

She immediately reprimanded me and said, "Don't ever speak about yourself in that way! There is great power in the spoken word–and you do not want to take that negative talk into your Mind or spirit." She went on to say, ***"Honey, the brain is very powerful- and so do not ever take a negative comment into your spirit, but rebuke it in the name of Jesus Christ and ask Him to erase it from your memory."*** Many parents have molded their child's future or destiny by negative words, comments and intimidation that will greatly influenced the outcomes of their lives. Their child may choose to marry someone that keeps them from growing into the person that God wants them to be...all because they chose someone who intimidated them and bullied them much like their parents did growing up.

We humans don't begin to start treating others well until we have fully accepted, understand, and love the person that God has created us to be. Most of the time- we are a work in progress. The fact is that we cannot fully accept and appreciate the differences in others until we have fully come to terms with who we are. This process takes time…so go easy on yourself.

I have worked for an employer or two that believe they will motivate their employees by "fear tactics" and "intimidation". In the end, it causes much damage to the brain to live in a constant state of fear and anxiety. If they only knew that their rage and intimidation would not produce the end product that they had desired. However, there will be a day when they will have to answer to our Creator for how they treated the precious lives that Jesus gave His life for and entrusted them with. (James Chapter 3 talks of the untamable tongue) There is no room for intimidation, manipulation or public humiliation of those around us. We are all God's children and we are all created equally. God will hold us all accountable for these instances where we may have recklessly and thoughtlessly treated someone with disrespect or perhaps devalued them in some way. These are times that we need to have a sense of self-awareness and ask God to show us how we come across to those around us. Increasing our self-knowledge and awareness will help us find our own path to personal freedom. ***A quote from "Courage to Change" pg 153, states, "I have the right to choose my own standards of conduct, but I do not have the right or the power to impose those standards on others."***

However, there is hope for us all! We, as God's children, have the privilege of praying to our Father in heaven and deciding NOT to take the harmful words into our bodies. Our Father is willing to intercede in our behalf if it is His will. Our part of this equation is to have faith and believe that God will act on our request pray for His will to be done!

We are very impressionable as humans and must constantly be on guard as to the things we see and listen to, and the people that we surround ourselves with. Joel Osteen tells a story of his own mother being diagnosed with cancerous tumor. He spoke of how she refused to take the doctor's diagnosis into her spirit or body. She began to pray to God and then addressed the tumor directly and told the tumor that God was shrinking it and transforming her body. She continued to pray these prayers of faith many times a day. She changed her diet and lifestyle and rebuked this tumor until she was Cancer free!

Mark 9:23 Jesus said, "If you can believe, all things are possible to him who believes."

Jesus was constantly giving encouragement and hope! "With God, all things are possible!" Mark 10:27

"Dear Father, each day can be a struggle as I try to put one foot in front if the other! Please be in charge of this day, because I can't do it without You! I pray that You would help me to treat others the way that I would want to be treated. Bring other brothers and sisters to cross my path so that I can give them words of hope, healing, encouragement and wisdom to live by! May they find a better path and greater peace in living their lives for You. Amen."

Chapter 13

"About...God's Grace"

*T*here is really nothing that can define the total awesomeness of true "Grace"! If you have been the recipient of true and unconditional grace, then I would say that you are very blessed! Usually this "Amazing Grace" deeply touches and moves the hearts of those that have experienced it. To describe this "Amazing Grace may involve tears, song and huge emotions from deep within the soul. However, Webster's Definition of GRACE is as follows:

a : unmerited divine assistance given humans for their regeneration or sanctification

b : a virtue coming from God

c : a state of sanctification enjoyed through divine grace

2

a : approval, favor <stayed in his good graces>

b archaic : mercy, pardon

c : a special favor : privilege <each in his place, by right, not grace, shall rule his heritage — Rudyard Kipling>

The song, "Amazing Grace... My Chains are Gone" by Christ Tomlin, has made an indelible impression upon my heart. I remember playing it over and over again and singing along with it...and then crying like I have never cried before. My tears were because I realized that Jesus loved me even though I was not perfect! I cried even more...because I realized that Jesus loved me for who I was right now!

It took me forty years to finally realize that that God's amazing grace is free to all who will accept it! There are millions of people today that think they will gain eternal life and be saved by how good they are. It grieves my heart to think that many people will die in ignorance, deceived by the false doctrine of working to earn God's approval. Grace is one of the most valuable things that you and I have ever had offered to us! It is FREE of Charge! It was bought and paid for already by Jesus, who died on the cross to save us from sin!

"Jesus, I accept Your sacrifice of Grace that You gave on the cross! I am blown away by what you have done for me! I accept your sacrifice in my behalf... and I want to get to know you so much better! Please come into my heart and live forever! Change me to resemble You in every way! Amen."

Do we have forgiveness without repentance?

Dietrich Bonhoeffer, the great theologian who was martyred by Nazis in 1945, argued against the "preaching of forgiveness without requiring repentance". He referred to such forgiveness as "cheap grace...which amounts to the justification of sin without the sinner repenting and turning from their ways."

Ephesians 2:8-10 "For by grace you have been saved through faith, and that not of yourselves; it is the gift of God, not of works, lest anyone should boast. For we are His workmanship, created in Christ Jesus for good works, which God prepared beforehand that we should walk in them."

The answer is "NO!" There is no grace unless we are repentant and sorry for what we have done! So, why are we not throwing our miserable selves at the feet of Jesus and asking for forgiveness? Grace is one of those things that we all have difficulty understanding. There are times in this life on planet earth, where we get glimpses of what grace looks like.

I was at a very low point in my life — and had experienced a women's "Weekend of Grace". It started out when I received an amazingly ornate invitation in the mail from a Christian woman that I had known for some time. Our children attended the same church school and we also went to the same church. She had invited a total of three other women, besides herself to participate in this progressive Weekend of Grace. The weekend started at a quaint little restaurant in town. She had arranged to bring in special plate settings, goblets, and each of us had a beautifully ornate card at our plate with our name on it. She had created a special gift for each of us with every meal. Meals and events were planned to the last detail the entire weekend. Our names were always set at the table with ornate dishes and beautiful gifts. We all were overwhelmed at the thoughtfulness and care that went into each meal as we spent valuable time together. The first evening after our first delicious and amazing meal, we followed our host to a beautiful two-story hotel suite where we got ready for bed and shared many vulnerable moments of emotional sharing and gratitude for each other. The gifts that were bestowed upon us at each meal were incredible. The feeling of what God's grace really feels like became absolutely overwhelming! We felt slightly unworthy of the showering of all of the undeserved gifts, love and attention. I truly believe that as we parted ways at the end of the "Weekend of Grace" that there was not any doubt of how God's unmerited grace looked. It is always there for our taking. The interesting part is that we began to realize that all we had to do was to "accept" it. It was our job to "feel the love" and to begin to "act like we are God's children". We ended up automatically confessing our unworthiness, our sinfulness and shed a few tears before we came to the realization of the lesson that we were learning! The lesson was one of GRACE...and that we are truly God's children.

I will never forget that weekend of Grace! God has great and amazing plans for YOU and ME! His plans exceed our wildest dreams. We, however, need to repent, turn from our sinful ways and "MOVE ON...out of our feelings of unworthiness!!" Because He has unmerited grace and gifts for you and me that we never dreamed possible! What is keeping us from throwing our sorry selves at the feet of Jesus!

"If we confess our sins, He is faithful and just to forgive us our sins and to cleanse us from all unrighteousness." 1John 1:9

"....Lord help me today to own my mistakes and repent when repentance is due. And more importantly, help me to learn to accept

Your Amazing Grace so that I may come to a full realization of Your Love and amazing blessings for my life. May You still find me useful to glorify You and Your kingdom! Amen"

How desperate are you for Jesus to save you from your sinful state?

After praise practice one evening, as I was on my way home I flipped on the radio and David Jeremiah was speaking. He was talking about the **"purpose of the storms in our lives**." He said that God uses the storms and trials of this life to help mold us into people that He can use. He mentioned that we should not be afraid of going through rough times...as long as we have a tight hold onto Jesus, the only one that can save us from ourselves and our past. David Jeremiah mentioned that these times create within us a "Desperation" for God!

In Derek Princes' book, "They Shall Expel Demons", Derek talks of a young man who came to him who was being harassed and tortured by demons. Derek Prince told this young man that he would need take a stand with him against these demons that were living inside of him. As Derek asked, "Do you want me to help you get rid of these demons for good"... the young man fell silent. Derek then said, "Come back when you are **desperate** to be delivered." Wow!! All we have is today! How many times have I been too proud, too ashamed...or even too worried about what others would think? How many times have we failed to humble ourselves before God and throw ourselves at Jesus feet and cry, "Lord help me...I have really screwed my life up!" I don't know about you, but it seems that we all wait until we are underwater or in the eleventh hour of our storm until we finally call on Jesus.... Jesus is always there and His direct line is open twenty-four/seven to answer and welcome us with arms wide open!

"Dear Father, I am desperate for You to come into my life! I so desperately need You in my heart and in everything that I do! I pray that You show me how to keep you at the center of my life! I believe that You can heal this wounded heart of mine. Show me Lord what I need to do. Please forgive me for not keeping my eyes on You and my feet on the path that You have for me! I repent from my evil ways and ask that You come and live in my heart. Amen"

Amazing Grace, How Sweet the sound that saved a wretch like me!

How come it is so hard to believe and accept God's Love and Grace? Tragically there are situations where we can become so wounded from our past and by placing ourselves in situations that wound us... that it is difficult to love others. Eventually...our hearts can become incapable of receiving true unconditional love. This can be reversed by running to God with everything- and asking Him to show us what we need to do. He will assist us in working through the pain and abuse of the past and by holding onto Jesus in Faith each step of our journey into the unknown.

John 3:16-17 "...For God so loved the world that He gave His only begotten Son, that whoever believes in Him should not perish, but

have everlasting life. For God did not send His Son into the world to condemn the world, but that the world through Him might be saved."

David and I sat in our pajamas one morning, drinking our coffee outside on the patio as we watched these beautiful birds come to the birdfeeder. We discussed where we had been five years ago and talked about the events of our first five years together. It became very apparent to both of us as we talked that God had grown us and we were more secure in His love and each other's love. David mentioned the fact that in our first year of marriage I somehow kept thinking that he had an agenda, much like some of the relationships that I had experienced in my past. I wasn't really sure if he truly loved me for me. It took some time to watch David's behavior that ultimately helped me to trust that he truly "was who he said that he was"! I remember dating these men that were very "smooth talkers". They were deceitfully charming, and would tell me what I wanted to hear to lure me into having and intimate relationship with them. They were the ones that did not want to be in a committed relationship. They would take what they wanted and then leave. It took a while for God to convict me that I was not looking for His guidance in my choices of men. I also remember being blown away with the fact that David didn't want to...or demand that we have sex before the wedding. I vividly remember him giving me a wedding band approximately 2 months after we had started dating. He said, "God convicted me that you need my commitment in advance...and without reservation." I remember the tears that came with David's amazing unconditional love. He said, "I know that you are the one that God has chosen for me!" The world tells us that in order to receive something, we must give something in return. However, in

God's world that is not the way it works at all! He died for my sinful self before I ever realized who He really was! He didn't expect anything in return. We all are in need of God's amazing grace! The power of His Grace is Incredible!

It seems that all too often we get so determined that we want to do things on our own that we lose sight of the fact that our Father places others around us to help us get through the hard times, to love us where we are at, and to help us grow. We can be so bull-headed and pride-filled that we stumble on ourselves! We might be praying and begging for a way out... when the answer is already right in front of us, just waiting for us to swallow our pride and say thank you!

Sometimes we have been so wounded by different things in our past that it is difficult to accept the help of genuine, loving people when God sends them into our lives to lean on. Many times we isolate ourselves from others in order to keep from getting wounded all over again. There is a world full of wounded people out there that need to see and experience God's amazing love and grace! The fact is that it is up to you and me!

"Dear Lord, Jesus, today I ask that You pour out Your Love and Grace upon me without measure. Heal my heart sufficiently so that I may help others around me! I want to be able to give away Your unconditional love and grace to those who have been wounded undeservingly. Lord help me to love those who are difficult, those who ridicule and hate me, and minister to those who believe that they are undeserving of Your wonderful Love and Grace. Amen"

Chapter 14

"About... Over commitment and Busyness"

For years... I know that I committed to doing way too much... in fact, I think that I probably still do! However, the difference now is that I have more of an awareness of what is driving my decision to be involved in various activities... and I have a husband that will not let me get too far off track! There is nothing wrong with doing good things for God and for other people, I just didn't know early on in my life- what my motives were and what was driving me!

I was an "approval junkie"! I needed to know that I was doing a good job, that I was doing it well...and that I was valuable. I loved to "show-off" my accomplishments, toot my own horn and was doing everything for the wrong reasons! I was '"invincible" and "self-sufficient" and had not yet come to the realization that I needed Jesus. I did all the right things and said all of the right things, however, I did not have a personal relationship with Him. I ran over a few people and probably wounded others in this process. I didn't know how to sit still for five minutes- let alone thirty minutes. I thought that sitting and reflecting was almost a "sin" and a luxury in itself. I remember looking at the beautiful couch that my ex-husband and I had bought...thinking, "Wow, it would be really nice to actually sit on it once in a while!"

Over commitment and busyness are usually all about "EGO", and "perfection". Busyness truly could have derailed me from the path that God had for my life! I am learning about the danger of our EGO from a wonderful friend who told me, *"E.G.O. Stands for: Easing God Out!"* Somehow, God got a grip on me...and I began to question every motive and every belief that I ever had! I started asking myself, "Why I did what I did...and why I believe what I believe!"

Busyness and over commitment can lead us to "Total Apathy" and can cause such a huge imbalance in our lives that we begin to wonder if life is even worth it! I pray that as you read these words, that you will be convicted to find some balance in your life! I know that your value and potential in God's eyes, far exceeds anything that you and I can comprehend! You and I will find a "new beginning" if we will only begin to sit at Jesus' feet a little bit more often! He will show you the road that leads to healing, fulfillment and ultimately your purpose in life! ...And I can tell you that it is NOT a life of "BUSYNESS"! He doesn't need a bunch of "busy-bodies" trying to find their purpose! He wants to be your B.F.F.- and the number one person in charge of your heart and your life!

Have you ever felt that your life is running out of control and that you can't ever relax?

"But seek ye first His Kingdom and His righteousness, and all these things will be added unto you." Matthew 6:33

I was reading a Chuck Swindoll book this morning there were several things that struck a chord in my heart! He said some profound things about "Busyness".

He said, "I have learned an ugly fact: Busyness rapes relationships. It claims to promote satisfying dreams, but ends in hollow nightmares. It feeds the ego but starves the soul. It fills the calendar but fractures a family. It cultivates a program but destroys priorities." One of Swindoll's late mentors once declared, **"Much of our activity these days is nothing more than a cheap anesthetic to deaden the pain of an empty life!"**

Wow! Powerful words! I too, have lived a very empty life at one point! I felt that my value was dependent upon my accomplishments, my job and my assets. It was only when my world fell apart – I experienced a divorce, lost my job and all family support,... eventually becoming homeless – that God showed me where my true value should come from!

The following is a list of things that you may want to look at if your life is out of control:

1. Admit that you are a people pleaser- and that you tend to fill your schedule way too full!
2. Stop it! Refuse every activity that isn't absolutely necessary! Stop feeling so important! Does this activity bring you closer to God?
3. Maintain it. Watch over time like a vulture! Discuss ways to invest in family and friends instead of laptops and smart phones.
4. Spend less time on face book and in front of the T.V. Just know that the things that we watch and listen to actually make us who we are! When deciding whether or not to watch certain TV programs, ask yourself, "Does it bring me closer to God?"
5. Share the benefits of your changed life with others.

We live in a world that has lost its way! Don't be influenced by it! Remember, your value is not based upon what you do, where you live, how perfect you are or look. Your value ultimately is based on the fact that you are a Child of the King!

"Dear Father, help us to bask in Your Presence as often as we can! May Your Holy Spirit help us resign from useless committees and commitments so that we can breathe in deeply and realize Your true love. Lord, help me to absorb the divine value that I crave to feel as Your child! Help me to grow in Spiritual things so that I may glorify You! Help me to realize that there is nothing "worthy" or "important" in this life that I will ever accomplish apart from You! Amen"

Are you one of those people that craves approval?

The bible says that Jesus made of Himself no reputation. (Phil. 2:7). We cannot always be God pleasers and people pleasers at the same time. In Joyce Meyers book, "God is Not Mad at You!" she talks about Paul...and the fact that if he had suffered from an unbalanced need for approval, he would not have fulfilled the destiny that God had in store for him. People who are addicted to approval frequently get burned out and are overcommitted. It can wear us out mentally and emotionally to constantly feel that we have to "keep up with the Jones', have our kids on the same soccer, softball or sports teams as the popular kids or have our house clean at all times. Living this way is not realistic and can create anger within us and make us feel trapped.

The pathway to God is not paved with perfect performance, peer pressure or societal approval. What is at the root of our fears? Why is it so difficult to step outside of our safe and limited perspective and try to do something that you have wanted to do forever? My challenge to you is to find out who God has destined you to be. You may mess up at first- and it might look like you are living in rebellion until you get a better grasp on God's plan for your life.

There are those that never realize the beauty of the person that God has created them to be, because they are either constantly being the person that someone else wants them to be, or they are too fearful or insecure to step out into the "Big Unknown" to find who they really are in Christ.

Our society tends to want everyone to feel that they have to look as beautiful and petite as those models or celebrities that we see on television. We tend to work our lives away to provide for our families and allow our driven lifestyle to dictate who we are. There are countless situations across our nation where "Baby Boomers" are tired of working all of the time and not knowing or understanding what a "Balanced Life" looks like. We are too often driven into sheer exhaustion and paralysis by the need to be successful, to "fit in" and be approved of. It is truly not surprising to suddenly hear of people that are having a "mid-life crisis". They have all of the sudden, left their family, wife or husband and have gone out on their own to experience some exciting adventure with a new partner. No one knows what single event may cause a person to give up everything they have worked all of their life for, however, it is very apparent that the lack of a balanced life can cause many problems with our health, our relationships and also with our integrity and our relationship with God.

Dear Father, I am on my knees asking you to change my heart! Mold me into a vessel that You can use for Your kingdom. I am at a crossroads in my life and I am questioning everything that I was ever taught or ever believed in! Please send your Holy Spirit to guide me and lead me into the true and right way to live. Please show me the things that I need to discard from my busy schedule- so that I can begin to enjoy life once again! Thank you for hearing my prayer and cries for help! Amen"

Are you way too "Stressed Out"? Did you know that as God's child, you and I are supposed to give Him our stress?

...Seriously!! "Easier SAID than DONE!" ....Psalm 7:1-2 " O Lord My God, in You I put my trust; Save me from all those who persecute me; and deliver me, lest they tear me like a lion, rending me in pieces, while there is none to deliver."

One day I was seeing several patients in various facilities. In the afternoon, I happened to run into a wonderful friend in the parking lot. We started catching up and he shared that his blood pressure had been off the charts.

As we discussed the environment around him, he mentioned that corporate had fired at least a half dozen people in the last month or two. He was fearful that he would be next. He had taken the right steps and was now on a blood pressure medication. However, I was surprised when he asked me to keep him in prayer. My response was, "Absolutely!" We parted ways and I sat in my car and prayed for his welfare.

Our Father in Heaven can come to our rescue and intervene in ways that we are totally oblivious to. He will "call out the armed forces of angels" to do whatever is needed. There may be times when we feel like He is not listening...or times when He doesn't come through immediately. However, trust Him! His timing is perfect! There are times when the things that we ask for are very self-serving and may not help us grow. However, I encourage you to try to simplify your life now before it becomes a crisis situation and there is no way out. It is way too easy to spread ourselves so thin that we are unable to function well at anything. Chaos should not be one of our personality traits!

Isaiah 41:10 "Fear not, for I am with you; be not dismayed, for I am your God. I will strengthen you, Yes, I will help you, I will uphold you with my righteous right hand!"

2 Cor. 12:9. "And He said to me, "My grace is sufficient for you, for My strength is made perfect in weakness." Therefore most gladly I will rather boast in my infirmity, that the power of Christ may rest upon me."

God is not mad at you or me; He is trying to get our attention through the chaos and the trials. He does want us to lean on Him, however, He also wants us to be wise and not overload ourselves with unrealistic expectations of perfection and desires of this world.

"Dear Father, I come before You today–humbled at Your love and grace. Lord, I pray that You be in charge of this day. Please remind me to run to You with my fear, anxiety and problems. Help me to learn how to say "No" and to guard my time with You and my family. Help me to not overcommit to things that will take me away from You. Dear Father, help me constantly ask myself 'who I am trying to please'! Amen."

Did you know that Busyness and 'Life in the fast Lane' has become a Cultural Epidemic? Living on adrenaline, caffeine and fast-food was not God's design for our lives?

Daniel 12:4 says before Christ's coming..."Many shall run to and fro, and knowledge shall increase."

I believe the majority of us are so desperate to find our "purpose in life", or our "identity", and we immerse ourselves in chasing the "American Dream" or we get involved in way too many other things! Ultimately it feels like we are chasing the wind as we try to please others. Our pursuit to find "significance" can start in many places; it might begin at work, or it may involve any or all of the following: music, home groups, church, women's groups, men's groups, bible studies, kids sporting events, fund raisers, charities, basketball, softball, volleyball and many other good things.

One day someone asked Dallas Willard what was the one thing they should do to get back to a vibrant relationship with God. His answer was to "ruthlessly eliminate hurry from their life." I love that answer!

By the time our days and weeks are done, we are way too exhausted to address, process or even talk about the good times, traumatic events, losses, thoughts, or feelings about our daily lives. Before we know it, our lives have gotten way out of balance..., causing depression, anxiety and fear of what tomorrow might bring! We soon begin to rely on caffeine, fast food, and live on adrenaline. How can we help anyone if our lives are so out of balance? Lifestyle imbalances over time can cause depression, anxiety, and health issues. Some people even turn to drugs, sex, alcohol or suicide to cope.

Last evening, David and I had the pleasure of talking with a wonderful missionary couple who had been called overseas to Honduras. As I spoke with Ashley, she shared with me that she had been so busy here in the United States, that she hadn't noticed the warning signs of her clinically depressed state. She said, ***"As long as I was busy, I was functioning."***

Ashley mentioned that it wasn't until they sold their cars, their house, and unloaded all of the obligations off their very full plates, that it suddenly ***"hit her out of nowhere!"***

It was only when she moved from our fast-paced culture that she was forced to sit and take the time to cry about the trauma and find healing and restoration for her soul. Ashley mentioned that she had become bitter about some things that she had not taken the time to talk with God about. She said that she had to get professional help to understand how to feel, grieve and process her own feelings. Today Ashley is definitely a joy to be around. She is now helping others find healing in Jesus Christ!

The million dollar question is this, ***"How can we find healing and peace in the midst of this cultural epidemic of fast-paced living?"***

1. **We must first be able verbalize and live like we know where our identity comes from!** (We are children of The King of the Universe, the Holy God who gave His Son's life on the cross to

save us!   Our identity cannot come from work, "what we do", our accomplishments, our education, our children, our spouse, or our parents. We are "nothing" unless we have Christ living in us! Only God's Opinion Matters!! (Galatians 3:5-9 talks about how we cannot achieve perfection through our own efforts)

2. **We must realize that our self-worth only comes from God!** It is not about how much money we have, our position or educational achievements. Ultimately our quest for purpose and significance will be fruitless unless it is God-centered. Only God's Opinion Matters!!

Galatians 1:10, Paul says, "For do I now persuade men or God? Or do I seek to please men? For if I still pleased men, I would not be a bond servant of Christ."

3. **We must realize that we were created to serve and glorify God!** We are beautiful or handsome and intelligent beings! God doesn't create "junk"! You were created in God's image! You can do all things with Your Heavenly Father Backing You up! If our ultimate goal in life is not to further God's Kingdom or help others grow, then we may need to have a long talk with God. Our entire purpose on this earth is to use the talents that He has given us, but ultimately we also need to be developing our own integrity and personality so that it is a mirrored image of our Heavenly Father's. **Philippians 4:13 "I can do all things through Christ who strengthens me."** We can do nothing in our own strength that will last.

When your life is void of quiet and you haven't carved out any significant time to talk with God or your family, it is definitely time to start asking yourself these questions about the activities that you are involved in:

1. Why am I doing this?
2. Who is getting the glory?
3. Is this building or enhancing my relationship with God or furthering His kingdom?
4. If I had limited time on this earth, would this be worth my sacrifice of time and energy?

"Dear Father, I really am horrible at keeping my life manageable! I pray that You step in and help remind me to say "No" to things that take my time away from getting to know You as my best friend. Please give me wisdom and discernment to protect my heart and mind and my time from the things that aren't honoring You. Amen"

Did you know that God's Word is the Spiritual nourishment that you must have in order to fulfill your purpose?

There is HUGE power in God's Holy Word. When God speaks... things change! This is why, as His child it is so important to memorize promises from His word. It is part of a life-long learning curve of "how-to" access our inherited and promised privileges and power as His children.

As Rick Warren said in His book, "What on Earth Am I Here For?", "The Truth transforms us! Spiritual Growth is the process of replacing lies with Truth." In fact the word of God also convicts us of areas in our lives that need to be softened. It can replace hard-hearted pride with humility, anger with compassion, stubbornness with flexibility, and selfishness with selflessness and love.

Charles Stanley, in one of His radio broadcasts said, "God's Holy Word can and has the power to transform your mind, your body, your relationships, and everything in your life! This transformation will happen only if you want it to! It is your choice and will definitely involve spending time in God's Word."

Our world today is plagued by overwhelming spiritual starvation and anorexia! We-the-people are too distracted and busy to reflect on God's word and His mighty untapped power. As a result of our imbalanced lives, we suffer from diseases, depression, bi-polar disorders, Crone's disease, GERD, Anxiety and ADD/ADHD. Suicide, bullying, cutting and emotional manipulation are now common occurrences on playgrounds, in schools, colleges and universities. If we could only slow down long enough to get a little spiritual nourishment and reflection! MOST CHRISTIANS today do not understand or even try to access GOD's amazing power in scripture! We do NOT take seriously His Promises to ACT in our lives!

John 8:31-32 says, "If you abide in my word, you are my disciples indeed. And you shall know the truth, and the truth shall make you free!" James 4:7 says, "Therefore submit to God. Resist the

Devil and he will flee from you. Draw near to God and He will draw near to you!"

At a very low point in my life, I was being attacked from all sides with finances, job-related issues, rejection, torment and abandonment by my own family and other Christians. I started memorizing promises from God's Holy Bible. I found promises that pertained to God being my provider, healer, and friend. I remember Matthew 7:7 being such a comfort ...and Hebrews 13:5. I began to memorize the promises that pertained to what I was going through. I wrote them out on index cards and took them with me everywhere. I would "crank" the praise music in my car and sing His praises at the top of my lungs while tears rolled down my face. I so remember feeling like "damaged goods", so damaged that I didn't feel that I was love-able. I remember realizing one day, that those people who were persecuting me were missing out! They had not fully accepted Jesus Christ! ...Suddenly I realized that I had a Father in Heaven and He wanted desperately to be a part of my life!!! I was not alone any-more because Jesus went with me everywhere I went. I realized and felt loved because My Heavenly Father gave His life for me! He actually wanted to love me and spend time with me!! I WAS and AM a CHILD OF THE KING! You and I are Royalty! We have access to more Power than the US Army, Navy, Air Force or Special Forces put together!!!!

God is alive and well! However, He is a gentleman. He needs to be invited into your life every day! He wants you to get to know Him by reading the instructions that He left for you! His Holy Bible is full of **instructions that... (2 Timothy 3:16) "...are given by inspiration** of God, and are profitable for doctrine, for reproof, for correction and instruction in righteousness."

"Dear Father God I pray that You lead me as I read Your word today! Re-align my thinking and purge the sin from my life! I want to be Your Child! I want You to come into my life and "clean my house!" Please help grow me into the person that You want me to be! I claim your promises in Matthew 7:7! I am now asking, seeking and wanting to find You alive and working in my Life. Amen"

Chapter 15

"About... Walking Worthy"

*G*od is looking for a few GOOD MEN and Women! Have you ever heard anyone say, *"Do what I say...not what I do"*? How impressive was that ....*NOT VERY*!!!! It is very important in the day that we live in, that we cultivate friendships with people that *"Walk the Walk!"* We all have hung out with and have rubbed shoulders with those who *"Talk the Talk"*...but are unable to *"Walk the Walk"*! **Proverbs 10:9 says, "He who walks with integrity walks securely, but he who perverts his ways will become known."**

What does it mean to Walk Worthy? It means to live out your values of truth, integrity, justice and light! The realm of psychology states, *"Believe Behavior"* , which is very true! Our behavior starts to change for the better when we start to put God first in our lives! God's Holy Bible can be used to direct us in "Walking Worthy". **2Timothy 3:16 says, " All Scripture is given by inspiration of God, and is profitable for doctrine, for reproof, for correction, for instruction is righteous-ness, that the man of God may be complete, thoroughly equipped for every good work."**

God's Word has incredible power ...ONLY when we put it to practice in our lives! This is the beginning of truly "Walking Worthy"! There are countless stories and verses of truth, integrity and light that we can read to help us in our daily lives! If you are praying for "wisdom"...and for "God's will to be done", then God's Holy BIBLE has exactly what you are needing for every situation that is happening in your life right now...because *"God's Word IS His Will!"*

The following are things that others will see in us when we are "Walking Worthy"!

- *Integrity*
- *Compassion*
- *Kindness*
- *Honesty*
- *Humility*
- *Wisdom*
- *Love*
- *Forgiveness*
- *Peace*

These are all "Fruits of the Spirit" that are manifested or seen in your life when you spending time with God, reading His word and letting His Holy Spirit into our hearts to change us forever! What do people see in you?

What is it like to be a productive Christian? Are you a person that "bears fruit"? Are you walking worthy?

Did you know that "productivity or productive Christian behavior" in the bible is referred to as "bearing fruit? *Martin Luther states, "Where there are no good works—there is no faith. If works and love do not blossom forth, it is not genuine faith. The gospel has not yet gained a foothold, and Christ is not yet rightly known."*

It takes time for what we learn about God to travel from our minds to our hearts so that it "bears fruit!" I have told my children that, "Talk is cheap!" Anyone can manipulate others and say the right things, however, you can always "believe behavior". Our actions will be the greatest sermon and testimony that anyone can ever see! (And ten times more powerful!)

I know that in the world of behavioral psychology there is a phrase that says, "Believe Behavior." If you can no longer trust mankind to say what they mean, then you can watch their behavior and it will tell you everything that you need to know. Jesus mentions this in scripture quite often.

Matthew 7:16- 20. "You will know them by their fruits (behavior). Do men gather grapes from thorn bushes or figs from thistles? Even so, every good tree bears fruit, but a bad tree bears bad fruit. A good tree cannot bear bad fruit, nor can a bad tree bear good fruit. Every tree that does not bear fruit is cut down and thrown into the fire. Therefore by their fruits (behavior) you will know them."

What behaviors or fruits do others see in you?

I was working at a Medical Center in Phoenix and my long 12 hour day was almost finished. I somehow was able to get things wrapped up early and headed into the report room to prepare to give report to the following shift. No sooner had I sat down at the table in the report room, when one of the CNA's came in and tugged at my arm. She said," I need you to come with me right now." I was somewhat annoyed and surprised at the same time because I was actually going to get out on time for once! However, I excused myself and followed this young lady out into the hallway. (I had continually felt a spiritual darkness at this facility and many of the staff had targeted me for unknown reasons.) As we entered the hallway she whispered loudly, "I need you to pray with me!" Suddenly my demeanor changed and I listened intently. She said, "I have seen how they have treated you so horribly and singled you out. Everyone here has made your life miserable!" Then she said, "I am in nursing school and some of my teachers are starting to do the same thing to me." She went on to mention that one of her teachers was trying to fail her for no reason at all. I gently said, "I will pray with you!" We stepped into the spacious linen closet across the hall and I began to pray with this sweet woman who had tears streaming down her face. As we finished, with tears in our eyes, I gave her a big hug and said, "It will be okay. You are God's child and He will protect you!" I found out several months later that she ended up passing this class with flying colors!

It is so good to know that our Father will show us at times, what others see in us...when we least expect it!

"Dear Father, I pray that You continue to help me bear good fruit so that I can be a tremendous warrior for Your Kingdom. I don't want to be stagnant anymore! I don't want to be just taking up space. Work on my heart so that I can be a useful vessel for You! Give me perseverance to walk with You during the times of great fire and trials. Help me to walk worthy! Amen"

Are there rewards and blessings for walking worthy?

Even though there is great cost when we choose to be obedient to Christ, there are also great benefits of being royalty and heirs to our Father's heavenly kingdom! Those who choose to spend time with their Heavenly Father definitely have his attention!

The following scripture pretty accurately describes that we need to rejoice while walking this path! We can't constantly focus on the daily trials and beat-downs that the world may dish out. *We must live in the moment and make each moment so beautiful that it is worth remembering.* We can't live in the past and can't be anxious about the future. All we have are the moments of here and now. We are so very blessed to hold onto Jesus' hand as we take one step at a time towards His plans for us!

1 Peter 1:6-9, "In this you greatly rejoice, though now for a little while, if need be, you have been grieved by various trials that the genuineness of your faith, being much more precious than gold that perishes, though it be tested by fire, may be found to praise, honor, and glory at the revelation of Jesus Christ, whom having not

seen You love. Though now you do not see Him, yet believing, you rejoice with joy inexpressible and full of glory, receiving the end of your faith the salvation of your souls."

These are quite a few benefits that we can claim as a child and disciple of Jesus Christ:

1. You have total access to the creator of the universe 24/7, 365 days a year. He always listens, hears our prayers, sees our tears and answers according to His will.
2. Total peace and rest in whatever each day brings. (Hebrews chapter 3 & 4, Matthew 6:25- 31)
3. Your Heavenly Father will never abandon or reject you–no matter what! (Hebrews 13:5)
4. You don't have to worry what anyone else thinks–because only Gods opinion counts!
5. He is our Healer! Total healing for your soul! God wants to heal your family through the generations if you ask Him. (Deuteronomy 20:5, 6)
6. Your father can move mountains if needed. (Psalm 46)
7. He can heal the sick! (Psalm 103:3)
8. He is our provider (Matthew 6:25-31)
9. He is our Father and wants us to ask Him for things! (Matthew 7:7)
10. Unlimited blessings are poured into our lives if we walk obediently. Jeremiah 29:11

Psalm Chapter 103 talks of all the benefits of God. They are too numerous to mention!

"Dear Father, I thank You for all the ways that You have blessed me. I continually am reminded of Your constant faithfulness, forgiveness and healing in my life. Help me to walk worthy as Your child and to always remember that there is no better place to be than to be walking within Your perfect will for my life. Amen"

Did you know that ethical principles are not flexible or negotiable? Genuine Integrity is not for sale!

"Character is created in the small moments of our lives."– Phillips Brooks

In his book, "Becoming a Person of Influence", John Maxwell says anytime you break a moral principle, you create a small crack in the foundation of your integrity. We all have seen instances where good people were taken down to prison level and poverty because they pushed the envelope too far! When we are under pressure, this is when our true character comes to light. **Character isn't created in crisis; it only comes to light during times of crisis.**

Integrity is not based on circumstances, credentials, and is not determined by reputation. Integrity is who we are and how we think when no one is looking. King Solomon of Ancient Israel said, *"A good name is more desirable than great riches."*

Where does integrity come from? I believe that true integrity comes from God. My integrity is the overall make up of how I live my life, what I read, watch, and expose my mind to and my accountability to

God when no one else is looking. It is a deep sense of a relationship to God and what God wants me to be. I truly believe that if more people in this world today were reading God's word ...instead of watching their favorite TV program, and if they were asking Godly friends to hold them accountable, they would find that their lives would not be falling apart.

The overwhelming lack of integrity and commitment in our world is displayed by a large number of single parents raising children, unfaithful spouses that are not living out their integrity or commitment, employees that are not trustworthy, and people that manipulate and try to control and take advantage of others for their own gain. I have told my children over and over to "Believe Behavior". If our words do not match our actions, then we have lots of "stuff" to work on!

Abraham Lincoln said, "When I lay down the reigns of administration, I want to have one friend left. And that friend is inside of me!"

President Dwight Eisenhower expressed his opinion about integrity in this way, "In Order to be a leader, a man must have followers. And to have followers, a man must have their confidence. Hence the supreme quality for a leader is unquestionable integrity." Integrity is the basis of trust.

The following are questions that may help measure your integrity:

1. How do I treat people from whom I gain nothing?
2. Am I transparent with others?

3. Am I the same person in the spotlight that I am when I am alone?

4. Do I change my opinion based on who I am with?

5. When I have made a mistake, do I quickly admit my wrong doing without being pressured to do so?

6. Do I make difficult decisions even if they come with a personal cost?

7. Do I put other people ahead of my personal agenda?

8. Do I have an unchanging standard for moral decisions, or do circumstances determine my choices?

9. When I have something to say about people, do I talk to them or about them?

10. Am I accountable to at least one other person for what I think, say and do? (Besides God)

"Dear Father, I pray that You come into my life and help me clean things up! I want to be that person who "walks the talk"! Please send Your Holy Spirit to prompt me when I am not talking or acting with integrity! Show me in Your Holy Bible, the stories and words of wisdom

to live by. I can't do this day or this life without You! Amen"

Did you know that part of "walking worthy" on this earth is not to "Lecture"..., but to "Love" others?

There is great power in "Living Out" your values and Integrity! Many people that you and I encounter will not care how much we know until we show them how much we care!

John 3:16 & 17 "For God so loved the world that He gave His only begotten son, that whoever believes in Him should not perish but have everlasting life. For God did not send His Son into the world to condemn the world, but that the world through Him might be saved."

I have witnessed many well-intended Christians giving "lectures" to others that they feel are in need of Jesus. I have also been guilty of lecturing others, including my own children, at times and letting them know of my disapproval in certain areas of their lives. I must emphasize the great care and love that our Savior had when approaching people. He truly was a "sermon in shoes". Jesus never beat people over the head with the Bible! He loved them where they were at! The greatest ministry You and I could ever have starts with 'Living a Godly Christian Life'! **Our actions and unconditional love are biggest sermon that we will ever preach. Our actions will either validate that we are truly Godly people...or they will ruin our reputation and invalidate any good words we might try to say.**

"Dear Father, I pray that You would bless me! Lord I ask you this day to increase my territory as You see fit! Lord, You live inside of me...,and I am so very grateful to be called Your Child! I pray that You would help me to see others through "Your Glasses" instead of mine. I thank You for all the blessings and for hearing my cries for help! I pray that you would pour out Your unconditional love and Your Holy Spirit upon me so that I can love others as You have asked me to! Teach me to love others as You do! Amen."

Are you living like you believe in Heaven?

This was the question that rang through my mind after watching the movie, "Heaven is for Real". It also brought to mind the tragic death of our beloved Robin Williams. I somehow wish that someone could have reached him and given him some words of hope! If we truly believe in Heaven, then why do we let the world's views creep into our lives and discourage us? The bible says, "**You are the light of the world. ...Let your light so shine before men that they may see your good works and glorify your Father in Heaven." Matthew 5:14-16**

You and I are a crucial part of our Father's plan of salvation for our lost world. It is up to us to show others that it is possible to have "a little bit of Heaven" on this earth. How do we do this you ask?

Matthew 22:37-39 tells us how to live and prioritize our lives. "You shall love The Lord your God with all your heart, with all your soul and with all your mind. This is the first and great commandment. And the second is like it: You shall love your neighbor as yourself." (On these two commandments hang all the Law and the Prophets.) There are reasons that scripture says these are the most important commandments! We aren't supposed to "Fake it until we make it"... Because if we just fake it, eventually we will wake up one morning and decide that this life is too difficult and not worth the trouble and heartache. We won't have truly built our life purpose on anything solid.

However, if you and I truly begin to love our Father in Heaven with all of our heart, soul and mind, we will find that the way in which we live starts changing! **The following are changes that we may be convicted to make:**

- You might feel like God is impressing you to turn the TV off and start reading the bible, go for a walk with a friend, talk with your spouse or spend quiet time with God.

- Maybe you have started listening to Christian radio instead of the other stations available.

- You might already be sitting at Jesus' feet more often and leaving the laundry or housework go once in a while as we sit at His feet.

- You may be feeling like God is asking you to live out your values and integrity. God will help you and me to, *"say what we mean and mean what we say!" -Harry Truman*

- It could be that you have lived with so much "judgement" in your life...and are feeling that God is calling you to start loving others right where they are at. This means that you aren't labeling people, judging others or making fun of them.

If the center of your world begins to become *"God-Centered"*, then your cup will begin to fill up from the inside- out! There will be an unexplainable love, joy, peace and hope inside of you! You will be prepared to love others and help those in need. God's desire is that we help others out of the overflow of our hearts. We cannot truly help others if our love cup is empty.

God's love has the ability to change even the hardest hearts and turn the worst situations into the most beautiful outcomes ever imagined!

"Dear Father, I am ready to change my life! I am on my face before You, I am so grateful for Your presence in my life. I am grateful for my family, church, and friends. I am on my knees, begging that You heal my wounded heart and fill it with Your unconditional love and Holy Spirit. Lord, please show me how to rebuild my life so that You are the center of everything. Help mend my brokenness so that I can make a bigger impact on others. Amen"

Have you noticed how easily people become "offended" these days? ...don't let their issues compromise your integrity!

Individual rights, patient rights, gay rights, government rights...Can you see how everyone wants their own way? Have you noticed that unconditional love and grace is becoming the exception and not the rule? Recently we have had rioting in the streets of Missouri over a tragic situation that has been turned into something racial.

Matthew 24:10-14 says, "And then many will be "offended", will betray one another, and will hate one another. Then many false prophets will arise and deceive many. And because lawlessness will abound, the love of many will grow cold. But he who endures to the end shall be saved."

It is very interesting and increasingly alarming to sit back and watch the general progression of all of the following issues that are infiltrating our government. There are things such as gay and lesbian rights and marriages. There is conflict over abortion rights, patient rights, women's rights, racial and ethnic rights, the right to bear arms, freedom of speech, freedom of worship and freedom and the right to celebrate Easter or Christmas. At work it seems to be the unspoken expectation that the word "discrimination" rolls off people's tongues as if they feel that they are exempt and not accountable to anyone...even the God that created them? Most people feel that it is "All about THEM"! Are we being brainwashed by the rules that were set into motion to protect the innocent? Have these rules been created because we live in a lawless, disrespectful, love-starved culture that doesn't love each other?   ....ABSOLUTELY!!!!

We live in a world that has lost its way! We live in a world that tells us not to offend anyone! We live in a world that has thrown God's words of truth out the window. We live in a world that tries to say God is dead when He is the only God that has overcome death! We live in a world that would rather worship animals, birds, Buddha, and Satan. In turn...we have exchanged the exclusivity of God and traded it in for whatever type of God that WE want! We have morphed and changed into a society that says life is "All about me"! Hospitals, businesses, churches, schools, and many other agencies have had to buy into these laws in order to survive and manage the offenses of society and uphold and honor their government and state laws.

The great part is that the Holy Bible says that when we live our lives with integrity, truth, compassion and love, God's spirit shines through us without even one word being said. We don't have to "beat people over the head" with scripture or advice, the bible says to "love people"! If we are trying to live out God's values, then we will automatically become offensive to some people. (We will have done nothing to provoke their wrath.) However, they will be able to witness and see "God's Truth" living in us. This Truth will have the power to convict others of the error of their ways if they are open and receptive to growth and healing.

Hebrews 4:12&13 says," For the word of God is living and powerful, and sharper than any two-edged sword, piercing even to the division of soul and spirit, and of joints and marrow, and is a discerner of the thoughts and intents of the heart. And there is no creature hidden from His sight, but all things are naked and open to the eyes of Him to whom we must give an account."

There are so many things that will never offend people! The bible tells us what those things are in **Galatians 5:22,23. ,"But the fruit of the Spirit is love, joy, peace, long suffering, kindness, goodness, faithfulness, gentleness and self-control. Against such there is no law."**

Galatians 6:1 says, "Brethren, if a man is overtaken in any trespass, you who are spiritual, restore such a one in a spirit of gentleness, considering yourself lest you also be tempted."

"Dear Father, as time unfolds, I pray that You keep my mind focused on You. I pray that Your peace will guard my heart and mind. That I will think about things that are pure and praiseworthy! As David

says in Psalm 39:1 Please help guard my ways lest I sin with my tongue! Lord, I want to honor You! Amen"

Did you know that we all need mentors? We all need people that will come along side us and help us to believe in ourselves again!

"Bear one another's burdens, and so fulfill the law of Christ" Galatians 6:2

"There is no more noble occupation in the world than to assist another human being- to help someone succeed."–Alan Loy McGinnis

I remember a time, not long ago, when I relocated to Arizona. I took a traveling nurse position in the heart of Phoenix. As I begin my first 13 week stent at Phoenix Indian Medical Center, It was very challenging to say the least. I knew no one. My life had changed in a flash. I went from the Midwest traffic to the I-17 and the 101 where it seemed that you were driving on a race track. My apartment was only furnished with an air mattress, an ironing board and the basics. I didn't know where God wanted me. I was literally living on pure adrenaline. I had no one that I could really count on. During this time God provided two wonderful, Godly women to mentor me from a distance. They lived in Nebraska, however, I was in contact with one or the other almost daily.

As the days and weeks zipped by- I was getting the feeling that God wanted me to seek His face,...for EVERYTHING! I knew that there was a huge reason for my situation of isolation. This reason was to get to know, "Who I was in Christ!"

In the bible God took Moses into the desert for a while to spend time with him and prepare him for His calling. There are times in this life when I truly believe that God calls us to spend time with Him in isolation so that we can better hear His voice.

It was somewhat different for me to spend so much time alone at first. I didn't have a ton of housework to do, I didn't have a TV and I didn't know many people in the town of Phoenix. I also didn't have a ton of extra money to run around and do other things- so, I stayed at home and dug into God's word. I started out having worship in the morning and would spend at least an hour in God's word. I loved listening to praise music and looking up God's promises and soon grew to crave and yearn for my quiet time at home with God. I started talking with Him out loud when I was at in my apartment and in the car on the way to work. I began to see God do amazing things in my life!

I remember times of great testing and stress as I worked at this Medical Center. There were times of huge spiritual attack. I remember feeling such a heavy presence of evil at work. There was one day when I felt so fragile and beat up, that I found the chaplain on the unit and asked her to pray with me because I was hugely under spiritual attack. I remember this female chaplain looking at me like I had lost my mind. However, she prayed with me and it seemed that the oppression was lifted.

There are many reasons that God has us walk alone with Him. He truly wants to grow us to become dependent upon Him, and ONLY Him. He may allow us to have mentors in our lives to help us get through the rough spots. If we can hang on and not get discouraged, we will begin to "Know who we belong to" and we will also "know beyond the shadow of a doubt, "who we are,(our identity as His Child) in Christ!" **Jesus wants us to call upon Him for our help. He wants to be the first one that we turn to in times of trouble...NOT the last resort!!** The time will come when your heart and life will be healed enough to mentor others when they are at a very fragile point in their lives. God will ask you to start 'bearing the burdens of others' when they are going through crisis. He will ask you to pray with them and point them towards our Heavenly Father!

"The influence of mentors will impact eternity- because there is no telling where their influence will stop!"–Unknown

"Dear Father, today I want to be that mentor, I want to believe in others the way that You have believed in me! Help my heart to heal completely of my wounded past so that I can be a powerful influence for You! Lord, I can't do this day without You! Amen"

Did you realize that science and research evidence is coming out with more and more facts that validate God's Holy word about the power of the tongue?

The bible states that the power of life and death are in the tongue!! (Proverbs 18:21) This is so true! There are reasons that we probably don't fully understand as to why we pray over other people and why we pray over our food! There are many reasons that we speak encouragement and praise over others also, however, I believe that you will be astonished to know that there is much more "power" in the spoken word than anyone ever thought possible! Our words have the ability to change other people's molecular structure...along with water, food, and many other things!

Dr. Masaru Emoto, alternative medicine physician in Japan, has a website that I encourage you to visit! He has photographed the effects of words, music and prayer on water molecules. After all, we humans are comprised of approximately 75-85% water. (You might also find his rice experiment quite incredible!!)

He has researched and studied the intrinsic vibrational pattern at the atomic level in all matter. This is what he calls "Hado". Our words and songs create vibrations that can molecularly alter someone else. I believe you will find this an amazing testimony to scripture! Dr. Emoto's website is: http://www.masaru-emoto.net. This definitely speaks volumes of how our words can effect another's growth and development. We can speak life and light into the lives of others, or we can also be verbally abusive or physically abusive to others, causing damage to their souls. Verbal abuse, intimidation and lack of respect is running rampant in our world. Ultimately we will never know what a powerful affect our words will have on others or what impact it might have on their spiritual journey.

"Dear Father, I beg of You to forgive me for those times when I have not encouraged others. Lord, help me to make up for lost time, so that I can be a vessel to bring life to those that I come in contact

with! Help me to be the encouragement that people need to help them along their journey. Please help me choose friends that You desire me to spend time with, because they will either help me or could potentially harm my future. Thank You for never leaving me or forsaking me. Lord, please bless this day! Amen."*

Were you aware of the fact that we all discover our role of integrity in life through our relationships with others? This is how we learn to "Walk with integrity"!

Solomon talks of the importance of friendships in **Ecclesiastes 4:9,10, & 12. "Two are better than one, because they have a good reward for their labor. For if they fall, one will lift up his companion. But woe to him who is alone when he falls, for he has no one to pick him up. ...Though one may be overpowered by another, two can withstand him. And a threefold cord is not quickly broken."**

God intended for us to fellowship with people at work, at the grocery store, at soccer games and any other places. However, His greatest desire is that you "belong" to His family! You are NOT on your own anymore! Jesus calls all of us not only to" Believe in Him", but also to "Belong to Him". To Belong to Jesus means that you are a part of His heavenly family!

This concept of friendship and spending time with others is a God-based idea. God knew that we could not grow and become who we were meant to be unless we came out of our isolated lives and started rubbing shoulders with other people. Others can help encourage us and strengthen us until we are strong enough with Jesus' help, to reach out and help someone else.

1 Timothy 3:15 says, "God's family is the church of the living God, the pillar and foundation of Truth." Unfortunately, we may miss out on many opportunities to use, find and maintain our spiritual gifts and DNA if we stop attending church or having fellowship with other believers at our local churches. Rick Warren mentions in his book, 'What on Earth Am I Here For', "***The first symptom of spiritual decline is inconsistent attendance at worship services and other gatherings of believers.***" Wouldn't you parents agree that when you sign your kids up for micro soccer and little league sports, that the main objective is to allow them to learn how to play, get some coordination, and learn how to get along with others? Well, in our adult world, our jobs, summer team sports, church functions and volunteer work all teach us how to interact more effectively with other people and with our creator. These places where we end up rubbing shoulders with others and meeting new people, have the potential of sanding off our rough, self-centered edges, developing character, and polishing our Spiritual DNA and servant heart for use by Our Creator, Savior, and King of the universe. Additional benefits are unending! By getting outside of our comfort zones and isolation, God will grow our faith and our service to others, our flexibility will become greater and ultimately our usefulness for God's kingdom! Jesus gave His life for us. John 3:16. Jesus has promised to build His Church. **"The gates of hell will not prevail against it!" Matthew 16:18**

-If we don't go and belong to a church family, God will bring someone
else to belong.

-Our church family will help build our spiritual muscles. We will learn
that not everyone is perfect or the same personality, or even in the
same spot of spiritual growth.

-We need each other in order to heal and grow!

-We must let go of pride and be vulnerable in confessing our sins and
shortcomings to each other so God can heal us.

-We don't need to be perfect to fellowship with others-just vulnerable and humble.

- We can reach out and help others who are in need by using our
spiritual and physical muscles!

-We can keeping each other accountable and on the straight and
narrow path.

*Dear Father, please renew my mind, create a right spirit within me!
Lord, help me not to be so proud and independent- that I isolate
myself from others! Show me how to be a vulnerable, humble and
transparent servant of You! Don't give up on me yet- Lord, I want
to be a part of the team that the gates of Hell will NOT prevail
against. I am humbled to be Your child. Amen.*

Why is irresponsibility rewarded in our culture?

There are those with the mentality of,*...*"but you don't have the right to hold me accountable."*

It seems that our society rewards irresponsibility. Our Government appears to reward laziness. People get paid to 'not have a job' while they draw unemployment. Some individuals get paid to have a bunch of children to receive more tax credits. However, anytime someone is irresponsible, someone else inevitably has to come along and clean up the mess. *The bottom line is that we are happier when we:*

1. Have responsibility.
2. Take responsibility.
3. Be responsible because you care about yourself and others.

The following are texts about responsibility:

Proverbs 28:9 says, "One who turns away his ear from hearing the law, Even his prayer is an abomination."

Proverbs 28:13 says, "He who covers his sins will not prosper, but whoever confesses and forsakes them will have mercy."

Proverbs 29:23 says, "A man's pride will bring him low; but the humble in spirit will retain honor."

What does it look like to be responsible in this world that we live in?

1. It means taking ownership of our behavior and not allowing our feelings to run our lives. It doesn't matter what we feel like doing or not.... God has called us to do 'the right thing'! (Start reading His Word when in doubt.)

2. It means paying your rent and bills on time and respecting authority. The current leadership of this country has been God-appointed. (Romans 13:1 "Let every soul be subject to the governing authorities. For there is no authority except from God, and the authorities that exist are appointed by God")

3. It means being respectful of my own boundaries. Say what you mean and mean what you say. Know that you are loved as a child of God! Know when to draw the line and say "no". Don't overcommit yourself. Get 8 hours of sleep. Drink plenty of water. Exercise regularly. Spend time with God.

4. It means being respectful of others' boundaries. Treat others how you would want to be treated. We are called to care about each other and love one another. We are to advocate for each other, encourage and edify one another. This means not drinking & driving. It means don't get someone pregnant and then leave them with the responsibility of a child.

5. Being responsible means that I will become the person that God wants me to be. I will start Living out my values and integrity from His Word.

Proverbs 16:3 "Commit your works to The Lord, and your thoughts will be established."

"Dear Father, We live in a world that has lost its way! It is so hard to lead a responsible and balanced life anymore. I pray that You fill me with the desire to live my life for You! I beg You, Father to forgive me of my trespasses and irresponsibility. Mold me into the person that You want me to be. I can't do this day without You. Amen."

Do you know that the Holy Spirit is not able to move freely in our lives when we are trying to live by the letter of the law?

Romans 7:6 "But now we have been delivered from the law, having died to what we were held by, so that we should serve in the newness of the Spirit and not in the oldness of the letter." (I encourage you to read Romans Chptr 7 & 8.)

IT IS All ABOUT Your Relationship with Your Heavenly Father! It is *NOT* about the *RULES!* It has taken the greater portion of 40 years for me to realize this!

I was typing out my testimony this week to share on Sunday, and it brought back a lot of my past life. I woke up one morning and turned to my husband and said, "That is it!" "That is why I never had a relationship with Jesus Christ until I left the lifestyle that I had been brought up in." The Holy Spirit had been working on my heart. I was deeply convicted that I had been way too focused on keeping all the rules perfectly*. He showed me that His Holy Spirit could not 'move' in my life freely until I started focusing on my relationship with Jesus Christ.*

I realized that I didn't have the right mindset or motivation when I was focused on keeping the rules perfectly. When I parted ways with this rule-focused life, at first- I went a little crazy. I started rebelling and getting off the path that God had in mind for me. I dabbled in things that I really shouldn't have even looked at twice! I got into relationships that weren't God-focused or pure. Jesus gave me a second chance to live my life for Him and He has asked me to walk worthy so that I can share the journey with you!

I am fully alive and well only by the grace of Jesus Christ! He is my reason for living! Every chore that I do is for the Love of God! Every devotional or text that is compiled is for His Glory! It is for His purpose and glorification that you and I continue to exist and live our lives. It is not wrong to keep Gods law. However, we will never be able to keep it perfectly without His help...so keep your eyes on Him!

Dear Father, please help me to keep my eyes focused on you as I am trying to live my life! Help me to realize that you want me to have "heart knowledge" and practical common sense when it comes to salvation. Help me to remember that if I can stop trying to be perfect and look into your face,... That you will take my hands and lead me the rest of the way home. Amen

Chapter 16

"About... Making Major Life Decisions"

*H*ow does one go about making major life decisions? Do you flip a coin? Do you cross your legs and hum a monotone note? What do you do when you are faced with something big? I would hope that you would consult those people that you respect and hold in high regard. But ultimately, I hope that you would ask your Heavenly Father for guidance.

Psalm 37:5 says, **"Commit your way to the Lord, Trust also in Him, and He shall bring it to pass. He shall bring forth your righteousness as the light, and your justice as the noonday."**

I must admit that I have made decisions with God in charge...and I have made decisions with Myself in charge! The outcomes were like night and day! I have learned through the years that I am not good at being in charge of these big decisions! I have learned that whatever these decisions are, whether they involve relationships, buying a house, moving to another state, jobs, buying a car or any major life decision, God is the one that I want to have in charge of it!

Proverbs 3: 1-8 says, "My son, do not forget my law, but let your heart keep my commands; for length of days and long life and peace they will add to you. Let not mercy and truth forsake you; Bind them around your neck, write them on the tablet of your heart, and so find favor and high esteem in the sight of God and man. Trust in the Lord with all your heart, and lean not on your own understanding; In all your ways acknowledge Him, and He shall direct your paths. Do not be wise in your own eyes; Fear the Lord and depart from evil. It will be health to your flesh and strength to your bones."

Did you know that your spouse, close friends and family are usually the people that will have the greatest influence on your life? If you are searching for a spouse, what are some important things to look for?

"Show me your spouse and I will show you your future." – Charles Stanley

Your spouse can either be your "Anchor" in horrible times...or they can steer you away from God and "Sink your Ship"! When you are dating someone and thinking of making a lifetime choice in a spouse, it is important to take a look at how invested the other person is in having a relationship with you and in knowing you deeper...intimacy can't exist without the safety of commitment. How important are Godly, Meaningful Marriages and Lasting Relationships to this person? The following questions are important things to ask yourself before plunging into a relationship with anyone.

1. Does this individual love God? If they don't love God with all of their heart, soul and mind, it will be more difficult for them to love you. They will most likely be self-centered and difficult to please.

2. Are they in a good place right now? Because it takes a certain amount of personal strength to provide love, grace and support to another individual. Anyone that you are considering getting closer to must have the ability to provide that fuel.

3. Are they willing to make a commitment to you? Are they willing to invest in this relationship? To invest is to devote a resource, in this case, one's love, attention, time, focus and energy. Vulnerable relationships are not drive-by relationships where, "I'll see you when I can." Healthy, intimate relationships involve a dedication of one's self to the betterment of the other. Committed, Godly relationships will not require sex in return for companionship. Most Godly people will not want to have sex before entering into a marriage relationship. This is something that God has asked of us in His word. Are they willing to give one hundred percent to the relationship?

4. Does this person that you may invest in, have internal integrity and moral character that will provide the foundation for a healthy relationship? Character is not about being perfect. Character is about doing the right thing to restore a relationship. It may involve "owning your stuff". He or she, if at fault, should display the maturity to apologize, change their behavior, ask forgiveness, seek therapy, or get in a support group to make themselves accountable. They may even say, "Tell me what I need to do so that I won't hurt you."

5. Does this person validate your point of view...or are they constantly invalidating your perception?

6. Is this person willing to support you through various trials, financial upheavals, and job loss?

7. Does this person have more than just good looks and a great body? Because if they do not love God, they may not be able to love you. Chances are if they are only worried about their looks, their clothes, or just getting their workouts in, they are way too self-focused and self-centered to even be in a relationship that will last. They are probably "takers" and not very giving or loving.

8. Is this person willing to pray with you through the tough times? Are they willing to point you back to Jesus?

You only have so much time and energy and emotional fortitude to invest in people, so evaluate the circumstances. You are not a cold-hearted or selfish person if you decide 'NOT' to take the relationship to a deeper level. This potential soulmate or spouse could affect your eternal destiny! Count the costs and kick all the tires to determine if this person is road worthy and willing to journey through life with you. They may not have the qualities that you need in a life partner or a spouse. Seek the advice of trusted, Godly friends. Pray and ask God what He wants you to do.

"Dear Father, I come before You today, asking that You reveal to me this person's true character. You have told us to ask and we shall receive in Matthew 7. I am asking, Father, that if this person is not Godly—that you would reveal this to me. Please shut the door

on this relationship if it is not of You. I pray that You would grow me and give me the patience to wait for the right person that You want me to be with. Thank You for answering this prayer! Amen"

Making a decision as to which church to attend is very difficult...and requires much prayer. When making this decision, however, please consider that God's churches are never perfect...and they may need you to be a part of the solution.

It is all about how each situation is handled that will "make" or "break" the situation at hand. Sometimes we win the battle and lose the war. We simply do not get the "Big Picture" because we are trying to defend our own turf! *Dissension and Disagreements within God's church are bound to happen because we are all very human and imperfect.*

Paul admits to persecuting the Church of God in **1Cor. 15:9. "For I am the least of the apostles, who am not worthy to be called an apostle, because I persecuted the church of God."**

How many times can you recall walking into a church, only to be chastised in a parental, hypocritical manner by a member of the church for something very petty? I recall one such occasion when I brought a friend to church with me one Sabbath and found out later that one of the "Matriarchal Pillars" of this small church had told my friend that her high heels were inappropriate for someone her age. (Her heels were only about one inch tall.) Little did they know that my friend had suffered from multiple strokes and a ruptured aneurysm. My friend had to learn how to walk all over again–and one of her greatest desires was to wear a pair of heels to church!

At another church I was told that I was going to go to hell if I wore jewelry or if I worshipped on any day but Saturday. I started praying for these people that were so judgmental and misinformed. Then I went back to God's word and read what He said about such things. I found that God doesn't want us to live under the law or by anyone's expectations but His. The more I read, the more I realized that all we are to do is love the Lord our God with all of our hearts, souls and minds. The rest will take care of itself as we grow in Him. Let people say and do what they will. What really matters is that we act like children of the King!

I am almost certain that you may have experienced some degree of hypocrisy, rejection or persecution in God's house also. As I recall my upbringing, I was definitely brought up with the Jewish law of Seventh Day Adventism. I have become acutely aware of the imbalance of emphasizing strict adherence to the "rules" without emphasis on "the relationship with Jesus Christ". For a long time I struggled with going to church. I kept asking myself why I even tried. In fact...before I met David, my husband, I remember pulling into a church parking lot in Phoenix, I was literally sweating and my heart was pounding. I knew that I wanted to go inside and worship, however, something inside of me was not wanting to be judged or rejected anymore. I started to pray to God for strength and then picked up the phone and called a strong prayer warrior that I had known for years. As I felt the tears starting to come, she said," Karen, you need to fight your fears...that is the Devil planting those fears

inside your heart. If you don't go to church, the devil will have suc-
ceeded." She prayed with me right then and there! My friend was
right! I went in and found wonderful love, acceptance and healing.

*The devil wants us to be wounded by other Christians and never go
back to church. He does NOT want healing to come to our lives. He
does NOT want us to share our testimony with others. He would
rather keep us too busy or too tired to go to church! That is part
of his "isolate, divide, conquer and kill strategy".*

There is no perfect church! In fact...if you are looking for the perfect church, you may never find it. (Because we are not perfect!)
Churches are actually meant to be hospitals for the spiritually, emotionally and even the physically oppressed! However, church should
not be just rituals without meaning. Church should not be a place of
judgment and boring sermons. Vibrant Churches are ones that are
filled with people that have a true, sincere, active love for others.
Did you know that **"You are the church"**?

If you experience any type of hurtful judgment or situation, the following things will help you to process it and eventually deal with it:

1. Pray about the situation. There is nothing more humbling
   than to fall on your face before God and to ask Him for help.
   God will reveal to you what you are to learn from this lesson
   if you are listening. Talk with a trusted, Godly friend about it.
   Do not gossip or talk with others about the situation. It will
   only get worse if you do and will not be honoring to Christ.

2. Apologize to the offended person or persons for any part you may have had in the misunderstanding or disagreement. There is nothing that can restore relationships quite like a sincere apology. People will respect you much more if you are able to humbly say, "I was wrong." Let it roll off your armor. Extend grace to the offender and start praying for that person. (They obviously are wounded and need your prayers.)

3. Be respectful of other's perception. (Our perception is our reality.) Don't demand that they see your point of view. Seek to understand them first. Once you understand the other person's viewpoint, only then is it even possible for them to see your point of view. Give them time to heal. Continue to ask God what He wants you to learn from the situation.

4. If healing and restoration doesn't take place after a period of time, don't stop attending the church unless you have God's permission. You may want to consult with the pastor and elders of the church as to how you can restore this friendship or relationship. God may have you at this church for the very reason of bringing awareness of a new and different perspective.

5. Always ask yourself, "What are my motives for feeling the way I do?" "Am I self-centered?" "Am I Christ centered?" "Do I have the other person's best interest in mind here–or am I just worried about my own agenda?" "Could I grow in Christ's will for my life if I stay and listen to this trusted, Godly advice?"

Hebrews 10:24-25 "And let us consider one another in order to stir up love and good works, not forsaking the assembling of ourselves together, as in the manner if some, but exhorting one another, and so much the more as you see the Day approaching!"

We were created in desperate need of a Savior. He designed us to need one another's encouragement, motivation, wisdom and strength in our lives. If you haven't found a church family in which you can use your talents, grow, and worship your Creator...then what are you waiting for? God will lead you to a place to worship Him. No man is an island.

Just remember that there is no perfect church. We are not perfect either! Each church on this earth has multiple members with differing personalities. Sometimes we may get pushed to the wall and hurt one another- or maybe our perception is totally different from someone else's. However, I pray that you and I are able to grow through these times of differences and ask God, "What do you want me to learn from this?" We absolutely need each other's different strengths in order to grow into the people that God would have us be.

"Dear Father help us to remember that our lives are really all about You and that we desperately need each other! Help us not to beat one another to death with the rules...but to love each other for who we are and confess our faults to one another and pray for eachother that we will be healed and whole. Amen"

Whose Opinion Really Matters?... Seek God's approval above all others!

Looking back at the journey that God has had me on, there was a time when I was overly concerned about "what others thought". It really drove my decisions and my life. I soon began to realize that I needed to do what God wanted me to do. **Matthew 6:33 tells us to..." seek ye first the kingdom of God and His righteousness."** You and I will always encounter worldly friends and influences that will try to persuade us to "do this or that" so that we will fit in.... People will ask you to be cool...or tell you that everyone else is doing it!" I am here to tell you that unless you are "grounded in Christ"...these worldly influences come along...and it will be nearly impossible to withstand the pressure that is coming at you. As a baby Christian, I thought that somehow I could mesh the values of my worldly friends with what God wanted me to do. I am here to tell you that I failed miserably. Instead of searching God's word for texts and promises that would help guide my life, I turned to worldly influences that instead...derailed my life.

James 1:5." If any of you lacks wisdom, let him ask of God, who gives to all liberally and without reproach, and it will be given to him."

God wants us to associate with people that are worldly, however, only after we have become strong enough in The Lord to clearly define who we are in Christ. My prayer is that we grow in Christ daily and hide his words in our hearts that we might not sin against Him. And that He constantly guides us and gives us wisdom so that we will influence multitudes of people for God's Kingdom! We are to **live in** this world but not **be of** this world.

In God's Word, He tells us, "Do not love the world or the things in the world. If anyone loves the world, the love of the Father is not in Him. For all that is in the world—the lust of flesh, the lust of the eyes, and the pride of life—is not of the Father but is of the world. And the world is passing away, and the lust of it; but he who does the will of God abides forever." 1John 2:15-17

"Dear Father, I come before You knowing that I have many times been too worried about the opinion of others. Please help me to remember that I am to worry about what You think first and foremost! Lord, help me to remember that I am to live in this world, but not to be changed by it! Thank You for walking with me today and every day! Amen"

Do you 'Wait on the Lord'?

Waiting on God is a very important of building a life of integrity. Did you know that some of God's children will never see or realize His amazing plans for them because...they didn't "Wait on Him"? I don't know about you...but I am truly horrible at waiting! However, I believe that I have missed some of God's wonderful plans and blessings because I was too "thick-headed" and way too "impatient" to wait on God.

Psalm 28:14. "Wait on The Lord; Be of good courage, And He shall strengthen your heart; Wait, I say, on The Lord!"

I have realized that most things in this life are based on TIMING… and it isn't our timing, it is God's timing.

This Life is very fast-paced and most of us are very busy. We usually want instant gratification—and it is very difficult to "wait".

Let us all be reminded, however, that <u>TIMING is everything</u>!

- in softball the batting success is all about "wait-wait-waiting for the ball."
- in sports in general, timing is everything.
- in marriage, it is imperative to wait for God to help choose a mate for us. If your intended doesn't have God's stamp of approval … Then run!! You don't want to marry them!

God does want us to "wait on Him." And while we are waiting, He usually is molding us or allowing painful events to occur in our lives in order to teach us lessons in faith or other things. "Waiting" is never a static event where one does nothing. It is always a dynamic situation where we are asking God, "What am I supposed to learn from this situation?" The goal is to "Become the kind of person that you would want to attract."

I know that both David and I feel that we "waited on God" to bring the right person into our lives. Even though it was difficult, lonely, and many times depressing. My husband, David, waited on God for over 20 years for the right spouse. I now know that if I hadn't been "actively waiting" on God and asking Him to mold me and change me into the person that He wanted me to be, I may have missed out on the opportunity of a lifetime of happiness. Don't be afraid to wade through the pain of the hard knocks of life. It is definitely worth it!

"Dear God, I know that Your plans are so much better for my life than anything that I could ever imagine or plan for myself! Please continue to nudge me when I try to take over. Lord, Jesus, help me to remember that the greatest privilege I have in this life is to live each day to glorify You! Amen" Jeremiah 29:11

Did you know that we "become" whatever we are committed to? Our commitments shape our integrity.

Rick Warren, in his book, "What in Earth am I here for?" He says, *"Nothing shapes your life more than the commitments that you choose to make. Your commitments can develop you or they can destroy you, but either way, they will define you."*

There are those that are afraid to commit to anything and just drift along through life. Others may make half- hearted commitments and get frustrated due to their own mediocrity...because they aren't seeing results. Others make full commitments to worldly goals, such as becoming rich or famous, having a big house or fancy car...and end up bitter and disappointed, and sometimes angry with God. It is so "Worth It" to commit to a godly way of life! *"Tell me what and who you are committed to, and I will tell you what you will be in*

twenty years!... "Wow! We actually become whatever we are committed to???? Scary thought!!..... So, are there ways to change our life and our commitments? ....ABSOLUTELY!!! Yes!

First we must change our thinking! The bible talks about our thinking. It says," Proverbs 23:7 "For as he thinks in his heart, so is he." If we start to read God's Holy Bible more and watch less TV. If we can put our IPhones down and spend some quality time with God each day, we will notice our minds beginning to change. There are a lot of us that get much more excited about our favorite sports events than we do about what God is doing in our lives and the lives of others. God wants us to live well- rounded lives, however, where is your time and energy going?

So, what are you committed to?

- are you in a committed relationship with someone?
- are you committed to healthy eating?
- are you committed to exercising regularly?
- are you committed to going to church routinely?
- are you committed to having a good work ethic?
- are you committed to being debt free?
- are you committed to getting to know Jesus Christ as your best friend?
- are you committed to talking to Jesus and waiting upon Him until you hear His voice?

`

Charles Stanley is constantly encouraging his congregation to **commit** to a life of godliness. He says, ***"There is nothing that you will ever accomplish on your own that will be of any significance, unless you are spending time on your knees committing it to God."***

Romans 12:2&3 gives great advice, "And do not be conformed to this world, but be transformed by the renewing of your mind, that you may prove what is the good and acceptable and perfect will of God. For I say, through the grace given to me, to everyone who is among you, not to think of himself more highly than he ought to think, but to think soberly, as God has dealt to each one a measure of faith."

We all are human and need our brothers and sisters in Christ to love us and pray for us. Sometimes I have needed to have my thinking re-aligned. I needed to be pulled back onto the right path- away from destruction by my mentors and close friends.

"Father, God, I lift my voice, my heart and my mind to You today! Please transform my thinking so that it is in alignment with You and Your Word! I am excited to see how You will work in my life! Please reign down Your Holy Spirit upon me today! I need Your hand to break the Strongholds that have derailed the important commitments in my life. I need You every minute and every hour. I can't make any commitments without your guidance. Amen."

Did you know that God has mentioned several times in the bible that we are to have no other Gods before Him? ...There was a big reason for this!

Exodus 20:3-6 "You shall have no other gods before Me. You shall not make for yourself any carved images -any likeness of anything that is in the heaven above, or that is in the earth beneath, or that is in the water under the earth; you shall not bow down to them nor serve them. For I, The Lord your God, am a jealous God, visiting the iniquity of the Fathers upon the children to the 3rd and 4th generations that hate Me, but showing mercy to thousands who love Me and keep My commandments."

One day, I was riding along in the car with a friend of mine. Our conversation was easy and pleasant and I eventually asked her about spiritual beliefs. She responded saying," I have somewhat of an eclectic belief system. I take a little from the Buddhists and some from the Native Americans, a little from Christianity and so forth." I was a little caught off guard and the only thing that came from my mouth was, "That is interesting"! I was not wanting to come across as being judgmental of her...and wanted her to understand that I loved her where she was at.

A short time after our conversation I was very convicted that if I was ever confronted with a response of that nature from her again... that I would have a solid response! Our Creator and God of the Universe tells us to have no other Gods before me for a reason. The world will tell us that it is okay to dabble in witchcraft, Buddhist meditation, Chakra healing, New Age practices and other things that are not of

God. When we dabble, we are automatically making choices to let evil get a foothold into our minds, bodies, homes and lives. We run the risk of compromise, double-mindedness, confusion, demon possession, mental illness and physical illness. (Isaiah 44:6-10)

I encourage you to start reading God's word and figure out who you are willing to serve. Our God and Creator wants us to Love Him with all of our Hearts! He won't ever leave us or forsake us!

"Dear Father, open our eyes to the fact that You are the one true God! Please lead us into Your Truth. Please destroy and get rid of any false Gods in our lives. As Jacob said, "Choose you this day whom you will serve! But as for me and my house, we will serve The Lord!" (Joshua 24:14&15) Amen"

Have you ever heard the saying..."Birds of a Feather... flock Together!" Or..."Show me your Friends...and I'll show you your future."

God's word has a lot to say about this subject. It is amazing how our choices in a spouse, companion or friends can affect our future! **2nd Corinthians 6:14 says, "Do not be unequally yoked together with unbelievers. For what fellowship has righteousness with lawlessness? And what communion has light with darkness?"**

Mark Twain said, *"Keep away from people that belittle your ambitions."* <u>Small people always do that, but the great people will always make you feel that you can and will overcome all obstacles and encourage you to keep trying!</u> Hope is the greatest gift we can give each other**! "Therefore my heart is glad, and my glory rejoices; My flesh also will rest in hope." Psalm 16:9.** I rejoice in you and what God is doing in your life!

Within the past couple of years, I had come to know a very sweet woman in the neighborhood. Upon entering her home for the first time I knocked on the front door and opened

it. I identified myself after knocking and then proceeded to enter the home. The house was hazy with smoke and unkempt. I followed the oxygen tubing to a back bedroom where this sweet woman was in bed and crying. Her live-in boyfriend was trying to console her. He was kneeling on the floor trying to console the patient as I entered the room. As I listened to this sweet friend and her boyfriend, I began to understand her life a little more clearly. She said that at one time, years ago, she had owned a business with her boyfriend and was doing very well. She stated that they had been together for approximately 15 years- and now were considered common-law partners for life.. She mentioned that her son, whom they were living with at the present, she was afraid of. She stated that he was an alcoholic and could get belligerent and violent. She proceeded to tell me that she preferred to have me come and visit her during the day while her son was away at work because she wasn't sure what he was capable of. When I asked her if there were any dogs or guns in the house- she said "no". As we were talking, she admitted to having post-traumatic stress disorder. She then started to cry because she wasn't sure what her son might do to her. When I asked her if she could move out, she said, "Well, he is not this way all of the time. He does have good days." She then went on to say that her past husband had shot her in the chest and she proceeded to show me scars on her chest. She admitted to smoking and needing pain killers for increased pain. She had developed severe health Issues.

In the years that followed, I watched as this sweet lady ended up in the hospital multiple times. She was constantly in crisis because of the people that she had surrounded herself with and the poor choices that she made. I remember on one occasion, I found out that she had been hospitalized and went to see her. She had experienced another medical crisis and ended up in the emergency room and eventually ICU on a ventilator. I asked her nurse if she could have visitors. Her nurse nodded and said, "She will have a difficult time talking because she is on a ventilator." As I entered her room, she was very weak and pale. I watched her gasp between breaths as the ventilator took over breathing for her, she grabbed my hand and whispered, "Will you please pray for me... I don't think that I am going to make it!" Tears started rolling down her face and onto her hospital gown. I began to pray for her and the tears started rolling down my face. I know that God was there as I begged for more time for her. She made it through this crisis to face another day, however, did not change her lifestyle or habits.

A wonderful friend of hers had found her affordable housing and offered assistance to move her, however, this woman was paralyzed with fear and unwilling to strike out on her own with God's help. She went back to what was familiar...even though it was killing her. She was very artistic and talented, but had never been able to reach the goals in life that she felt God had for her.

We live in a world that has lost its way. My hope is that today each of us will prayerfully consider the choices that we have made in our circle friends and even in potential dating relationships or spouses.

"Dear Father, I get way to comfortable with things in my life that are detrimental to my spiritual growth. Please, Lord Jesus, I beg that You show me what I need to change in my life so that I can grow. Help me re-evaluate my friendships and get rid of those friends that are not lifting me up to walk the path that You have for me to walk! Please place a protective hedge around me, open my eyes to the battle that is going on for my life! I can't get through today without You in my life! Amen."

Who are the friends that God has brought into your life to help you?

It was Charles Stanley that said, "Show me your friends and I will show me your future."

My life has been so blessed by the people surrounding me with support of encouragement and prayer. I have realized the importance of Godly friends and have prayed long and hard for God to bring people of integrity, wisdom and genuine love into my life! **Proverbs 17:17 says, "A friend loves at all times, and a brother is born for adversity."** My concordance says that a true friend is constant, and a real brother helps in times of stress. I remember, during a very dark period of my life, praying for a Godly mentor who would teach me to pray and would give me wise counsel. God did hear my prayers for help! He has brought many wonderful people into my life at just the right moment to guide and direct me to the path that God had for me.

One evening our praise team gathered to practice at the church. As we gathered to sing, it was as if God was tapping me on the shoulder, saying, "Look, There are wonderful and amazing people surrounding you!" Then I heard Him whisper, "Pray with each other and for each other and love one another and I will pour My Holy Spirit out upon you all and richly bless your church!" "I will bless your friends and family and enrich your lives"! When God brings us mentors, friends and people to mentor, He also expects us to be willing to get involved and support one another! Eventually, to complete the cycle of learning, it is our role to "become" the mentors and help the next generation become the people that God created them to be!

John Maxwell has said, "When we help others reach their goals, we also fulfill and meet the goals that God has for us."

"Dear Father, thank you so very much for my friends, the worship team, our church and pastor. You have blessed me with an amazing spouse, family, children, church family, mentors and awesome co-workers! Help me Lord, to come along side others when needed. Please guide me and show me how to support others with encouragement, prayer and whatever You ask me to do. Amen."

Chapter 17

"About... Being Humble"

"The Lord lifts up the humble; He casts the wicked down to the ground." Psalm 147:6

James 4:6 says, "God resists the proud, but gives grace to the humble." "Humble yourselves in the sight of the Lord and He will lift you up." James 4:10.

The bible talks about how humility cures worldliness. In this day that we live in, it is all too easy to get caught up in the mentality of "You deserve it"...or "It is all about Me". The bible tells us that this is not a Godly trait. The sin in this world began when Lucifer, began to think that he was the best thing that ever happened to the universe. Our EGO is not to be bigger than God.

As I had mentioned before, E.G.O. stands for Easing God Out! It is the opposite of humility.

Humility may look like the following:

- When someone does things and does not expect anything in return and just does acts of kindness out of the love in their hearts!
- When someone lets another into a line at the grocery store or when they wave a car to go in front of them when traffic is heavy.
- It is putting someone else's needs in front of their own.
- It is making coffee in the morning for your spouse.
- It is making the bed in the morning when your spouse is in the shower.
- It is pitching in and washing the dishes when your spouse is sick and unable to function very well.
- It is picking up the slack at work for someone that you work with...without making a big deal of it.
- Donating your time at the church to help clean, teach, sing, play an instrument, wash dishes or prepare food- without asking for any recognition in return.
- Helping someone in need with their utility bill or giving someone a nice warm bed for the night with a warm meal.
- Worldliness may look somewhat like this:
- When someone does something and then has to advertise it all over CNN.
- When people cut in front of someone at the grocery store or when driving- they cut someone off and are not thinking of anyone but themselves.

- Most self-centered people will be much more worried or concerned about how they look then they are about the welfare of others.
- Worldly, self-centered people will not donate their time to help a good cause unless there is something in it for them... or unless it makes them look good.
- The worldly mentality is usually, "What is in it for me?"...or "What do I get out of it?"

Have you ever wondered whether or not it was okay to promote yourself...or toot your own horn?

Did you know that self-promotion equals self-destruction? This is exactly the opposite of what the world tells us! The world says, "It's all about me!"

"Humble yourselves under the mighty hand of God, that He may exalt you in due time." 1 Peter 5:6.

It seems that "Power" can change people. As God's children, we can look forward to each opportunity that He gives us to serve others. No matter what our title or position in this world, we can rest in the fact that God wants us to succeed! **(Jeremiah 29:11).** However, it is up to us to **"...Commit our ways unto The Lord" (Psalm 37:5).**

A few years ago, I had a friend that asked me, "Karen, what do you think about 'tooting your own horn'? She went on to say that she didn't feel that she would get any recognition at work if she didn't do a little boasting about her own accomplishments and abilities. Interestingly enough, I mentioned to this awesome friend that I really believe that we all have the need to feel like we are amazing individuals and that we are multi-talented. However, I went on to tell her that it has been my personal experience that God will exalt us in due time. I mentioned that He is where our confidence, self-worth, approval and identity need to come from. We all will have times in our journey where we feel that all of our needs are sup- posed to come from our spouses, our friends, our family and people from our church or work. However, to be real honest, Satan wants us to buy in to this concept of being "self-made" people....because we will end up like "hollow shells" of humanity walking around trying to find meaning and worth outside of Jesus Christ. He is the only One who can make us whole, complete and full of integrity, kind- ness and humility.

We many times do not see... that the evil one has a plan of worldly temptation that will not lead to satisfaction, contentment or peace. The world has not filled itself with the Holy Spirit or developed good habits to create Godly character. Friends, spouses, family or co-workers will not be able to meet our need for Jesus...even if we ask them to. This is why it is so very important to spend time with our creator and savior, Jesus Christ. We can also surround ourselves with emotionally and spiritually healthy and mature individuals and friends who will hold us accountable. Scripture talks about how our identity is to come from our Heavenly Father and creator. Our jobs and the things that we do are merely the "vector" in which God can work through us if we let Him. The true sign of a "spiritually mature individual" is that they don't always have to be the center of attention or they don't have to get any credit for things that they have done. Maturity usually has the hallmarks of humility, grace and selflessness. There are very few of us that can just "Be". We all seem to talk of our accomplishments, talents, possessions, careers and all the material things that the world has to offer when we are asked "what we do." We don't even remotely consider the option of saying, "I am a child of the King of the Universe", for fear that someone may think we have lost our minds.

Even the great rope walker, Jim Wallenda, admitted," After my last victory walk across Niagara Falls,…to keep myself grounded and humble, I went and picked up trash left by the crowds of people that had come to watch." He went on to say that picking up trash helps him realize that I he is no better than anyone else. We also remember that Jesus washed the feet of His disciples. Wow!! Servant hearts are truly rewarded by God!

Charles Stanley has often emphasized that "True, sincere humility" can keep you from being derailed from your God-given path. He states, <u>"The thing that constantly kept me humble and with proper perspective, was the Holy Spirit whispering in my ear, 'Remember that this is not happening because of your ability!'" Stanley then said that He would fall on his face on the floor daily and spend time in prayer before God.</u>

"Dear Father, I struggle with pride and various other temptations. Lord, I don't want to be like Lucifer—and think that I am better than anyone else. Father, please help me to remember that I am "Nothing" without You! I humbly fall on my face before You, Lord

Jesus and thank You for all that You have given to me. You are my provider. You are the source of everything good in my life! I am so very grateful for Your love dear Father. Amen"

Did you know that we are created to "serve" others? "Every saint has a past...and every sinner has a future." -16th Century Poet.

Matthew 20:26-28 , Jesus says,"...Whoever desires to be great among you, let him be your servant. And whoever desires to be first among you, let him be your slave. Just as the Son of Man did not come to be served, but to serve, and to give His life a ransom for many."

There is no Christian that "has arrived" at perfection. All goodness that is in us comes from God. I recall a season in my life before I really knew Jesus Christ. I claimed to know Him...and I was such a "hypocrite" about my faith.

I remember a point in my life where I felt that I was better than the homeless person on the street. I remember being very judgmental of anyone that was divorced or anyone that had HIV/AIDs. My "take on it" was that in these situations, the person had "brought it upon themselves." Whew!!! God had His hands full with me! He allowed me to be taken to the bottom of the Pit to "break my stubborn self-sufficiency and judgment" so that I could see that I really needed Him. He brought me through the very things that I was judging others for. He brought me through a divorce, through homelessness and healed me of AIDS. It is very plain to see years later, that His Love is still alive and dependable for all of us. If you are searching for success, greatness, or the cutting edge on leadership... the answer can be found in "servant hood" and service to mankind. The key is "Descending into Greatness instead of Ascending into Greatness. This was God's plan all along as you find him washing his disciples' feet and caring for their needs. We are only truly "alive" when serving others. If you find yourself as a janitor, as a care-giver for a disabled parent or family member, please realize that God is in the middle of it and is growing your wonderful heart to be just like His!

James 4:6 "God resists the proud, but gives Grace to the Humble".

"Dear God please continue to mold my life so that You can use me. Lord, give me a servant's heart so that I can better see the needs of others. Pour Your Holy Spirit out upon me. Please take the wheel and driver's seat of my life. Lord, help me to look closely for what others need before they even ask. Help me to love those that can't even love themselves. May Your Holy Spirit be alive and well in my heart today!
Amen"

Did you know that God can use you in many ways to heal others? However, Humility is very important... giving God the credit.

Isaiah 61:1 "The Spirit of The Lord is upon Me(you), Because The Lord has anointed Me(you) to preach good tidings to the poor; He

has sent Me(you) to heal the broken hearted, to claim liberty to the captives, and the opening of the prison to those who are bound;"

Wow! This is amazing!!!! Yes, God can use you!! You are His Child... whom He absolutely adores and loves! His children's prayers have always carried **"clout"**!

1 Peter 3:12 says," For the eyes of The Lord are on the righteous, and His ears are open to their prayers; But the face of The Lord is against those who do evil."

I have learned, that when you have sold yourself out to Jesus and you believe in Him, He hears your prayers! I remember being at the bedside of a patient that was suffering from migraines. I had taken over this patient's care half way through the shift. The nurse that had been assigned to this lady was mysteriously transferred to another unit. The doctor had ordered a very strong narcotic, dilaudid, to be given intervenously, every 2-3 hours for her headaches. When I walked into the room to assess this patient, she was very groggy with shallow respirations. She was not able to answer any of my questions, so, I then turned and talked with the patient's two daughters. The patient's daughters were very concerned about their mother. I found out that they were just passing through Phoenix, and that their mother had suffered from migraines for many years.

I ran and got the daughters some chairs to sit in and then found them something to drink and some snacks. I overheard them saying that they were Christians and that they had relatives praying for them. After getting them settled comfortably beside their mother's bed, I explained that this dilaudid was a very powerful narcotic, and that after my assessment of their mother, I felt that the doctor needed to be called. I mentioned that I would ask for a drug called narcan. I explained that this was a medication to reverse the narcotic effects of dilaudid. I came back after phoning the doctor with the narcan in hand. I asked the daughters to pray. As I pushed the narcan through her veins, I felt God's presence rush through me. I had goose bumps all over my arms and down to my toes. I talked to the daughters and told them that their mother should be waking up soon and asked the daughters to push their nurse call button if they needed me right away. I sent a nursing assistant in to check her blood pressure and vital signs while I checked on my other patients.

Approximately ten to fifteen minutes later, I re-entered this lady's room and this woman was alert and sitting up; laughing and talking with her daughters. She motioned for me to come to her side and grabbed my hand and pulled me to sit on the bed beside her. She asked, "Have you ever given this medication before?" I told her that I rarely give it... and only in emergency situations. She said, "When you pushed that medicine through my veins, it was as though fire was shooting through my entire body." She said, "Then three faces shot out through my eyes and landed on that curtain over there." My eyes filled with tears. I prayed with them and left to care for my other patients. I told my Godly friend about this event later that evening. She started praising God and said, "That was a modern day version of Jesus using you to cast out demons!" What a privilege to be used as a vessel for the healing of others! I pray today that you are sold out for Jesus Christ. He will hear and answer our prayers when we call on Him! **It is amazing what God can do when we don't care who gets the credit!**

"Dear Father, keep me humble and help me to be willing and obedient to Your bidding. Use me today to help someone in need. I know that my very purpose on this earth is to serve You and make life a little more bearable for those around me. Thank You for the privilege to be used as a conduit of compassion, love, grace and healing for Your kingdom. Amen"

Chapter 18

"About... Doubting Your Worth as God's Child"

*H*ave you ever doubted your worth...and wondered why God ever created you? Have you ever wondered why you were born? You are not alone! I also have shared in the very center of that negative mentality. I felt like "Damaged goods" ...that no one would ever want.

However, **I know that God has a purpose for your life!** I know that you were born for many reasons! I applaud the fact that you are searching for healing and working to find a way out of that mentality! Don't accept these negative messages into your heart, mind or body! You are Valuable and Loved! I urge you to tell yourself the following words as many times per day as you need to- until you start believing them! "I am valuable and loved by God. I am God's child and I accept His love for me today!"

Many years ago... God showed up and talked to me as I sat on the floor of my apartment sobbing. And as I cried... I begged God to show me why my own parents could not accept me as I was. I pleaded with Him to show me why they could not love me. I asked God a whole lot of things that day- and used up a whole Kleenex box in the process. As I sat there in my P.J.'s grading papers, these are the words that He spoke to my wounded soul. I wrote them down and saved them to my computer. I hope that these words speak to you and give peace to your wounded places. You are loved!

My Child,
I Have been..
Right beside You!

My sweet Child,
I have never left you
In the valleys of depression and despair.
I was right beside you to guide you.
I whispered softly – words to comfort
...through the turmoil and indecision-
-it was me who gave you vision.

My precious Child,
You were made in my very likeness,
-no matter what others may say,
You are unbelievably beautiful both inside and out!
Just remember that....I...CHOOSE...YOU!!!
And I have given my very life for You!

My dear Child,
I will never leave you,
I will never abandon you or forsake you!
I long to meet you in every morning!
Your ears are slowly –
Becoming attuned to my voice with each hour
That we spend together!
I am the Father that you have longed for,
-I am the parent that you never had.
I love you with every fiber of my being!

My precious Child,
I have been your biggest fan!
I have given you thoughts of encouragement-
-or sent friends to cheer your countenance.
I have orchestrated your path to cross another
At just the precise moment needed.
-You- My Child, have reached out to others
-and given encouragement and support- even
When you had nothing left to give!
I am so blessed to be your Parent!

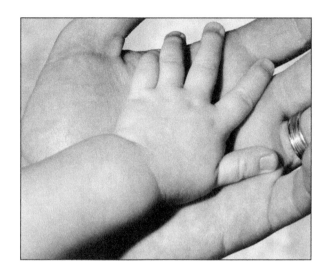

My Blessed Child,
I now continue to offer unconditional
Love and support in every aspect of your life!
Enjoy knowing that I am here forever!
Nothing you could ever do would make me
Love you any less.
I will not disown you or treat you like a
-second-class citizen.
Because your heart is marked with my Love-
..and compassion.
You are Royalty! You are MY CHILD...and I love you so deeply!

So, My amazing Child!
When you are tempted to think of yourself-
Less than the Masterpiece that I created,
Read this again.
Lift your eyes to the heavens
And meet me in your special place of prayer.
For I will lift you up!
I will carry you on my shoulders through the rough times.
I am your Father- and I never want to loose
You ever again!

I am so proud to be your Father!
When I hear your name- I get so excited to see you
Appear! When asked whose child this is- I boldly step
Forward to claim You!...my wonderful child!
Your value is immeasurable!

Remember, that I am only a prayer away!
You can call on me anytime of the day or night!
I will always hear You!
You have a heart designed to Love me..
-and to love others!
Continue to keep your eyes on Me!
Don't fall prey to the prison walls of your own
Making. Don't listen to the old tapes of
-Low self-esteem and victimized thinking.
..Because now you are MY CHILD!!
So, claim your place beside me and hold
Your head high! Because I love you and died
That you might live!

So, live your life to the fullest!
Don't wait another precious moment!
Bask in My Love for You!
You bring me such Joy!
Go Ahead!!!!
Start Your Own Journey of Joy!—
-It all begins with your own acceptance of the
Inheritance that was given for you!
You are an amazing and wonderful child
With talents and personality beyond belief!

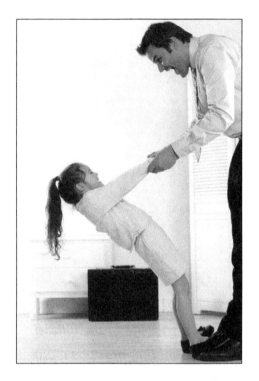

I Love to watch you Grow!!
Wow!! The journey that each day will bring!
-Don't forget... I will be waiting for you –
...to listen, guide and nurture you.
See you in your special place in the morning!
My Love for you may be difficult to understand.
I love you to the heavens and beyond!
Your loving Heavenly Father,
Jesus Christ

Author -K. Land.

My hope is that these loving words will change your life forever... as they provide comfort, wholeness and healing in your life as well!

Bibliography/ Works Cited

References

[Radio broadcast]. Flagstaff: David Jeremiah.

Amen, D. (n.d.). Spect Scans of the Brain. Retrieved March 5, 2015, from http://www.amenclinics.com/

Iron Man III [Motion picture on DVD]. (2014). Vivendi Entertainment.

[Television broadcast].Oprah.

Bonhoeffer, D. (1959). The cost of discipleship (Rev. [i.e. 2d] & unabridged ed.). New York: Macmillan.

Chapman, S. (2014, January 1). Retrieved March 5, 2015, from http://www.youtube.com/

Crabb, D. (n.d.). Connecting.

God is not dead [Motion picture on DVD]. (2014). USA.

Henderson, D. (n.d.). The Seven Most Important Questions You Will Ever Answer.

(2014, January 1). [Radio broadcast]. PHX: Charles Stanley.

Hybels, B. (2002). Courageous leadership. Grand Rapids, Mich.: Zondervan.

Interview with Dr. Bernie Siegel.(Interview). (2006, January 1). Townsend Letter for Doctors and Patients.

Maxwell, J., & Dornan, J. (1997). Becoming a person of influence: How to positively impact the lives of others. Nashville, Tenn.: T. Nelson.

Maxwell, J. (2013). How successful people lead: Taking your influence to the next level. New York, NY: Hatchet Book Group, Center Street.

Meyer, J. (2002). Battlefield of the mind: Winning the battle in your mind. New York, N.Y.: Warner.

Meyer, J. (2013). God is not Mad at You (First ed.). New York, NY: Faithwords.

Meyer, J. (2010). The Confident Woman (First ed.). New York, NY: Faithwords. Pgs 40, 175, 176

Muller, G., & Matisko, D. (1984). The autobiography of George Müller. Springdale, Pa.: Whitaker House.

Batman begins [Motion picture on DVD]. (2005). Warner Home Video.

Prince, D. (1998). They shall expel demons: What you need to know about demons—your invisible enemies. Grand Rapids, Mich.: Chosen Books.

Reba McEntire songs. (n.d.). Retrieved March 5, 2015, from http://www.youtube.com/playlist?list=PL9A3DCECD4571B4E9

Stanley, C. (2005). "God's Grace is the Starting Point" In Living the extraordinary life: Nine principles to discover it. Nashville, TN: Nelson Books.

Story, L. (2014, January 1). Song—"Blessings" Retrieved March 5, 2015, from http://www.youtube.com/

Tozer, A. (1982). Following Hard After God. In The Pursuit of God (p. Pgs 13,14, 4,45,76,77). Camp Hill, PA: WingSpread.

Venden, M. (1986). How to make Christianity real. Siloam Springs, Ar.: Concerned Communications :.

Warren, R. (2002). The purpose-driven life: What on earth am I here for? Grand Rapids, Mich.: Zondervan.

About the Author

*K*aren M. Land has her BSN and is currently the Director of a Home Health Company in Arizona. Karen has been in the nursing profession for over twenty years. She has taught Med-Surgical and Pediatric/Obstetric nursing at a community college. She has been a Director of Nursing at two Skilled Nursing Facilities in Nebraska, and also has done Hospice nursing, ER, Med-Surg, ICU, Orthopedic and Rehabilitation Nursing. Karen took a job in Arizona as a traveling nurse with Indian Health Systems and fell in love with the Arizona climate. Her innermost desire is to help others that are facing trials and difficult times and point them to Jesus Christ! In the last 10 years, God has brought Karen full circle; through homeless-ness, abandonment, rejection, financial ruin and AIDS. She is total healed of AIDS and God has rebuilt her life! She is now living the life that God has planned for her. She is now married to the Love of her Life and has wonderful family and friends surrounding her! "Never underestimate God's power to act in your life!"

Further Reading/ Website Information

You can go to "http://www.walkingworthywords.com" to access my website. I do have plans for the next book! I welcome your comments. Please e-mail me at "sharokm@hotmail.com". I would love to hear how God is working in your life! May God bless you and keep you close to His heart.

Walking Worthy

Who's in Charge of Your Life?

Are you FORFEITING all of the BLESSINGS and BENEFITS that God might have in store for your life by deliberately NOT inviting HIM into your heart?

What are the benefits of living a life where God is in charge?

- God won't ever lead you down the wrong path.

- God can protect you if you pray to Him and ask Him to.

- God promises to never leave you or forsake you.

- God promises that if you go to Him with everything that He will make things end well.

- God can heal and restore you and give you the ability to be victorious. (This means spiritually, mentally and physically)

- God can give you hope and a reason to live.

- God can give you a testimony that will help many people find their way.

""There is absolutely no reason for anyone to live a powerless, unsuccessful life. God can turn any 'Mess' into a 'Miracle',...and any 'Test' into a 'Testimony!' "
— K. Land

"Matthew 6:33 "Seek ye first the kingdom of God and His righteousness, and all of these things shall be added unto you." "
— Holy Bible, NKJV

""Never underestimate God's ability to ACT in your life!" "
— Jamie Rassmussen, senior pastor of Scottsdale Bible Church

Devotional Coming Soon... *available by July 2015*

Once published, books will be available on www.Amazon.com
"Anywhere With Jesus I Can Safely Go..."
New Volume One, of a Series of Devotionals!!
**A compilation of heart-felt candid experiences with scripture
that are intended to
lift you up out of the "muck" and give encouragement
through each day.**

Book Coming Soon!

"Don't Just Settle!"

"Show me your friends and I will show you your future."–Swindoll

This book will be coming out soon- and is for anyone who might be really bad at choosing the right people in your life, or just 'settling' for relationships or friendships that are mediocre. God wants you to "hold out" and demonstrate "Confident Expectation" for His plans for you! (They are much better than our own plans for us!)

""Wait on the Lord; be of good courage, And He will strengthen your heart; Wait, I say, on the Lord!"

(The Hebrew word for wait may also be translated to 'hope'. To hope in God is to wait for His timing and His action.)"
— Holy Bible NKJV

Flagstaff, AZ, United Statessharokm@hotmail.com
Managed by Nick Sharon

CPSIA information can be obtained at www.ICGtesting.com
Printed in the USA
BVOW11s0143190515

400896BV00002B/3/P